THE SCIENCE OF CHARACTER

LUDWIG KLAGES

THE
SCIENCE
OF
CHARACTER

*Translated from the Fifth and Sixth German Editions
by* W. H. JOHNSTON, b.a.

**First Published in German under the title
"Grundlagen der Charakterkunde"**

ROGUE
SCHOLAR

First published in 1932 by Sci-Art Publishers
This edition © 2021 Rogue Scholar Press
All Rights Reserved

ISBN 978-1-954357-07-5

AUTHOR'S PREFACE TO THE FIFTH AND SIXTH EDITIONS

The new edition is in the main unchanged, for this work has received its definitive form (for the time being) in the fourth edition. Only Chapter VI, dealing with "Faculties for Impressions and Directions of Apprehension", has been considerably enlarged, two Directions of Apprehension being added which had to be passed over last time in spite of their importance, from lack of time. The first three editions of this work were small, the fourth large. In spite of this it was exhausted in rather more than two years, although the text requires study rather than reading; which seems to indicate that instructed readers are beginning to go to the sources in spite of the unpleasant clamour of intellectual speculators who, much to the disadvantage of science, are preparing to create a new fashion in characterology. We venture therefore to send out this new edition accompanied by the pious wish that the tares may perish and the wheat endure.

June 1928

AUTHOR'S PREFACE TO THE
FOURTH EDITION

This book is the outcome of lectures which were given by the author on various occasions at Munich between the years 1905 and 1907. External difficulties, however, stood in the way of its immediate publication, and it did not appear until 1910 under the title of *Principles of Characterology*. At first it was neglected, but afterwards quickly went through three editions, the third of which was soon exhausted. The demand grew considerably later, but some five or six years had to elapse before this new edition could be published. For the author discovered that he could not escape from the necessity of completely recasting his work, while his time was completely occupied. The reasons which compelled him to recast the work are briefly set out below.

He found that he could no longer read his own book, from a violent dislike of the innumerable foreign words which it contained. The dislike may have been due to the general tendency of the times or to a personal change, and in any case might have been remedied fairly easily; nor could the fact that he had been forced to change his views in some comparatively unimportant points suffice to explain the profound transformation which he found himself bound to effect. The decisive cause was and still is something else. His investigations during a period of at least ten years had been turned almost exclusively upon the doctrine of the nature of consciousness. Compared with the results of these, his former text necessarily seemed to him partly incomplete, partly as groping prophetically rather than firmly grasping, and finally as in need of greater depth. Although the principles and the fundamental classification remained, it was impossible to make good these deficiencies by patchwork, and the only remedy was to write a new book. The old book was not perhaps epoch-making, but still it had done pioneer's work for the characterological point of view; it had won friends, and even passionate friends, who were inclined to consider it the most important work of its author; yet in fact it contained more than one page the contents of which the author did not trust himself to set down with the old vehemence. He therefore had recourse to a remedy which thinkers a hundred years ago were also in the habit of employing: in the new book he has *quoted* all the parts of the old which appeared valuable—by pages, paragraphs, or sentences, admitting minor changes of style, transpositions, and improvements, but leaving the matter unchanged, and using special inverted commas (<< >>) in order to provide an immediate means of distinction from other quotations.* This also affords all readers who cannot obtain the former edition an opportunity of testing in what respect the fundamental views have remained the same and in what respects they have developed.

Everybody knows that the intellectual atmosphere has undergone considerable changes since then. In 1910 the name of "characterology" met with smiles; today it is a commonplace. It must not be expected of the author that he will explain his standpoint with regard to contemporary undertakings of a similar nature. There are three classes of the latter. The results of one would not exist at all, or not in the shape which in fact they have, but for the "stimulus" (to use a favourite term of the day) which they received from the *Principles of Characterology*; but they try to hide this very fact. Such performances are valueless if only because they necessarily distort and caricature the good which they appropriate, in order to make it look original, and it would be waste of time further to deal with them. Books of the second group expressly refer to the investigations of the author and try to utilize them for special scientific ends. Here, then, there is no need of words. The third group has a different origin and different aims. If controversy were our intention, evidently a separate book would be the proper

---

* These have been omitted in the English version.—TRANSLATOR'S NOTE.

means to that end, and not a work which sets out point for point original results which form one coherent system. Finally, we wish to say with regard to those students of the day, or of the most recent past, who have afforded us stimulus or help which is reflected in this work, that each of them is named, and that further the attempt is made to designate their significance and value, as also their limitations, so far at least as seems at all necessary; and to pay the thanks which are their due, while giving the reasons which have induced us to travel a different road.

April 1926

AUTHOR'S PREFACE TO THE ENGLISH EDITION

Psychology outside Germany has concentrated upon experimental investigation of the inner life, frequently with successful results. The question which is beginning to become important to German science is in principle of a different nature: it is the question how far the individual peculiarity of the living entity must be made the basis for interpreting every manifestation of life, and what means we possess for an intellectual penetration of individuality as such. It was our work which in 1910 gave a new direction to investigation; accordingly, in later editions of the German text, all parts which remained unchanged have been picked out by inverted commas. For the reasons just stated, these have been omitted in the English edition with few exceptions.

An author's book is always accompanied by his good wishes, whether expressed or not; and we would therefore express the hope that the reader will set it down to the novelty of point of view if he thinks that he meets difficulties in certain places. For criticism can be fruitful only when it is preceded by readiness and understanding.

August 1928

CONTENTS

CHAPTER I

The Science of Character as a postulate of every science of spirit. Failure of school science. False views of soul-"element" and soul-"datum". Experimental methods are fruitless. Former psychology a doctrine of intellectual processes. Why its excursion into characterology must fail. Antecedents of the characterological view. Particular significance of Nietzsche. Main characteristics of psychological mental attitude. Morphology of characters and its relation to physiognomology.

CHAPTER II

Threefold meaning of the word "character". Examples. Peculiarity of the most universal meaning. Definition of personality. Problem of discovery of alien character. Similarity as condition of unreflected understanding. Strangeness as condition of self-reflection. Importance of contact with men for development of self-knowledge. Polar differences. Self-knowledge the foundation of study of character. Principle of Participation. Vanity as source of self-deception. Life-envy can be discovered—Why does this not conflict with the principle of participation? Abstractive self-reflection.

CHAPTER III

The most general procedure of abstracting self-reflection. Main obstacles of self-understanding: too great proximity, trivial nature of experiences, emotional relation to these, need for self-esteem, too great distance. The action of the substrata indispensable, their work. Dividing and distinguishing are different. Characterology of the will. Personal energy. Personal ease of will. Personal will-capacity of feelings. Kinds of self-control. Life-envy. An investigation of names necessary. Definition a means of discovery in characterology. Pseudo-types. The method of taking literally.

Examples of soul-skilled wisdom of language. All relics of culture in principle capable of interpretation. Incalculable nature of human mutations.

CHAPTER IV

Talents as quantitative properties. Their totality the material of character. Driving forces or interests as properties of direction. Their totality the nature of character. Why every driving force is also a disposition of feeling, and conversely. Driving forces and inhibitive driving forces. Dispositions governing the course of emotions as properties of relations. Their totality as the structure of character. Indications relating to the structure of character and the properties of behaviour. Relation of driving forces to urges.

CHAPTER V

Distinction between memory and capacity for recollection: the former a vital and the latter a spiritual fact. Prelude to their schism—examples. Chief functions of vital memory, viz. recognition, habit of attitude, expectation of impression, acquired character of impressions, imagining. Recollection—how far is it remembering? Strength of memory and ease of capacity of remembering. Criteria of each. The process of impressing. Recollection of experience and of objects.

CHAPTER VI

Distinction between impression and act of apprehension. Participation in the latter of impression-memory and of judgment-memory. Personal receptivity for impressions. Personal fullness. The "Trace of Impression" as function of growth. Contrast of full and empty. Personal warmth of the material of intuition. Contrast of coldness and warmth. Personal motility of the material of intuition. Contrast of ease and difficulty. Degree of the action of apprehension. Vital and spiritual direction of apprehension. Dependence on Life, and on Spirit, of the manner of apprehension: the difference in Goethe's and Schiller's nature used to explain this. Application of the contrast to the sexes. Subjective and objective direction of apprehension. Importance of the feeling for actuality for the objectivity of apprehension. Greater objectivity of woman in estimating persons. Direction of apprehension turned upon persons and upon facts. The former more characteristic of woman, the latter of man, and why. Greater partiality of woman due to indifference to universal values. Concrete and abstract direction of apprehension. The former more characteristic of woman, the latter of man, and why. Close-focused and far-focused direction of apprehension: contrast between artistic and inartistic natures used to explain it. Glance at the intelligence of primitive races. Formalistic direction of apprehension. Its growing importance for the modern age. Connection with financial development. Parallelism between this and the development of mathematics. Essence of formalistic thought and criteria of formalistic talent. Impending retrogression of consciousness a consequence of formalism.

CHAPTER VII

Personal capacity for stimulation of feelings. It is distinct from particular capacities for excitement and from the strength of feelings. Examples of easy and difficult capacity for stimulation of feelings. The ambiguity of each. Formula. Personal capacity for stimulation of will. Comment on doctrine of four temperaments. Changes in meaning causing choleric and melancholy temperament no longer to correspond to the modern sense of temperament. Contrast between sanguine and phlegmatic temperament is one of degree and is based on the manner in which experiences run their course. Personal constant of temperament. Distinction between the side of impulse and of mood in feelings. Relation of event of willing to the former. Formula. Soul-resistance indispensable to the arising of striving. Flighty and inhibited striving. Types. Advantages and faults of extremes of temperament. Relation to manic-depressive insanity. Combination with opposites of the capacity for stimulation of feelings. Objections answered. Neutral actions and their importance for the discovery of capacity for stimulation of will. Temperamental differences between peoples and races. Personal capacity for expression. Formula. Evolutionary development of the fact of resistance to expression. Its importance for the development of specific talents. Relation to "spirits".

CHAPTER VIII

Capacity for expression and impulse for expression. Inhibition of expression accompanied by feeble impulse for expression, and its consequences. Origin of hysterical desire for representation. Hysteria. Introduction to doctrine of the reality of images. Impulses as the attractive force of images. Feelings, weak and strong, in image. Distinction between original man and animals, and between historical and original man. Growth of will at the expense of the image-creating capacity of Life. Hysterical suggestibility. Noticed and unnoticed attacks of imagination. Impotence of the formative force of the organism as formulative of Hysteria. Contribution to the history in Europe of the severance of images from impulses. Vampiric nature of spirit. Why the hysterical tendency towards representation aims at the production of symptoms of disease. The hysterical personality. Relation between caprice and Hysteria. Impulse after representation of Life the main driving force. Relation to the spectator. Explanation of Pseudologia phantastica.

CHAPTER IX

Fundamental concepts of psychology: Sensation, motor-impulse, intuition, formative impulse, act of apprehension, act of will. Independence of vital centre, dependence of the Ego. Details about sensation and intuition. Superiority of volition over cognition. Contradiction between feeling and will. Relation to the contrast between "heart" and "head". Ego passive in feeling and active in volition. Will essentially negative. Explanation of how it can nevertheless serve affirmative emotions. Difference between impulsive movement and action. Realization of goal effected by will the consequence of the exclusion of the living entity from the context of the world. Interpretation of the paradise-myth. Contrast of definite and indefinite fear. The former always fear of death in general, the latter (in animal) never definite fear of death. Man inhabited by the latter and by the consciousness of perishability. Cause: his Ego. Only a being having Ego is conscious of time. Urge after existence the immediate condition of every event of willing. Chief connections between act of will and act of apprehension explained. The thing a projection of the Ego. Derivation of chief principle of classification of all driving forces. Self-assertion and self-devotion. Three forms of subjection to Life. Dependence of volition on Spirit and on Life. Acts of self-devotion only rendered possible by the negation of negation. Examples. The contrast between assertion and devotion must be postulated already in feelings. Feeling as messenger between Ego and It. Ecstasy. Strivings of feelings arise from desire for ecstatic release of the Ego. Oscillating nature of all feelings. The spiritual world and its opposite. Dual nature of the soul-substances of man. Division into Spirit and Soul resumed. Personality as a specific mixture-relation between the two. Varying predominance of the two substances in the course of history. Spirit and the Ego. Ego asserts itself not only against Life, but also against the world of objects, the foreign Ego, and partial claims of itself. Why the personal Ego is a spiritual as well as a vital fact. Essential inharmoniousness of the personal Ego. Difference of psychical from sensuous devotion.

CHAPTER X

Development of the concepts of Release and Bond. Spiritual Bonds. Meaning of theoretic aesthetic and ethical reason. Dangers of the Ethical Bond. All ethical claims are claims of the will to power of Spirit. Proofs from Kant and Stirner. Meaning of self-assertion. Egoistic Bonds. Neutral and particular egoisms. Psychology of the rogue. The man of action. Relation of the moral man to him. The segregation of sex. The will to have and to excel.

The urge to collect. Passions as slavery. Meaning of every such slavery—Selfishness. Urge to count for something. Need of applause. Ambition as the male form of vanity. Feminine desire to please. Spontaneous passive and reactive egoism. Obstinacy as driving force for rehabilitation of the self. Sensitiveness, desire of revenge, envy, and jealousy. Isolated egoisms and their relation to lunacy. Unscrupulousness, severity. Releases of Spirit and Releases of Ego. Profound difference between the sexes. The forms of self-control and of lack of self-control. General difference between the side of Releases and the side of Bonds. Works as monuments.

TABLES

TRANSLATOR'S NOTE

Each of the English words shown below has been used to translate the German word set over against it. All the German terms are used by the author in a technical sense: in order to indicate this, their English equivalents have been written with a capital wherever it seemed that there was any risk of ambiguity.

Act of Will	Willensakt
Bond	Bindender Antrieb
Event of willing	Wollung
Impulse	Antrieb
Life	Leben
Memory	Gedächtnis
Nature	Artung
Passion	Sucht
Recollection	Erinnerung
Release	Lösender Antrieb
Spirit	Geist
Striving	Streben, Strebung
Urge	Trieb
Vital	(adjective corresponding to compounds of "Leben")
Volition	Wollen
Will	Wille.

PATHIC.—This word is used to translate *"pathisch"*, which describes that passive disposition of the soul by which the man in whom it exists is made susceptible to cosmic influences, while his spirit is stimulated to profound intuitions. The nouns "Pathos" and "Pathiker" (translated by *Pathos* and pathic type respectively) have similar denotations.

W. J.

THE SCIENCE OF CHARACTER

CHAPTER I

SCHOOL PSYCHOLOGY AND ITS RELATION TO CHARACTEROLOGY

The first chapter of this book has a significance in mental history; and further the school-methods applied to psychology which it criticizes still persist in wide circles even after the expiration of sixteen years: for these reasons we give what bears upon these points in much the same shape as before.

Suppose that it were asked of psychology what would be the minimum of knowledge to which it ought in fairness to offer a key; for example, what has been the nature of the change in mind since the classical period; the distinction between civilized and "natural" man; of what vital facts the ruling religions, the various castes and races are the index; what constitutes a statesman, a priest, a strategist, artist, or scientist; what are the laws which govern jealousy, greed, or selfishness; how to lay hold of his enduring characteristics behind the changing actions of man, and how to lay hold of true motives behind the mask of his politeness: suppose that these or similar questions were asked, then the inquirer would not only be disappointed by the tendency of our day, but must needs believe himself to be asking in the wrong quarter. For to his disappointment he would hear of sensations, perceptions, imaginations, judgments, Strivings, acts of will, feelings—in short, of the commonest characteristics of mental existence, or of the nature of our organs of sense (the admirable nature of whose physical structure is not disputed). He would be instructed how conclusions are drawn; how something is remembered; how concepts are formed; and his study of history, law, or religious consciousness, of the forms of mental sickness, or his interest in understanding practical life would be enriched but little more than would be the botanical studies of a lover of flowers who should be instructed that these are spatial bodies fixed in their places, capable of growth, requiring certain food, and dependent upon light.

We do not desire to combat modern psychology and its openings (some of which show promise): the more so, as we shall call upon its aid successfully more than once in the course of our argument. For reasons which will be touched upon later it is least of all what its etymology implies: a science of *soul*; still, we are fully aware of what it really has accomplished, and of the analytical training, hitherto perhaps without parallel, which it brought with it.[1] But the time has come to remember that the course upon which it has entered never leads beyond a somewhat restricted range of questions, that it is possible to treat its subject by other methods, and that it runs the risk of exposing itself dangerously if it persists in raising those foolish objections to a loftier conception of psychology, the commonest of which will be disposed of now.

Under the influence of the curious belief that its favourite concepts—that sensations, imaginations, feelings, and the like are the psychically simple, or data, atoms so to speak, of which the mind is properly composed, Psychology believes that it ought to reject as premature and unscientific any dealings with the questions of characterology. We do not now ask whether it was ever seriously hoped to solve the problem which lies, for example, in the name of Napoleon, by analysis of processes of thought and of the commonest estimations of value. The objection in any case is invalid. For nothing is less immediately "given" to observation than the fact, simple enough in the meaning of modern psychology, of the perception of *red*. A red ball a yard distant from my eyes appears different to a child and to an old man; to myself when rested and when tired; to instantaneous and to protracted observation; to a hungry and a full, to a merry and a sad man; it appears different under changing illumination, and if placed before a white, green, or red background; quite

2

apart from the feet that unconscious if not conscious comparison is required in order that the same or even a similar redness shall be recognized in a raspberry, the evening sky, red wine, blood, a brick, a tiger lily, and a coral. Redness, and even a redness more closely determined, is a structure of thought; it is extracted through the elaboration of contents of perception, but it is not itself content of perception; and whatever we might succeed in establishing with regard to the perception of red, it would never furnish us with a brick with which to build personality.

But even if it were a conceivable task to translate personality into the language of such universal concepts as must be developed in order to elucidate the processes of perception, this still would demand the closest acquaintance with personality. Once we possess this, we may perhaps be able to derive peculiarities of personal colour-perception, and to test experimentally the correctness of our conclusions; otherwise we look for them in vain from any theory of colour-perception, however perfect. The case is similar to that of cytology, for it is certain that most of the processes with which that science deals belong to categories which are proper partly to physics and partly to chemistry, but are much more complicated, from the standpoint of those sciences, than any chemisms known to us. Here, too, then, a warning might be made against the study of cells on the ground that chemistry is not yet sufficiently advanced in order to cover with its formulae all the phases of germ-formation, cell-division, etc. Fortunately man's search for knowledge has disregarded such out-of-date impediments: with the best results it has made the cell the centre of a science of its own, which now is even preparing a resurrection for the *vis vitalis*.

The concept of a cell can be defined as exactly and unambiguously as that of light, sound, heat, magnetism, chemical affinity, etc.; and it demands to be considered independently because it appears as the medium of those innumerable processes the totality of which we call life, and which we must know before we can undertake their interpretation in terms of physics.

A comparison of the cell with the Soul seems relevant in more than one regard. Like the cell, the Soul is the substratum of certain processes of the inner life, of which the modern analysis of the facts of consciousness reveals little more than would be revealed of the life of a cell by a consideration which should demonstrate in it the laws of physics and of chemistry. Naturally the concept of the cell, like that of character, is reached through abstraction. But it would appear inconsistent with natural thinking to use the vital processes merely to illustrate chemistry, and similarly it must cause surprise and even amazement that the "science of the Soul" does in fact do something quite similar, in neglecting all the qualities of character, and eliminating the nature of the substratum, and finally allowing validity only to those which remain as differential signs of mental existence. We ask with astonishment how it was possible, before making any attempt at the exploration of character, to proceed towards that maximum of abstraction which was so hostile to man's original interest in man. This remains to be explained later, and we now already remark that the unnatural direction of this development is the reason why today the science of psychology and the soul-skilled wisdom of all times and peoples are strangers to one another. But although the former direction may perhaps be justified, still the latter is closer to real life; a deeper need requires it and it admits of more unlimited progress. The dangers which threaten a scientific treatment of its material, as opposed to the objections which we have refuted, are due to the inclination to plant the ruling notions in the ground which is to be freshly ploughed. But here we touch upon, and negate, certain instructive excrescences of modern psychology.

The more it was believed that unanimity existed about the fundamental facts of consciousness, the more attention was paid to the differences which must in the nature of things subsist in the capacities of individual minds for imagination, apprehension, Striving, and the like. It was

4

hoped to effect a reversion of the process, and to construct a kind of individual psychology from permutations and combinations of the universal characteristics. But here it appeared, as was inevitable, that the crucial question was unknown, and that the means for solving it were lacking. First, it was overlooked that it is not the distinction in these processes (a distinction which generally is pretty unimportant) which is the goal of investigation, but the permanent disposition, which may be discovered through the distinction, but not through it alone.[2] A wrong track was reached, which led not to personality, but through a weary waste of its disjecta membra, scattered abroad (so to say) in the shape of degrees of sensitiveness, operations of association, comprehension, of observation, combination, judgment, and reactions—showing no law which might unite them, and still less the "spiritual bond".

At the same time the experimental method, whose validity in the mental sciences generally is open to doubt, was applied to the sphere of characterology, where it is entirely useless. The inevitable constraint even in neutral experiments for testing perception, judgment, and reaction may modify the mental disposition of the medium and invalidate the result; all security must vanish when it is no longer permissible to neglect the peculiarity of the object, since it is precisely this which is to be ascertained.[3] It must, moreover, be considered whether experiments can ever teach us what we ought to know first of all—whether a man is envious, covetous or devoted, whether faithful and true or capricious and flighty, whether of a happy disposition or gloomy, brave or cowardly, bold or timid—and what is the nature and operation of these and similar qualities.

The wrong formulation of the question produced a corresponding fiasco all along the line in the results—which we would pass over in silence, but that it seems more fitted than any other fact to reveal the traditional limitations of the modern handling of psychology. We select as example no obscure lesser light, but an authority rightly acknowledged by everyone. Kraepelin is a student who must not only be treated with great respect in his special field of psychopathology, but is also a master of the art of clinical classification. As fundamental qualities of personality he posits capacity for training, for stimulation, and for fatigue.[4] That is, the difference, for example, between Diocletian and Gregory VII must be reduced to differences in capacity for training, stimulation, and fatigue. Criticism is superfluous.

From this not only the fundamental strangeness to the facts of life of this kind of thought is obvious, but also its particular interest. The question here is, not the qualities of personality, but the inner causes of its effectiveness. And even effectiveness is not estimated in its totality, for then initiative, inventiveness, intuition, and what else borders on the sphere of creative impulses would have to be investigated: here the only quarry is, the conditions of power to work; as indeed is proper to an age which has long grown unaccustomed to the view of great individualities, and has replaced nobility of blood by the dubious honour of professional fitness. Man, as such, is no longer seen or known, but only an intellectual mechanism, the servant of an external purpose, and having for criterion a hypothetical "end".

This end was unknown to other ages. A Renaissance busied with psychology might perhaps have considered man's faculty of action as worthy of investigation; a mediaeval period, the strength of his faith, a classical period—in part at least—his capacity for happiness. Such traits have lost their value for the modern psychologist; they are not even regarded at all, and industry has remained as the only virtue with its satellites, ambition and success—a complex, that is, which the Ancients would never have hesitated to relegate to the lowest of men, to pariahs and to slaves.

Others may applaud an advance to sober poverty: this is certain, that science should remain neutral, and turn a deaf ear to the suggestions of an ochlocratic idealism. But instead, it is completely hypnotized by the latter's standards of value, and the practical nature of its apparatus is completely in harmony with tendencious partiality in the impulses which point the way. But this does not apply to psychology alone, but to all the philosophy of the last centuries, in so far as it is attached to names traditionally famous. The development briefly was this.

After the Reformation had undermined mediaeval piety, morality appeared as the true kernel of Christianity, and now appears stronger than any idolatrous form of superstition. From it not only all systems since the beginning of the modern period received a moral tincture—atheism most of all; but also it governed the exploration of the facts of natural and mental sciences, which to this day denies neither in method nor in results its origin from the Christian dogma of the kingdom of God. But spirituality without metaphysics becomes a faith in reason and finds itself referred, both in truth and in error, to the two foci of logic and utility— otherwise also called "the good".

We do not, of course, here follow the development of rationalism, or the belief in the essential rationality of the world-process; which would mean to write the history of spirit from a wholly novel point of view; we only mention what is essential for an understanding of the development of psychology. After the first assault of mechanistic thought, which naturally was directed upon the universe, and won those great conquests of physics (Copernicus, Galileo, Keppler, Huyghens, Newton) which the nineteenth century could do no more than perfect, there followed a self-reflection of the organ of thought, mediated by the question of the range of the use of understanding and the reasons for the inviolability of its results. The self-analysis of reasonableness, which sometimes took a speculative and dogmatic, and sometimes a purely analytic turn, was given the somewhat too narrow name of "critique of cognition"; and, since Kant, no small credit was taken for a renunciation of metaphysical desires. Now modern psychology in all its modifications is a particular form of this critique of cognition. Its object is not man, but rational man, i.e. a being which can think logically and act in a utilitarian manner; and the mainspring of its investigation is not an interest in life—

which is the intent of psychology—but in the capacity for thinking and willing—which is that of logic.

But in view of the singleness of its fundamental aim, it is of little importance whether it finally masters its tasks with or without "soul", whether it attributes great or little importance to the grey cerebral cortex, and whether it clings to experiment or devotes itself to the art of definitions. Among the unpleasant results we shall always find an amazing ignorance of the urges and passions which, as "lower", are hardly considered worthy of notice; helplessness in the face of the unconscious, or the psychical substratum even of reasonable actions, of which for years we learned nothing save the vague "Laws of Association"; uncritical acceptance of moral judgments, which at the least encourages a superficial classification; a foolish misinterpretation of every non-social human type as a differential form of unnatural "sport"; and complete failure before the problem of individuality or inner multiplicity of times, peoples, castes, strata of culture, and of everyday life. In parts it commands respect for its achievement in its critique of cognition and its masterly analysis of the processes of apprehension, but it appears as the sickly offspring of average common sense when it is taken as what it professes to be—a science of the inner life. The entire achievements of the so-called science in this respect is outweighed by a single page of Goethe's or of Jean Paul's psychology; and it is impossible to evade the bitter truth which Novalis already has summed up, when he says that so-called psychology is one of those idols which have usurped that place in the sanctuary where true images of the gods should stand.

But even today the "inner life" is somewhat deeper than it appears in the mirror of psychology, and consequently gives individual impulses to the investigating mind which lie beyond its general considerations: in reality, therefore, it has not achieved the first thing which might rightly have been asked of it: to lay a critical foundation of the "sciences of the spirit". Philology, the science of history, the study of peoples, psychiatry, and practical knowledge of mankind alike looked to it for help in vain—as was shown at the beginning; and therefore in time a new treatment of the material must come to the front which, while retaining the more exact knowledge of the processes of cognition, makes it its task to understand the whole wealth of forms of the life of the soul.

But such a treatment lacks neither precedent nor yet a certain tradition, even if we neglect the sages of all times and peoples who never practised psychology in the sense of intellectualism. The impulse of psychological investigation is most active in that epoch of German spiritual life which is called the *romantic*, whose later period contains the name of the physician and thinker Carl Gustav Carus. It suffices to mention this name, which, though not the greatest, yet denotes a man in whose nature the roaming element of those days found prudent caution enough to allow it to condense into a doctrine which still awaits elaboration and extension, instead of exhausting itself into prophetic imaginings. But he, and similar essays of contemporary minds, together with many fruitful germs of the thirties and forties, were swept away by the course of development, so that now the chain must be linked afresh and across a gap of time.

But all this could not be done with so sure an eye for every elective affinity without the mighty achievement of that man of the most recent past whose coming, even if it allows no new hope, still crowns with a proud lustre the decay of ageing peoples—the achievement of Friedrich Nietzsche. Reasons, the analysis of which would here lead us too far, cause the ardour of metaphysical intuition to feed in him almost exclusively the stream of criticism, giving it a piercing quality never reached before. The instrument of his prophetic power is the gift, armed with the arrows of acutest understanding, of "discrimination of spirits". For the first time since the Middle Ages at latest, and in the more familiar forms of the most immediate present, he furnishes us with an example of that millennial flower, the great piercer of souls and knower of spirits, who, unlike the poets, does not bury under flowery meadows of fanciful sentiment the outlines of fire-born truths. It would require a separate section, if justice were to be done to his significance for a possible future psychology.[5] Here we merely state a fundamental fact, and now pass over to the next chapter by designating the essentially psychological attitude by that symptom which emerges most clearly especially with Nietzsche.

The real scope of his philosophy is the devaluation not only of ethics but, further, of intellect, of which, for the first time in the known "history of the world", paradoxically enough, the disposition, that is, in this case, the biological value, is scrutinized, without prejudice or favour, by the eye of spiritual hostility. "That it is false is no objection to a judgment"—a proposition the consequence of which may be followed in its more positive counterpart—correctness alone does not make a judgment valid, truth is no value in itself. Even the organ of thought, whose mainsprings are reasons and causes, proves to be conditioned by its urges, and its criteria are subjective. It is possible to side for or against logic, and (this is Nietzsche's most important application) the latter is done when we take the side of Life which is unspiritual and non-logical. Life and Spirit are distinct, and as Nietzsche apprehends it, Spirit is a diseased form of Life.

It is possible to take a further step, and this will be done in the chapter which deals with the Metaphysics of the distinctions of personality: and, although the shattered autonomy will be restored, this will be done only to widen the gap until it becomes the fundamental dualism (which appears as a necessity of thought) between Life (element, Soul) and Spirit. In fact Nietzsche continually makes use of this, although he still takes Spirit as a by-product and tries to treat it too anthropocentrally—as derailment and *lusus naturae*. Before him there was no student of the Soul whose analysis, however subtle, did not end with a new "rehabilitation" of man; for example, even the methodical scepticism of Stirner has for its ultimate pole an ideal of personality which (although alien to most) might be described as the "domination of consciousness of uniqueness". Nietzsche, on the other hand, takes up his position outside man or, in the most literal manner, "beyond good and evil" as is evidently fitting in one who makes man the object of his study. In this way alone he was able to reveal the envy of life ("ressentiment") at the roots of every moral judgment and to lay bare the atrophy of instinct which, in the disguise of numerous "ideals", distorts the view of man— especially of modern man—when he looks upon the world.

We must stand opposed to ("gegenüberstehen") that which we would understand; this is a necessary condition of all cognition, as the name of object ("Gegestand") irrefutably proves. We remain within the metaphor (which in fact is more than metaphor) if we add that the survey is hindered if the object is too close and that philosophy rather demands a "distance", however little we may like a name which since the time of Nietzsche has become a favourite with writers. For proximity fixes the eye upon one point and isolates the object of this contemplation at short range; it leads inevitably to that atomism of thought which was exemplified by the school-science; whereas distance, as it widens the horizon, demands, so to say, a roving eye, which opposes to the belief in the isolated entities of the object the totality of an image.

We emphasize the meaning of the word "intuition" as a kind of cognition which is cognate to contemplation; then follows next the "world-view", which has now become somewhat rarer. The image, or vision, alone rises to the acid test of attention, and compels the spirit with an irresistible force of conviction. But distance causes the incomplete actuality of objects which have merely been "focused" to plunge back into a totality of contemplation; consciousness, whose eye merely *distinguishes* in the light of common day, borrows from it something of the *synthetic* foresight of the prophetic eye. The profundity of truth varies with the seeing power of the spirit which seeks it.

Now the study of the Soul concerns itself with facts which in themselves are non-sensuous; the individual finds within himself the material needed in order to interpret them. Consequently the Spirit must be able to achieve a relation of exteriority in order that it may experience the personality of which it is a part; it must in a sense dehumanize itself in order precisely to look upon this human quality; and it must even have the skill to remove itself so far from it that the individual traits of the inner life coalesce into an image for it, whence it may read partial characteristics as the corporeal eye reads the position of a particular place on the finished map. But images, whether they be dreamed or perceived, are spatial-temporal actualities. Consequently we state the facts more exactly in saying conversely that a gift for studying the Soul rests essentially upon a capacity for seeing in the phenomenal world its meaning. But to see its "meaning" in it means just to see the phenomenon symbolically. And indeed it is an implicit trait of the πάθος φιλόσοφον, which it shares with that of the artist and the poet, that, following an irresistible compulsion, it apprehends things symbolically: herein (in spite of the enormous difference) it resembles the spiritual disposition of the "savage".

Now it is not only the fascinating, but also the essentially true element in Nietzsche's mental attitude, that he thus sees individual persons as entire peoples, cultures, and epochs according to the analogy of pictures. For example, he speaks of the "nordic gloom" of "haunting thought and thin blood", he calls the southern soul "an abundant fullness of sun and irradiation of sun" and discovers "clumsiness and peasant gravity" in the Englishman: in short, he uses convincing traits of its sensuous appearance to stamp each character, or rather he finds in the visible world the key of the invisible, and draws from the actuality of the symbol its conceptual element.

Formulated as a principle, this means that we must have the whole before we can successfully undertake to study the parts. It is possible, of course, to analyse the former into the latter, but to compose the former out of the latter is impossible, unless the idea which is to guide in the process of composition has already been extracted from the whole.

New and fruitful thoughts always arise at some point of that profoundest dividing line of the spirit where the symbolism of phenomena ends, and they begin to be symptoms. The romantic philosophy is wholly dominated by the symbol—by the fact, if not by the concept. The world is taken as a vast symbolic language, which must be deciphered by speculative absorption; we do not observe facts, but look on their face and ask what vital pulse, what secret constructive impulse, or what evolution of the soul seems to speak in these lines. The doctrines of the growth of plants or of crystals or of cosmic movements are treated as a kind of physiognomology of the universe; and conversely Carus characteristically enough gives the name of "Symbolism of the Human form" to the physiognomy of man in the title of his chief work on that subject.

This leads us to revert to the importance of the image as a starting point for the study of the Soul. In the sense which has been laid down by us, this must primarily be a morphology or doctrine of the forms of the Soul's anatomy. But forms in the proper sense are external forms, and no science of the inner life could afford to renounce to be guided by its sensuous manifestations without risking to lapse into amateurishness. We consider the psychological manner of contemplation as not only cognate to the physiognomical, but as fundamentally identical with it. The new intuition, whether reached by the most circumspect thought or by lightning illumination, always has its source in an extension of an understanding of the symbolism of the external world or in the progress in spiritual assimilation of physiognomies hitherto alien. However, we have thus given a shape to the contrast between our own and the traditional point of view which, detached from its place in the logical sequence, would appear as capricious paradox. We therefore meet an impending misunderstanding, and end by throwing light upon this formula (which in truth must be taken literally) from another side.

An especial effort on the part of modern students was needed in order to master the heresy that a knowledge of the inner life is increased by investigation of the nervous system. No more than twenty years ago it was seriously believed that a study of the anatomy of the brain afforded instruction in psychical processes. In proportion as this un-philosophic hope vanished, "pure" psychology grew up by the side of "physiological" psychology, and the provisional thesis of the psychophysical parallelism established itself. Our demand that the psychical is to be construed out of its phenomenal form might therefore be misinterpreted as constituting a relapse into a direction to which in fact "pure" psychology stands much closer. For it is not of essential importance that we shall discuss extra-sensual facts in a preponderantly physical, or, on the other hand, in a preponderantly psychological language: the only question is whether such concepts have, or have not, their origin in a view of the totality of the organism. Ganglia, nerves, the convolutions of the brain and the like are, within the body, only disjecta membra, so to speak, as, in the sphere of the inner life, are perceptions, imaginations, processes of sensation, and so on. In "intuition" must of course necessarily be one of the body; but the symbolism of the body is so far from coinciding with any concepts of the anatomy of the brain that the latter must be completely forgotten if we would reach the former. The Soul does not reside in the brain, but in the form, and, if a paradox be permitted, we would recommend in place of a study of man's nerves, a study of his superficies. We end with a sentence of Novalis, who anticipated the truth here as he so frequently did elsewhere: "The seat of the soul is at the point of contact of the inner and the outer world."

CHAPTER I NOTES

[1] In this connection the name of Theodor Lipps must be recalled. Quite undeservedly he is beginning to be forgotten, and in fact it is not easy to do justice to this student. Of the results which he reached, hardly anything remains, apart from some discoveries about the observation of space and the psychology of Metrics. He had a predominant tendency to take actuality as the manifestation of a world-Ego—a tendency which bears the imprint of the liberalism of the sixties, and so restricts his vision that one is tempted to say that it is bounded by his desk. But within a horizon which, so to speak, is spaceless, he has an eye of microscopic power, and this eye actually is turned inwards. If the *Psychology* of Wundt, with all his reading, is compared with any one of Lipps' works, it will be clear after a few sentences that the latter practised genuine psychology, even if it was no more than the analysis of contents of consciousness, while the former practised everything under the sun, but never psychology. (To put it somewhat forcibly, Wundt's psychology consists in the fact that he uses the adjective "psychological" half a dozen times on every page.) In short, although his *Weltanschauung* has already been forgotten, Lipps alone (so far as we can see) among the popular professors of the last generation was enabled by his method (at least attempted) of self-examination to anticipate and prepare a way for the study of Appearance, which now has once again become practicable. In order, however, to give a name to his merits in this connection, we would recall that it was he who, with an accuracy hitherto unattained, taught how to distinguish the connection of facts of consciousness to which self-reflection bears witness and, again, their demonstrable dependence upon the peculiar characteristics of the conscious entity, from that causality by whose aid we make calculable the sequence of processes in the world of things; and that he, at any rate, prepared the explanation of the assumption of causality by applying to extra-spiritual actuality a certain manner of experiencing, namely, that of the activity of will which causes action. Compare his work *Bewusstsein und Gegenstände.*

[2]   The new branch was even given the learned name of "differential psychology", which is evidently as reasonable as to call cytology a differential chemistry, or optics, acoustics, and thermics, differential mechanics.

[3]   In fact it is rather funny when, for example, French investigators meticulously avoid the traditional nomenclature and make the grand discovery, based on descriptions by pupils of pictures shown to them, that there are some four types of apprehension: type *déscripteur, observateur, émotionnel, érudit.*

[4]   *Psych.,* Arb. I. More exactly, the following categories: capacity for performance, for practice, for retention of what is practised, special memory, capacity for stimulus, for fatigue, for recovery, depth of sleep, capacity for distraction and for habituation.

5   It would rather require a book, which we have written since: *Die psychologischen Errungenschaften Nietzsches*, Barth, Leipzig.

CHAPTER II

CONDITIONS GOVERNING THE DISCOVERY OF CHARACTER

Any definition of the limits of characterology must depend upon a definition of character: a word which has at least three meanings, only one of which, however, is suitable for scientific use. Its narrowest meaning is employed (for example) by Goethe in the often quoted lines:

> A talent forms itself in quietness
> A character, in the stream of the world;

and this is always intended when an express distinction is made between intellectual and artistic qualities, qualities relating to talent generally (and especially to the so-called genius of a man), as against that "character" which has "strong" and "weak", or again "good" and "bad" for predicates. The first of these contrasted pairs clearly points to will, the second to the moral value of motives. Here "character" is equivalent to "moral will", whence it is quite consistent to denote the completest want of moral strength by "lack of character".

But the use of the word in a wider sense, so as to mean not one side of personality but personality itself (and in this way alone we have to consider it), is not inconsistent with current usage. Personality in general, for example, is referred to in the contrast between "differentiated" and "undifferentiated", or especially in the popular contrast between "normal" and "abnormal" characters, which, although primarily it may apply to the life of urges, yet in very numerous cases serves also to distinguish (for example) intelligences. In this use of the word, character thus coincides with personality, a name of which here the definition is only partial and will be completed after a discussion of the widest meaning of the word "character".

Personality is the abstract which is complementary to the concrete term of "person", and in so far it certainly has the characteristic of unity. The Christian dogma of the triune nature of God would not have met the lively opposition which it often did meet had it not at the same time demanded that God be thought of as person. When this unity vanishes temporarily (as in hysteria, somnambulism, and so on) it is suitable to speak of a "division of personality". This unity then is not a unity of the body, but a unity of its livingness; at this point then we define personality as vital unity or individual. But sometimes even a thing may fall for us within this definition, and thus we reach the third meaning of "character".

The expression that two people agree like cat and dog presupposes an incompatibility in the character of two beings to whom nobody would attribute "personality". We also speak of the character of a people—of a thing, that is, which consists of many persons. Further, nothing prevents us from speaking, even of the character of the dialect of this people, or of the character of a building, a landscape, or of an event like a tempest, storm, or revolution, or finally of such abstract concepts as number, line, unity, geometry, or monarchal constitution. If it were contended that character here is simply equivalent to property, it might be objected that all properties, for example of the desert (for instance, extension), do not by any means belong to its character, and that in order to characterize a thing some of its distinctive qualities are preferred to others. Finally, if such a phrase as "the character of the desert" is compared with "the nature of the desert", it will be felt that the former has a certain poetic tincture, since it attributes to the desert an inner life, as though it were an individual.

The fact that we can speak of the personality, even of inanimate things, reveals a part of the history of our past. Originally every object of apprehension was taken as containing a soul: the reason of this was the immediacy of experience, which even now acts powerfully in the child and struggles to make itself heard even in the man as soon as the criticism of the intellect grows tired. Originally every apprehension is the seizing of living unities, and the separation of the world into a dead and a living half is the result of later experience which, in detail, never comes to an end. Language has preserved this epoch of our past when it describes innumerable events of the extra-human world of perception, and even static facts, as though they were vital processes and activities: not only does the rain "lash" the tree, but the path actually "runs" across the meadow, and the house "casts" a shadow. We shall revert to this below. Here the fact that the "character of objects" survives unimpaired in language is to prepare us to realize that the "Soul" cannot possibly be identical with the foundation of consciousness in thinking man. The assertion that the stone has a soul would certainly meet with sympathetic understanding if not with belief, and it is equally certain that nobody would admit even a poetic justification for reference to the *personality* of a flint, plant, or cloud. Therefore, something must be added to the living entity in order that personality shall result.

This we discover by comparing man with the next kindred form of life, the animal. We do not doubt that the animal has sensations, feelings, and perceptions that (at least instinctively) it imagines, judges, and forms conclusions, that it has feelings, passions and impulses, that it dreams and recognizes: but we doubt, and must doubt, that it has consciousness of itself. In the animal too (since it is a crystallization of more universal life) life is an assimilative process, and consequently leads on and on to preserve the body which it inhabits, and which finally must nevertheless perish. But among all the actions which animal instinct executes in order to preserve, continue, and defend life, there is not one which could force us to assume that, like us, it is aware of its own mortality. If an urge of self-preservation is posited, this represents an application of the specifically human feeling of existence to other—and particularly to animal—life, an application which is not so much poetical as logically quite inadmissible. The plant too "preserves" its form; and yet in respect to a plant we must doubt whether it has anything akin even to our sensations.

Personality is not only vital unity, but also an ego: more briefly, it is the individual self, and characterology is the science which treats of it. Thus we find two elements clearly distinct already in the process of defining our subject, and upon these we rely later in order to develop methodically the system of Driving Forces. One element is the foundation of the *universal* normality, according to which life-processes coagulate into thought-things independently of personality. The other (which is creative) provides the material for its exclusively "regulative" activity, and this element we follow immemorial usage to call *Soul*: here the personal Ego (= individual self) resembles a chemical combination having for elements the universal spirit and an eternally particular soul.

We conclude these considerations with regard to the definition of personality by pointing to a fact which has an approved convincing force, namely, that with reference to this concept the name itself already indicates the duality of the terms which constitute its meaning. "Person" is the Latin "persona", which is derived from "personare" = "to sound through", and originally denotes the mask through which the ancient actor speaks, then the part he has to play, and finally "character" or "personality". Thus the Latin name for the tragic mask has taken root as standing designation for the essence of man; the mask which begins to live only when the actor's voice sounds through it. We do not ask here in how far this peculiar duality affords a useful hint even to the metaphysics of the duplicity in question, and are content to record that the original etymology in fact uses "person" to denote something two-fold: a face which is lifeless in itself, and a voice which sounds through it, which in original drama is the voice of a god.[6]

It follows that the first task of characterology must consist in the completest possible characterization of the individual selves: the question then next arises how this knowledge is to be achieved. This question again resolves itself into two: how the individual self enters into appearance in the external world, and how we investigate it in and for itself, that is, neglecting, or, rather, presupposing, its appearance. The answer to this question is the main object of physiognomology in the narrower sense: the best cultivated regions of this science we have elsewhere surveyed so thoroughly that a short reference may here suffice.[7]

Apart from the forms of the organs, whose meaning, though undemonstrable so far, may be understood by a prophetic feeling, the inner life manifests itself in the movements of the living entity, and in their permanent traces. Apart from the almost wholly internal function of the lungs, heart, and intestine, and the purely reflex functions of sneezing, coughing, and blinking, many of these indicate a will and all a psychic process: all therefore are expressive. Expression as such serves to discover personality, and so-called action, which is a partial component of it, limited by purposes, aids us in substantiating our judgment. How we set about to recognize in certain movements definite mental dispositions, or, again, definite processes of willing, is an important question on which the reader may instruct himself in the work just cited. Now we are concerned with a fundamental condition which precedes such discoveries, which promises to lead us to the discussion of a second question—how character may be investigated by the help of its symptoms and precipitates.

We perceive no living man without also perceiving *that* he is a living man, which means that we do not only perceive a body in movement, but in and simultaneously with it something alive: and we do not only perceive something alive, but, in addition, something alive in a personal manner. We repeat that at first any given object is apprehended analogously to a living entity, or even to a living person. A child says, and, further, means, that the knife bites, and, without judging, judges about this imagined biting in a manner not essentially different from that in which it judges about the biting of which it is capable itself. And if it knocks itself against the table, it hits the table in essentially the same way in which it would hit a companion from whom in reality it had taken a hit or push. But a grown-up, as having *outgrown* such a state of consciousness, by no means experiences a biting dog like a cutting knife or a biting person like a biting dog; and experiences the water flowing from the tap in the kitchen as living at most metaphorically, but not with a serious belief, although it is in restless movement. He has learned internal differentiation and accordingly he does not find *himself* in a jumping or running dog, still less in plants, and not at all in atmospheric phenomena or in tools.

Thus the world of perception originally is like a mirror which reflects for man his image a thousand-fold, and we must be on our guard all the more not to enter the blind alley of the so-called projection theory. What in fact we project *into* a phenomenon serves only to deceive, and only that which we correctly extract *out of* it serves cognition. A lover returning from a happy meeting finds all the people he meets happier and more lovely than commonly: he has projected into them his own happiness and perfection, and has deceived himself just to this extent about their real mental disposition. Rightly considered, the phenomenon of "mirroring" shows us something quite different. Essential cognition, or, more briefly, understanding, is possible only by virtue of *some* similarity between the perceiving self and the perceived object; and as dissimilarity grows, understanding gives way to a failure to understand, which at first is only felt but later is known—except in so far as by virtue of mere projection the gap is filled by misunderstanding. Hence we cannot be immediately certain when the "savage" adores stones, trees, and animals that, instead of having projected something non-existent, he does not rather manifest a deeper understanding than ours. For it may be that his vitality is more vegetable in proportion as he has less personality than we, and in that case his judgment, or rather attitudes, would have sprung from greater similarity or closer kinship, and this would have expressed something about the essence of stones, trees, and animals—albeit in mythical language—to which we later men have no road of approach, because we have become strangers to it. Be this as it may, we proceed to convince ourselves in greater detail of the decrease of immediate understanding with the decrease of similarities.

Long before it can speak a little child responds readily to an amiable smile or tender whisper, and responds with fright to the voice of scolding, and, later, to the mere face of anger; but it has to *learn* that a dog by wagging its tail denotes friendliness, and by putting its tail between its legs, fear. In us grown-ups, such manifestations of the moods of our domestic animals have, through repeated experience, become so familiar that we imagine that we perceive them as immediately as those of man: but if we carefully examine ourselves we must admit that without special previous experience we would not know (and partly do not know at all) what mood is expressed in the neighing of a horse, the bleating of a sheep, the roaring of a stag, the screaming of a monkey, the rattling of a porcupine, the clapping of a stork, the shrilling of a cicada, the croaking of a frog, or the humming of a bee. Without previous instruction it is impossible even to guess that with horses, dogs, cats, beasts of prey, and monkeys, the action of laying flat the ears against the head denotes savage readiness to attack—and many town-dwellers do not know it even when grown up. Once we are convinced of this from broad examples, we shall not overlook it in more refined. The face of a Mongolian or Japanese tells us less than that of a European, our countrymen are more familiar to us than members of a foreign people, and we are best capable of understanding our equals.

We must remain a little longer at the stage of unreflecting awareness, but we may remark in advance on one circumstance which confirms what has just been recited with regard to the lowest stage of reflection. Everybody assumes at first those motives in another which would guide himself in the same case, and thus *has* already presupposed the peculiarities of his own character in that of the other. A malicious and selfish man is distrustful and suspicious, because he considers his fellows, too, to be malicious and selfish; a liberal and good-natured man inclines towards confidence, because he attributes the same good nature to his fellows. If, then, we resume what has been hitherto discussed in the judgment: "Our own nature gives us the material for understanding foreign natures", then we easily observe that this cannot possibly comprehend all the conditions of a faculty for understanding. In everyday life everybody takes into consideration those peculiarities of others which precisely are not his own; a lazy man the industry of the energetic, an insolent man the patience of the long-suffering, a cunning man the simplicity of the honest; and one who eminently knows mankind has the skill to use for his ends the most diverse characters. Thus, obviously, differences form no barrier to an apprehension which hits the mark at least instinctively, and we are even forced to ask how and in what way this is compatible with our previous result. We are here forced to insert a more general observation.

That which we call the world, and, on more advanced reflection the outer world, could never be experienced, still less known, as that which it is without its alien character; and if Goethe truly declares

> The eye could never see the sun
> Were it not of sunlike nature,

it is no less valid that seeing and shining are as certainly and as fundamentally separate as it is that they must in spite of this be cognate. Accordingly, when we said that originally man rediscovers himself in the external world, this means more exactly that he finds, by means of self-mirroring, the significance of the content of an image of intuition, alien to himself, and therefore (for example) immediately numerically different from him. We immediately take a further step, however much it may appear to take us away from our goal. The saying which tradition has handed down from ancient times, that astonishment is the beginning of all philosophy, announces with epigrammatic brevity the indisputable truth

24

that it is precisely the unexpected (that which is dissimilar to the content of an expectation) which is pre-eminently fitted to stimulate reflection and perhaps prepare it for discoveries; and the whole history of thought is there for proof. Especially a fresh understanding of the nature of an alien character is invariably due to the fact that some animal or man did on some occasion behave in an essentially different manner from that which would have corresponded to our instinctive assumption.

If we transpose into judgments that which has in fact taken place many times unconsciously before it finally becomes conscious, and if we select a definite example, then the process appears as follows. On coming into a room I remark jokingly to a person of my acquaintance that it is in a state of perfectly heroic disorder, and observe in him, to my great surprise, every sign of injury. (We will assume that the facts are clear beyond dispute, and that there is no danger that my remark may have revived an unknown event in the life of the other person.) I mentally put myself in the place of the other, and it suddenly is borne upon me that, if I were very proud of my methodical nature and considered orderliness my prime duty (which is far from being the case with me), then there might be one reason at least why I might be quite annoyed if I were found guilty of lack of order. The manner of realizing a conclusion which has here been analysed takes place like a flash, and even its result need not necessarily take the form of a judgment. It has taken place, even when the new discovery manifests itself merely in a change in my manner.

It would be a task equally difficult and stimulating, but also one which would lead us too far from our subject, if we were to look for those aptitudes which guarantee a knowledge of mankind proportionate to the degree in which they exist; we may only remark this in passing that it is not the simple but the complex frame of mind, not the amiably assenting but the critically negating, and especially not the harmonious but the dual, which in this respect produces greater gifts and promises greatest results. Men of action, and not contemplative minds, have ever excelled in masterly exhibitions of knowledge of man; and the soul-reading wisdom of Shakespeare, Goethe, Jean Paul, Stendhal, or Nietzsche cannot be compared for unreflecting acumen with the readiness of Cromwell, Richelieu, Frederick, Napoleon, or Bismarck. Knowledge of man and study of character are two distinct spheres, having but a small region in common, and lying quite apart for the rest. Knowledge of man does not imply, though it does not exclude, the passing of judgment about men: but when this is done it occurs as each case arises and with reference to the given individual person who passes through the practical field of vision, and it remains indifferent whether and to what extent universal laws may be extracted from such judgments. Conversely the student of character pays very little regard to the individual persons of his environment, and the results which he reaches are never due to a practical need, but exclusively to the peculiar direction of his search after knowledge: the goal is, definitely, to reach universal propositions, which we shall discuss later at length. But we now return to the problem of the discovery of the essential character.

Elsewhere we have distinguished between two kinds of reflection, namely, reflection upon the alien and upon self, and we have proved that the former precedes the latter all along the line.[8] What has so far been adduced about the nature of man lies within the sphere of reflection on the alien. I refer myself to something distinct from myself, whether I speak of the fading of the fear or judge that somebody is of suspicious nature. The apprehension of things necessarily precedes that of my own existence, and the apprehension of alien characteristics that of my own traits; and a masterly knowledge may be acquired in the sphere of things as well as that of beings without any considerable admixture of self-reflection. But if, from real or imaginary acquaintance with the suspicious disposition of another I find myself drawn to inquire what suspicion really is, with what other characteristics it may be connected, then, apart from my skilled knowledge, I should have entered into

26

the sphere of the study of character, and henceforward shall advance only by virtue of self-reflection. Before, my material had come to me by virtue of unconscious transposition into my object: now I try to bring it into consciousness, and it appears that the material of my own nature is sufficient to construct innumerable characters largely and even completely different from my own. To revert to our previous example: the immediate discovery of a methodical nature as the basis of a sense of honour is now the starting point for a profounder process of thought which tries to penetrate to the general grounds which make possible such a mental disposition: thus I am now no longer engaged in putting myself in another place, but in abstractive self-reflection. The reflected discovery of essential character, and consequently the whole science of character, is based upon this, and therefore we must now examine its most general condition, and, in the next chapter, its methodical aids.

If knowledge of self is acquired exclusively through knowledge of others, then in order to develop it requires that its subject shall come into contact with others, and then self-knowledge does in fact coincide almost exactly with the presuppositions of knowledge of men. A contemplative absorption in the landscape does not serve at all, and a struggle with nature serves only to produce partial reflection: solitude will be the echo of our fullness or emptiness, but, for the rest, will be silent about our qualities. If we resign commerce with mankind, we may become mystics, pedants, or hairsplitting metaphysicians, but not masters of characterology; and the danger of self-deception becomes enormous. The famous *tat tvam asi* does perhaps strike some prophetic chord; but only weary men's love of solitude could help to spread a saying whose delusive profundity hides the fact that the world is immeasurably greater, richer, and more manifold than that part of it which fits into one poor formula. Qualities which are to enter into our consciousness must have been exercised; and the most important are exercised only among men. A man may have greater capacity for jealousy than most, and may never know it until the day when he falls violently in love. Many town-men overestimate their physical courage, because town life rarely gives occasion for a serious test of courage. Goethe is never tired of insisting that only the "active" man learns to know his strength and weakness.

But, while he who knows men immediately sets his aim at the other person, is constantly in need of fresh experience, and tends towards width, the reflection of the student leads into the depth, for he can hope to master the multiplicity of his impulses only by exploring himself. With him, too, numerical quantity serves to demonstrate: but he receives the impulse towards discoveries from some few individuals, or, in fortunate circumstances from one single personality with whose genius he has to strive hard and long for his own world-picture: and if he carries it through to the end he gains knowledge of the scope and limits of his own nature. This may lead us on to show up an even more important condition, which, though it too is universal, emerges only at the stage of reflection, and allows us finally to resolve the apparent antinomy which we struck above.

If it is certain that apprehension of any character would be impossible without some degree of understanding, it is equally certain that the grounds of understanding must be distinguished from those which change an instinctive grasp into conscious cognition. There are many conditions which we thought it necessary to assume on principle in order to explain the possibility of that automatic procedure of putting oneself into a place with which the instinctive grasp operates: among these conditions there is one group which may fittingly be considered from the point of view of a peculiar kind of contrariness, that of polar similarities or, more briefly, polarities. The preliminary question, why a desire is experienced immediately, and, probably, justly to apply the notion of polarity to such different cases as positive and negative magnetism, right and left, and man and woman, is probably answered sufficiently by reference to three points of congruence. Poles are similar: the positive end of the magnet is more similar to the negative than either is to the un-magnetic bar; the appearance of the right half of the body is normally more similar to that of the left than the appearance of the whole body is to that of another member of the genus; and the mature man to the mature woman than either is to the infant. Within the range of their similarity poles are opposite to one another; this needs no further explanation. Poles cannot exist independently, but each only in connection with its opposite.

It is true that the third characteristic, which is called the complementary principle, seems (in the case of man and woman) to conflict with the corporal independence of both: and it is certain that this separation of two sexual organs which, strictly, are not polar, but opposed in some other manner in two living subjects which are numerically distinct, corresponds to differences in character which cannot be exhausted from the point of view of polarities. But if in spite of this we cling to a true polarity of the sexes (to be found perhaps in its corporal aspect in the nature of the blood), then this would mean that every man contained not only the male but the female pole (only normally with a lesser development) and every woman, besides the female pole, also the male (only, again, less developed). Thus contrariness (a contrariness of emphasis, so to speak) would include similarity by virtue of participation, and thus would admit the possibility of an understanding. If we add that this *must* be the case, in so far as there can be any understanding between man and woman, then we have shown in a fundamental example why the condition of understanding (similarity) is compatible with polar contrariness, and how far the latter is at any rate no obstacle to the act of putting oneself into another place. And we may state the more general principle, that a difference in nature is no bar to reciprocal understanding in so far as it goes with reciprocal participation, and, as participation decreases it renders understanding more difficult until in practice it may reach the point of zero, although in theory it always has a value different from zero, and positive, for all living beings. Thus on the assumption that we are right in applying the concept of life to plants, for example, then, by virtue of our participation in life in general we may potentially understand something of the soul-life even of plants, however rarely the exceptional conditions may be fulfilled which allow this to be realized.

Perhaps it was Goethe who first indicated that reflection is due to some interruption in experience: and Carus wrote these pregnant words: "the external ground of cognition is conflict with other ideas". We have seen that Nietzsche provides us with the prologue to a philosophy of the hostility to life of consciousness in general, and we ourselves have systematically completed the theory that reflection is to be considered as a phenomenon of interruption in experience, and cannot be understood otherwise. Our own nature gives us the material of a foreign nature, but to that guiding rule we now must add that what helps us to reflect upon our own nature is *interruption* due to other beings; interruption especially caused by contrary characteristics, to which we owe the consciousness of our own; and we learn to understand other characters by applying our knowledge of our own.

A frank nature, in order to be aware of the frankness which inspires its actions, must at least once have been the victim of a lie. However paradoxical it may sound, it understands the liar by virtue of its own frankness, and on this latter in turn a light falls from the understanding of the lie. Every impulse which urges me to *do* something affords the mind means of judging the inhibition which might cause me to *refrain* from doing it. The unvarying "naive" benevolence may at first be no more than an instinctive tendency to assent and approve; but, once stimulated by collision with cunning and malice, it becomes henceforward also a tendency not to deny nor to hurt; and, as such, it has absorbed knowledge of denying and hurting. Here we are not dealing with polarities, but with heterogeneous differences, to which we devote separate consideration.

Benevolence and malevolence, taken as qualities, generate feelings of a peculiar oppositeness which are further related as having opposition of degree. If a man had both dispositions in equal strength, now following his benevolent and now his malevolent affections, and if we assume benevolence to be vanishing progressively, then his malevolence would grow proportionately; and conversely his benevolence would increase as his malevolence decreased. Such a relation to other qualities does not exist. A very benevolent man may also be extremely fond of pleasure, or again very sober; a very malevolent man, very sober, or again very fond of pleasure. We cannot tell by inspection of either quality whether it is better fitted to accompany benevolence or malevolence, and would have to wait upon experience to give us enlightenment in that direction. On the other hand, benevolence in relation to malevolence is also a minimum quantity of the latter, and so with malevolence in relation to benevolence, and it is precisely this minimum of benevolence which the malevolent man must have experienced (or felt) in order that he may comprehend the benevolent, and the minimum of malevolence which the benevolent must have experienced in order that he may understand the malevolent; and each of the two must have reflected on this before he can undertake the investigation of the other.

There may be some inclination to credit even an exceedingly malevolent character with some capacity for benevolence (for example towards his children): but people are not equally ready to attribute to themselves even that minimum capacity of malevolence which is the condition of any understanding and further investigation of malevolence. This is one of those regrettable self-deceptions which are inspired by moral prejudices, and are the most insuperable of all obstacles to the investigation of character. Whoever has not only read his Nietzsche, but also studied and pondered each aphorism, is instructed once for all about this dishonesty against oneself, which is the basest "false coiners' " shop. It is certainly an exaggeration when Nietzsche says in the *Fröhliche Wissenschaft* (200): "To laugh means to rejoice at misfortune, but with a good conscience"; but even the most benevolent of men, if he is at all skilled in self-examination, would have to confess to himself that a small dose of such rejoicing was an element in a thousand laughs, and that the faintest mockery, the least irony, and even the harmless and "good-natured" teasings of childhood and youth contained some part of this same malevolence of which pharisees claim that they are free and without any taint. The study of character is not for those who cannot be persuaded to make this confession, and they should keep clear of it; or we might say it more gently in a sentence written a generation ago: "Before a study of mankind could develop on a grand scale, philosophers must learn to forget to be ashamed of vanity, selfishness, envy, malice, fear of death, and forgetfulness."[9]

But there is a means for refuting those who think themselves perfect in their generation. If a man had never been capable of the least malevolence, he could not have the least understanding of malevolence; and in that case he could indeed be sensibly irritated by the effects of malevolence (as, for example, he might be by a wasp's sting); but he could not feel hate or contempt or even repugnance of a moral colour (so to speak) against rejoicing at misfortune, malevolence, quarrelsomeness, cunning, intrigues, and secret poisoners of wells, any more than he has such feelings against the wasp, or the dirt into which he has stepped, or the soaking downpour which overtook him on the way to a party. But if he cannot deny the occurrence of peculiar antipathies, to which his endeavour to consider himself incapable of even the least malice clearly bears witness, then he *has* understood malice, and thus is acquainted with it from his own interior, in however small a degree, and on however harmless occasions.

If children under ten years are carefully observed, it will be possible to establish two terminal groups of extreme cases, apart from a broad stratum of mixed cases: the group of infinitely good-natured children and the group of infinitely ill-natured children (of the kind which Wilhelm Busch liked to treat as normal). In dealing with the former group (which in our experience, in spite of everything, is by much the greater), it is practically possible to speak of absence of ill nature, and with the latter, of absence of good nature; and here it sometimes appears with the utmost clearness that so extremely good-natured a child is in fact incapable of understanding the ill nature of very quarrelsome children, and thus, therefore, when (for example) he has been pushed or kicked from behind, he never thinks of revenge or of attacking the enemy, although pluck is not wanting at all; rather, he cries a little, but, especially, is sad, and becomes pensive about something incomprehensible. This attitude changes only with the years—which shows that now a capacity of malevolence—although pretty feeble—has arisen in the child.

The opposition of degree which exists between good and bad nature is repeated in an indefinite number of pairs of qualities, and in the end is applicable to any such quality, although in fact there may not always be a word to denote the opposite term. It does not matter whether we succeed in discovering among the names of qualities one which seems to denote the absence of a sense of duty: in any case we cannot speak with any meaning of a sense of duty without equally envisaging the fact that character is bound by a sense of duty, and that when this is wholly absent, character is loose; whence it is clear that the formation of ideas of qualities implies acquaintance, for each example, of the opposite in degree, and could not have taken place without it. The example which we selected before may serve to elucidate in principle the nature of abstractive reflection. Unless I, too, had experienced that order can be agreeable, and disorder a nuisance, I could not understand the meaning of the expression "a sense of order", and would be unable (for example) to reflect on the fact that I myself am lacking in this sense. But if I can do so, then my immediate notice *must* be due to the fact that I have some share in this very quality which I seemed to lack; and I shall be able to discover its nature and its conditions in so far as I cross out (so to speak) internally those qualities which hitherto have obstructed its growth within me.

THE SCIENCE OF CHARACTER

In order to reach the general part of our subject we must finally consider a class of cases which form a real exception, and therefore demand a special explanation. If we consider the degrees and different kinds of envy, then the following main classes of envy appear, in accordance with the kind of object to which envy applies. *A* envies *B* his property, his "luck" (*A* being generally an unlucky creature), his bodily advantages (for example his beauty), and, finally, his talents (in whatever sphere it may be). The reader may make it clear to himself that there is no difficulty in applying the principle of participation to these cases. But there is one envy more active, evil, and devastating than all the other kinds together, which presupposes that the envious subject is totally excluded from his object: this envy should therefore be altogether incapable of existence in so far as understanding demands some degree, however small, of participation. This we call life-envy, while Nietzsche (whose work in the main is an entirely original investigation of its activity in the formation of ideals) has designated it as Revenge upon Life ("Ressentiment").

In order to understand the issue, what follows must be known. No man makes his character, but finds it as a natural datum, and it is indifferent what use he knows to make of the latter: and this character implies a certain ration of capacity for depth, breadth, warmth, passion, sincerity, comprehensiveness, greatness, etc. of experience, of which he may fall short a thousand times, but which he can never surpass. Granted now that he envies another man his incomparably greater depth, breadth, warmth, etc. of experience, then, first, it is obvious that he can effect a radical cure of such emotion only by expurging the object of his envy—and that would be the man he envies himself, together with the recollection of his advantages; and further, it is obvious that he must have envied the envied man for something from which, by hypothesis, he was completely cut off. If an experimental attempt were made to evade the difficulty with the remark that a shallow experience is a lesser depth of experience, and therefore again participates in its opposite, then this would be a delusion due to verbal ambiguity. For deep experience is distinguished from shallow experience, not by degree alone, but also by wholly new qualities by which the totality of experience undergoes a change *in kind*. Let us bring in a comparison from the sphere of the sensuous: depth of life is related to shallowness of life not so much as great to less clearness of vision, but as capacity for hearing *and* seeing to that of hearing alone: whence it follows that the poor in life can know no more of the *differentia* in the manner of experience of the rich in life than a man born blind can know of colours.

But if now it were objected that in this case it would be altogether impossible to speak of greater or less depth of experience, or to consider from the view-point of intensification a set of circumstances where it is impossible to intensify, then this question would indeed have touched the far wider question the solution of which would bring us the solution of that now before us. We have comparatives for everything: bright—brighter, dark—darker, warm—warmer, cold—colder, hard—harder, soft—softer, sharp—sharper, blunt—blunter, pretty—prettier, ugly—uglier, good—better, bad—worse, clever—cleverer, dull—duller, firm—firmer, etc., and, if we carefully consider it, we cannot really say to what the imaginary difference in magnitude relates. We here give the solution as briefly as possible, partly because we elsewhere treat it in greater detail, and partly because the means of a better understanding of the case will accrue by themselves later.

In so far as man is not only a living subject but also an Ego, and in so far as the latter quality (we say this by anticipation) manifests itself in the capacity for two acts, that of apprehension and that of willing, the original world of living or inspired images of intuition has changed radically, since now it is forced to reflect not only his Soul, but also his capacity for judgment and will. As reflecting his capacity for judgment, it appears as a world of non-living objects (or things), and as reflecting the will, it appears as a world of disembodied forces (or resistances). One event of willing in relation to the rest is solely stronger or weaker, and similarly one force in relation to the next is solely greater or less. If we abstract and scrutinize the Ego capable of willing, and ask how the world must appear to the entity which it inhabits because of *it,* then the answer is, as a system of forces resisting or attacking with different degrees of strength; and, faced with this world, the subject must necessarily endeavour to make it the material and instrument of his intentions. So far as he fails in this he experiences, and treats, it as a rival, and it is clear that he may experience rivalries as painful long after he had become insensitive to the extent of spiritual deafness and blindness, to the particular shape of that which causes him offence.

Suppose a Stock Exchange speculator, empty of soul and suffering boredom on the shores of the Mediterranean, to see a person whom the spectacle of the sea evidently transports with joy. He does not know what this person experiences, and the conclusions he reaches about this by analogy of his own shallow pleasures will certainly be wrong. But the fact, obvious for him too, that this person experiences pleasures denied to himself suffices to make him the malicious rival of his disposition—a rival whose enmity is the stronger since he has no source of experience left save in the breaking of opposition. The opposite procedure, by which a student of character, untouched by life-envy, succeeds in unfolding the "ressentiment", will be touched on in the next chapter. This explanation of the reason which allows life-envy to be discovered, although sketchy, may perhaps suffice to remove the difficulty which seemed to stand in the way of the principle of participation. We now turn in greater detail to the procedure which enables us to mobilize the essential material, which we contain, for the purpose of cognitive penetration of alien characters. This is abstracting self-reflection.

CHAPTER II NOTES

6   In the first edition of this work (1910) it was mentioned that the Greek word πρόσωπον (prosopon) was used in exactly the same double meaning— that of mask, and of character or personality. Meanwhile, classical scholars have asserted that the *Latin persona* must be taken as a corruption of a form "prosopon" borrowed from the Greek. This is possible, but improbable; and, until better reasons are offered us than have been offered so far, we shall continue to consider the old derivation from "personare" the more probable. But even if some day it should succumb to philological arguments, this would not alter our reasoning, which is interested solely in the fact that the old name for mask furnished the term to denote both personality and its character.

7   Compare our outline of the science of expression in *Ausdrucksbewegung und Gestaltungskraft*.

8   In our work *Vom Wesen des Bewusstseins*, Barth, Leipzig.

9   *Graphologische Monatshefte,* 1899, p. 29.

CHAPTER III

PROBLEMS AND METHODS

Let the problem be the investigation of the characterological conditions of murder with robbery. Everybody knows the pleasures of possessing material goods, and can look back on actions having love of gain for motive; he has also experienced a stronger or weaker manifestation of this love, according as opposite motives, like sense of justice, of duty, or affection, counterbalanced it more or less. He need merely imagine the driving forces of sympathy and sense of justice as put out of action, and he will possess, if not all, still some of the most important of the premises needed for an understanding of one who murders with robbery, whose action accordingly would be explained less by the strength of the conditions of certain impulses than by the weakness of the dispositions for certain inhibitions. One preliminary result would then be this, that the inner conditions of murder with robbery would consist in the combination of considerable greed with diminished capacity for feelings of sympathy and an almost complete lack of sense of justice; but in applying this to real events we would soon have cause for reflection. For, on the one hand, we would find these conditions pretty well realized in many industrial and financial magnates who never felt tempted to commit a proper theft, much less a murder with robbery; and, on the other hand, we would find examples of murder with robbery which our formula would appear to fit less well than that of Nietzsche (which is equally incomplete): "He thirsted after the joy of the knife" (*Zarathustra*). But whatever extensions or restrictions we may effect under the guidance of examples, our method would always be the same: we first pursue examples known to us from personal experience; next attempt to recollect exactly what we did in fact experience whenever we felt inclined to follow such a motive, and finally we isolate the foundation of this experience by separating it in thought from the context of the conditions of our experience. Thus we succeed in forming the notions of distinct "driving forces", forces or entities resembling forces, the effects of which we can calculate, if not arithmetically, yet still by methods of a similar kind and, as in arithmetic, without the aid of further observations—like the action of gravitation on two masses of known magnitude and distance.

Of these methods, the first generally operates automatically, while the second demands an aptness, intensified by training, not in self-observation (which does not exist), but in faithful recollection of the colouring of our own experience, and particularly of experience due to small causes. Here the capacity mentioned above for "distance" is required, which cannot further be explained, but can be characterized somewhat more closely, especially by indication of those faults which are avoided by its aid.—If one stands too close one does not see the wood for trees, sticks to details, and strives in vain to find connections.— Important events are usually interpreted better than trivial: for it is incomparably easier to know that on such an occasion I felt fear, or fright, or embarrassment, than to have a clear notion as to what parts exactly of a certain case are present to the mind, or what shade of feeling accompanies the use of the particle "but". On the other hand, events which are rich in emotion have the disadvantage that, when recollected, they again master us and more or less suspend the state of observation, not to mention that our need for self-esteem is always operating to embellish our picture of ourselves, thus finally engendering distortions of memory which are unparalleled in the field of immediate self-recollections, and far surpass the grossest illusions about facts. We will scrutinize the two separately and begin with the case of a strongly emotional relation to the object.

Both love and hate are much too near to their object and only see one side of it, hate that which is judged bad, and love the "good", neglecting the rest. Even the particular degree of closeness manifests itself in the corresponding degree of the falseness of the judgment inspired by the feeling: and here love which unites is even a worse guide, in otherwise equal circumstances, than hate which alienates. "Hate is partial, but love even more so", says Goethe, an excellent authority on such questions. Hate aims at rendering the opposition more acute, and at any rate keeps its eye on its object which it judges from one point only, but, from that point, correctly; but love requires no more than a fact of negligible slightness to found on it a fiction which mocks reality. Hate criticizes, but love is the true element of illusion.[10] The second source of error, less considered but perhaps more dangerous, is found in the measures taken by the impulse of self-esteem to ward off any diminution threatened to our self-estimation.

A man of sufficient conceit who has been greatly irritated on some occasion will be inclined to describe his condition to himself as rage or indignation; and in doing so has entered the path which inevitably leads to complete distortion of the facts. Now, by analogy with all other processes of growth, a metamorphosis of character too is presupposed instinctively, and so a man faces the judge within his breast the more boldly, the more the event which is to be judged belongs to the past, and this is the reason why the comparatively unskilled psychologist esteems more rightly his state of some years ago than his present state, and why history judges the more fairly—where the information is equally complete—the more distant are the facts with which it deals. But, as events vanish away with the past, not only our recollection of them, but also that of our own feelings fades; and thus it is in fact the ordinary course of events that the spirit, in reflecting upon past experiences, experiences them once again in a weakened form, and that, conversely, it has also ceased to have for object that which it can no longer experience (as is the case for many men of middle years with the state of consciousness of their youth). The capacity for recollection can be trained for every sphere: but also we may expect in every sphere the best results when the talents are the best. The faculty which is the foundation of self-recollection might be compared to an intenser wakefulness, as Goethe in fact does, who glorifies it in passionate words with reference to the poet (in *Wilhelm Meister*). "Sown in the soil of his heart the lovely flower of wisdom grows up; and when others dream waking and are frightened by monstrous imaginings from all their senses, he lives the dream of life awake; and for him the rarest happening is at once past and future."

The technique of "detaching" (abstraction) begins only with the third of the procedures enumerated above, and with its completion the science of character automatically completes itself. But before taking an example to explain it, we reject any misunderstanding due to the school of "sensualism" which has introduced unending confusions into science generally and characterology in particular: we mean the popular opposition to the notions of substrata. There still are people who think that they have said a weighty word when they substitute for the concept (for example) of the body the concept of a "bundle of sensation-contents". We answer them by saying that this would in fact create an invalid concept, but that even in the opposite case the suitable concept would have had to yield to an unsuitable and even foolish concept.

We speak of properties (accidentia) in so far as we have mediately or immediately experienced their effects, and we call the conditions of these effects properties in so far as we refer them to something which is supposed to unite them all. If we refrained from distinguishing the condition of effects and the effects themselves, then we would at the same time be refraining from passing beyond our contents of intuition and would not have the right ever to think about them. But if, on the other hand, we are resolved to think and to investigate, then we must make this distinction, which, however, already implies the distinction between properties and their substrata. What is the peculiarity of the properties of the red ball before my eyes? It is that its redness, roundness, hardness, shape, and weight belong together in a manner governed by law (hence "concrete" = "grown together"), and therefore guarantee under given conditions a behaviour of the ball which may be subjected to laws and foretold. We do not mean by the ball the sum of its properties (a sum which can never be arrived at)—far from it: we do mean the ground of the coherence of its properties, and this exists in fact and without any "as if" as soon as ever we start our consideration from properties. If instead of them a "bundle of contents of sensations" is posited, then the word "bundle" merely denotes in a different and clumsy way that which must be added to the properties in order that it shall be even possible to think them as such.

But further this circumlocution contains a mistake, or rather two mistakes. A bundle of twigs is a broom from which individual twigs can be drawn out: but the body is not a bundle at all from which individual properties can be extracted, but an original whole whose properties are merely distinguished from the latter. We will soon deal with this point. Further, the twigs do not coalesce into a broom of themselves, but only by means of a band, and it is precisely this band and not the bundle which we denote by substratum-notions like body, thing, material, and so on. With his horror of substratum-notions the sensualist proves that he is in the toils of the very prejudice which he pretends to abolish, namely, that the substratum, which is the condition for the co-existence of the properties, must be discoverable itself, like a property. This, of course, he can never succeed in doing, and therefore he denies its existence —"mocks himself and does not know how". The deeper cause of this curious error in taste lies in the fact that he is a secret Platonist; for him properties float in empty space, or rather in Nirvana, as independent essences. "Idealism" and "sensualism" are only two aspects of the same thing.

Those who, with Heraclitus, have reached the conviction that actuality is independent of any consciousness, and knows neither things nor properties, have in this philosophy a better starting point for characterology than in the opposite: but if anyone for this reason indulges in the belief in any *thought* which should be independent of consciousness, then he is involved in an extremely humorous self-contradiction, and to be consistent, should present his discoveries in the shape of propositions consisting solely of predicates. On the other hand, the doctrine of Heraclitus, rightly understood, allows us to distinguish in our judgments the elements due respectively to Spirit and to actuality, and, in our concepts, to keep apart their function of pointing to the ever-changing and therefore inapprehensible content of experience, and that of distinguishing the mutable by means of centres of coagulation implanted in the latter. Once we know that all understanding consists in the distinguishing, and in distinguishing alone, we have eradicated once for all the disease of scepticism which has endured for three thousand years, and place the question of "true or false" on the knife's edge without being troubled by the secondary thought that the keenest distinctions, correctly drawn, must presuppose as incomprehensible both that which is to be and that which has been distinguished.

Now it is true that essences are not things, and the tendency to identify them with things has done almost as much harm as the Platonic identification of properties with things; but both essences and things completely agree in the fact that they are substrata of properties. The widespread hesitation to use substratum-notions in characterology rests, as has already been indicated, on a clumsy confusion of properties with parts. Parts can be separated, properties distinguished. One property can be taken from out of the rest which make up a character no more than the shape or colour can be abstracted from a leaf; and they can be distinguished with precisely the same exactitude as can the leaf's shape from its colour. This provides us with a suitable transition to the method of abstraction which renders possible the development of characterological concepts.

Let us imagine that the question is asked, What are the chief differences of will (capacity for willing) in different men? and let us accordingly begin with the kind of willing familiar to us from our own experience: the first thing which will occur to us is the feeling of exertion which accompanies it. Self-reflection bears testimony that we felt our volition most strongly the more we had exerted ourselves, and conversely: and we often have had to acknowledge a limit to our capacity for effort, beyond which will would fail. Now it is true that the number of different properties which we discover in ourselves is identical with the number of properties of characters in general which we are capable of comprehending; and that the number of the degrees of the efficacy of a property which we discover in ourselves is identical with the number of degrees which the property can manifest in different characters. We have no other means of developing concepts of properties of character and of their degrees, but it also appears that abstracting self-reflection in every instance opens a vista on literally infinite varieties. If I find in myself will characterized by automatic exertion, then I am justified in assuming will power; if I discover in myself degrees of exertion on different occasions, then I must consider that will power admits of intensification; if, finally, I find limits to my capacity for exertion, then I must apply the property of personal energy—in the sense of a varying characteristic limit to the capacity for exertion. At the same time the fact that exertions can be intensified leads me to a graduated series which I can extend at will beyond the range of manifestations of energy which is characteristic for me personally: in one direction practically to zero (*aboulia*), and in the other to a multiple of my own will power: only the magnitude always remains finite.

If we were to confine ourselves to degrees of energy, our wisdom would soon be at the end. Will and power are not the same thing; but we would not have the least acquaintance with will if will did not so often pass over into performance. Force of will is clearly related to force of action, but the latter is by no means based entirely upon the degree of personal energy alone. We can recollect that we performed a task (for example, in arithmetic) sometimes with great expenditure of energy, and sometimes with the utmost ease. In the first case, obstacles seem to surge up between desire and performance; in the latter we sped towards the goal as though on smoothest rails. Hence we conclude that there are personal differences in ease of will or talent of will (in the narrower sense). Thus, for example, many men must always force themselves to concentration, while others have continually a mind present, concentrated, and collected. The same is the case of some peoples and races in relation to others.

But this would not lead us to the end even of the preliminaries of a characterology of will. If we consider the automatism of volition we are forced to remark that it appears threatened by innumerable sensations. A rough observation, let fall in a moment of angry irritability, is no manifestation of energy but an expression of anger; and if immediately afterwards I must admit to myself that I was a fool, then I realize that the remark came not only without, but against my intentions. More generally, whatever plans I make I shall be able to execute only in so far as I forbid my feelings to come into play or else make them serve my intentions as far as possible. And, again, it appears that I succeed in this sometimes more and sometimes less easily. Now the event of willing, too, has some vital foundations, and is accompanied by characteristic feelings which for the sake of brevity we will call will-feelings, and therefore the taking of a resolution, and more particularly persistence in executing it, depends among other things upon the relation of my will-feelings to my other feelings. Accordingly we must assume that there are personal differences in the will-capacity of feelings. On this depends (for example) the contrast known to everyday speech between the "man of action" and the "man of feeling".

This little practical example of self-reflection has furnished us with some results which are not quite obvious. The customary distinction between strength and weakness of will is now seen to relate to two somewhat complicated states of affairs. So-called weakness of will may be due to lack of energy especially, or to lack of ease of will, or to diminished capacity of the feelings for will, and the reverse is true of strength of will. Thus whole series of new questions come within the horizon of reflection. The so-called capacity of the feelings for will comprehends a capacity for suppressing the emotions, or more briefly, a capacity for self-control: but we immediately remember also that self-control at one time serves to realize external events of willing, and at another is ensued for its own sake. The self-control which a "saint", a Yogi, or an ascetic requires, great as it certainly is, is still a very different matter from the self-control which a Napoleon needs on a thousand occasions in order to realize his plans for conquering a world. We do not prosecute this matter further here: it is enough if this example has shown that, and how, systematic self-recollection may be the key to a veritable universe of characteristic traits in an alien soul.

We may mention here, by way of supplement, how a skilled student of character could reach a derivation of life-envy without himself sharing in it or having hitherto experienced its effects. It is true that, unless he knew from personal experience the emotion of envy, he would not even understand its name, still less the composite phenomenon of life-envy: but if he has had that experience—and there is no historical man who has not, in however slight a degree—then there is no difficulty in delimiting the groups of objects designated above, and in positing life-envy as a characteristic possibility with regard to the last of them. If now the process of detaching turns to the impulse for self-esteem and to feelings of rivalry, then the question inevitably emerges, What must be the form of a type of envy which stands against a background of irremediable and, so to say, fated impotence? Now the student of character is familiar with this sensation from thousandfold experience (one need only think of the inability to remember of one's schooldays, and the limits of bodily power, so often experienced); and therefore he is able to estimate not only the particular anger, the particular jealousy and loathing revolt of envy suffering from this impotence, but also its tendency towards hiding from and transvaluing itself: and thus he gains an insight into a class of experience, which in itself is hidden from him, sufficient to allow him to deduce numerous forms of judgment and attitude relating thereto. To check his results

46

he may use any given character, and, further, universal history, beginning with traditional deeds, notions of law and customs relating to general views of life, and of ideals and proceeding to the ancient coinage of wisdom laid down in writings, legends, and turns of speech as a material awaiting interpretation which either eludes his theories or else confirms them when it serves to throw light upon them. About two-thirds of the unparalleled discoveries which we owe to Nietzsche about the capacity of "ressentiment" for discovering epoch-making "ideals" can be found after the event implicit in the pretty fable of the fox and the sour grapes.

But we must not recollect ourselves alone, but also recollection itself, if our science of method is not to have a dangerous lacuna. School learning has employed great subtlety in inventing cunning apparatus to spy out the Soul, but generally does not realize sufficiently that the master-instrument is speech. If, as we have just done, we speak of willing and of will, then we must not forget that we have not discovered these facts, but at best have rediscovered them, unless, indeed, we took them on trust, relying on the traditional linguistic designations, which in themselves are no guarantee for the existence of these facts, still less throw any light upon their nature. The ancient Greeks had no word even approximately equivalent to our "feeling" and "sentiment" (meaning moods of the soul), and therefore their whole philosophy remained unacquainted with the threefold division of psychical processes into thinking, willing, and feeling which to us has become almost axiomatic, although it has gained real currency only since the sentimental literature of the eighteenth century. The word "to understand", [German, *verstehen*] which we prefer to psychological apprehension, together with its derivative "sympathy" [German, *Verständnis*] and, especially, "understanding" (meaning capacity for apprehension and judgment generally), nowadays implies complete spiritual penetration, but also and particularly it means the grasp of the meaning of *words*: a foreign language is (or is not) *understood*, and one asks, "Have you *understood me?*" in order to know whether the listener has grasped the meaning of a statement. Thus if our language at least testifies that understanding in general coincides with linguistic understanding, this may serve as a new reminder that the hidden force which pulls the wires of our self-recollections is a language which came to us before consciousness; thus we reach our judgments by way of prejudices, and would hardly escape serious errors in our conclusions without a parallel study of names.

Hereby the task of conceptual definitions set to psychological investigation receives a very particular meaning. The problem is not to hold fast just anyhow the results of experience, but to do so with the help of linguistic designations which have grown into their status and bear the burden of all the richness of their age. The logical utilization of our discoveries has to measure itself against the witness of language, and self-analysis is complemented by the art of definition, now almost lost. It may be admitted that this is a turn towards scholastic, or rather towards classical methods, which, with their tendency for finding the explanation of things in their name, were on the right path with respect to the explanation of problems of the inner life, however numerous were the false etymologies which they committed.

Much is said about the poverty of language, and it is said that words are wanting for our deepest experiences; it is perhaps more correct to speak of poverty of experience, which in innumerable instances borrows only a semblance of significance from the display of words in which it arrays itself. Life, which has coagulated into speech, in fervour and wildness and in spiritual range leaves far behind the ultimate heights and depths in the life of the individual (apart from the dim feelings of earliest youth); and for this reason alone it still has the power, once it is stirred, to transport the Soul even now with almost supernatural magic, carrying it into a whirl of super-human experience unattainable otherwise: and a great poet leads us into an unknown fairyland wholly because he is blessed with the genius of language.

Indeed, it is not only undesirable, but absolutely impossible to escape while thinking the impulses which continually come to us out of the vocabulary of the language in which we think; the real danger is not that we may disregard the mould into which pre-existing language presses our meanings, but that we may accept it uncritically because unconsciously. Nietzsche, the first of modern psychologists in this respect too, that he follows the traces of language with insight and acumen, never wearies of mocking those metaphysicians whom he holds to have been its unwitting prisoners since the beginning. "An invisible charm drives them around the same old track: however independent they may feel of each other in their critical or systematic intentions, there is something in them which guides and drives them in a fixed order one behind the other, namely, this inborn machinery and relationship in concepts. ... The curious family likeness of the whole of Indian, Greek, and German philosophy is explained simply enough. Where there is a linguistic kinship, it is inevitable that, by virtue of the common philosophy of grammar—that is, the unconscious domination and guidance of identical grammatical functions—the way is made plain for a similar development and sequence of philosophical systems *ab initio:* just as the road here seems barred to certain other potential world-interpretations ..." *(Beyond Good and Evil,* chap, i, §. 20).

But if the wisdom of schools, although for different reasons, thought it necessary to construct a technical language for its ends, then it is following an illusion which more than ever places it at the mercy of an uncritical dependence upon traditional units of meaning. The instrument of psychological discovery—unlike those of physics, chemistry, astronomy, and so on—namely, self-recollection, lies ready at hand throughout the existence of historical humanity, and has been active through an equal period from generation to generation in rendering precise the meanings of words whose growth is organic. It would be the denial of an immemorial erosion, the extinction of earliest history, and the false assumption that a fresh beginning was being made of something which in fact had reached its end, if an attempt were made to cast off or out the real or imagined psychology which we have inherited with the language with which we grew up. The German language gives us at least four thousand words to denote the simplest as well as the most complicated processes, conditions, and properties of the inner life: it would be an act of intellectual hubris to wish to *invent* a psychological terminology. What do the alien neologisms perform? They misinterpret where they do not distort the meaning of the older words. A belief that the matter is settled by the mere avoidance of verbal appearance leads inevitably to those traps which beset higher reflection in common language. The "trace of memory"—a term of current if not of popular usage—loses nothing of its hidden directive force in the investigation of the capacity for recollection, if the learned "engram" is put in its place: but it does escape a quiet weighing of its claims as an instrument of cognition; and "emotion" (which is dog-Latin) merely repeats, but in a false key, the meaning of "movement of the mind".

It is one thing to be the servant of language and another to make use of its hints. An apprehension of the inner life necessarily takes place by the help of traditional words, and therefore we consider it a decisive step in psychology that this necessity be present to the mind permanently, and consider a critical treatment of the names of properties of character as the necessary compensating moment of self-recollection. Of the problems which result we enumerate those only which are of the greatest fundamental importance.[11] The investigation of names must decide first how far they can be adequately defined, and which of their component parts might be spared in order to obtain a more rigid statement without surrendering their main meaning. A good many words and turns of current speech are thus lost to scientific thought, but still more, as being sufficiently certain in their meaning, act as pioneers, setting curious problems, and giving hints for their solution.

A first question which cannot be avoided is this: when there are experiences which are denoted by terms which though evidently related are not interchangeable, then in which respects do these experiences coincide, and in which do they differ? "Passion" certainly means something *similar* to "enthusiasm"; but in many sentences it cannot be substituted without changing the sense. But the infallible method of attaching adjectives immediately guides us to a distinction in meaning which will cause high intellectual tension in every reflective mind: we say "violent passion", but not "violent enthusiasm"; and "high enthusiasm", but not "high passion". Instead of beginning with self-recollection, we might begin with two words of everyday use in order to elucidate the experience which they call before the mind; and, with sufficient talent and tenacity, we could finally reach results of almost incalculable importance, with which we shall deal in a later chapter. Or again—what are the distinctions in the meanings of the following cognate words: sensitive, receptive, impressionable, delicate, tractable, impulsive, sanguine? Have they all something in common? Which of them belongs to narrower groups? Or what is the meaning of "benevolence" as against "good nature", and of both as against "tender-heartedness"? Or, again, let us consider the perfectly irritating wealth of names for formations, degrees, and manifestations of egotism. What modern psychology could boast that it possesses the means for placing the following classes of meanings, which we enumerate here in a certain order: self-confidence, self-esteem, exaggerated self-esteem, megalomania—self-reliance, self-certainty, self-justice—pride, nobility—haughtiness, insolence, conceit, arrogance, pomposity—ambition, vain-glory, vanity—self-satisfaction, self-sufficiency, self-delight—selfishness, self-love, self-admiration!

Another problem of fundamental importance is the analysis of names which denote not the main forms or shades of the faculties of the soul, but the results of the joint activity of several of these. For example, adaptability is not a property, but the typical result of properties which may vary greatly from case to case. Our question must be, What properties of character involve adaptability or are its inner conditions ? Similarly we may seek after the premisses of consistency, faithfulness, honesty, gratitude, loyalty. What are the components of "heart"? Language in these words gives us pseudo-types to which certain complexes correspond, which experience shows us: hence analysis, in so far as it is successful, often discovers laws governing the co-existence of faculties. Thus, for example, the word "pertness"* allows us to guess by itself that inquisitiveness often goes with boldness of judgment.

But the testing of names for their immediate psychological content is a more important task than either of the two just mentioned. The process of growth excels in wisdom the bare action, and the organism an artificial structure: and similarly language, a growth, excels in unconscious insight the acumen of the most talented thinker, and we contend that whoever, having the right talent, should do nothing but interrogate the words and phrases which deal with the human soul, would know more about it than all the sages who omitted this, and would know perhaps a thousand times more than has ever been discovered by observation, apparatus, and experiment upon man. Since the classical period thinkers of standing have engaged this problem, though none perhaps with greater trust in the revealing capacity of language than the author of these lines, who, from real or imagined insight into the *reason* of this state of things, has applied to each of his psychological discoveries the test of the philosophy of language—by which latter method, indeed, he reached most and probably the best of his results. We have offered many examples of this at another place (some of them above, "object", "person", "understanding"), and must adduce some later: here therefore we are content with a few.[12]

---

* German *Naseweisheit*, literally "nose-wisdom"

It is a still debated question whether "intelligence" is more peculiar to the male or to the female character: most thinkers have declared for that party to which they belong—obviously because they esteem intelligence—namely, for the male party: on the other hand, a Nietzsche, for example, who deduces understanding from timidity, reaches the opposite result, namely, that cleverness is at home among women, and that the superior thinking power of men is due not to greater understanding, but to a more powerful passion behind it. We will not here decide the question, and only remark without proof that it is not one of degrees but of kinds of cleverness. There is an elegant illustration of the advantages which investigation could draw from a consideration of language in the use of the somewhat obsolete "wit" in the sense of "understanding ... ,"* For if we find the compound "mother-wit" in current use for natural common sense, with no parallel "fatherwit", then we see that the genius of language, or at least of our language, looks for unsophisticated gifts of apprehension chiefly on the female side, and have thus obtained an invaluable hint for the more subtle classification of capacities. And further, who could deny that he had gained in insight when he considers that "irony" originally meant "pretence", and that "pretence", in turn, exemplifies a state of affairs where something by its position is covered up and changed; or when he realizes that "to lose one's temper" implies that a man in a state of angry excitement has lost his *edge*, and therefore has lost certain conditions of self-assertion?

Among older students of language L. Geiger, in his incomplete work on the *Origin and Development of Human Language and Reason* (1868) held the view (which is correct in fact, though very ill developed by him, and until this day unappreciated) that the development of language, and therefore of the whole of human thought, takes place under the main guidance of the sense of sight. Now, if it be granted

---

* A line is omitted here, giving untranslatable examples of this use.—TRANSLATOR'S NOTE.

that, for reasons connected with the science of consciousness, we held this assertion to be correct, we would certainly not reject the confirmations which the testimony of language affords in the following cases, which are few among many. The German "wissen" (to know) leads back to the Indo-Germanic root "wid", which in almost all Indo-Germanic languages means interchangeably "to find", "cognize", or "see": Sanskrit vid = to find, Greek ἰδεῖν = to see, Latin videre = to see, Gothic witan = to observe. Accordingly, in German the chief words for the most important function of intellect and their results are taken from the sphere of sight: *view, insight, intuition*, and also *aim*. On the other hand, the development of the Latin cemere passes from "to sever" by way of the abstraction "to distinguish" to "to perceive with the eyes", and to "clearly to see a thing": and such examples, which might be easily multiplied, illustrate the inner connection between power of judgment and of sight—that is, according to the "spirit of the language".

With the derivation of names we now enter on the province of the history of life in man, and thus acquire from it immediate instruction only with regard to the change in human character in the course of ages; but it will be admitted that this precisely is the source of invaluable contributions for characterology. The *full* meaning is never present to the mind when a word is used, and different times take a prevailing interest in different shades of meaning: thus the content of a word is, as we know, in continual flux, sometimes impoverished by expansion, sometimes enriched by contraction, and occasionally undergoing a complete change in the course of centuries. The most powerful lever of this development is seen in social sympathies and antipathies, which constitute the expression, in the shape of philosophical or religious conviction, of the needs of the ruling caste. The word "simplicity" conveyed praise and was almost synonymous with "piety" so long as strength of the faculty for faith determined (in the estimation of priests and knights) the value of man; while the complexity of an intellectualistic period like ours speaks of a "simple" man as being just a stupid. Now it is certain that characterological nomenclature must do justice to the present meaning of words and not to that of some past period: but still it will do its part to prevent the mechanization of terms of speech which once were important, and to preserve the best part of its original content in a more rigid frame. "While the formulae remain, the meaning may at any time revive", says John Stuart Mill in his excellent chapter in the *Logic* on the requisites of a philosophic language. "To common minds only that portion of the meaning is in each generation suggested of which that generation possesses the counterpart in its own habitual experience. But the words and propositions are ready to suggest to any mind duly prepared the remainder of the meaning." This notion contains the plan the execution of which would be the duty of a complete characterology.

Among the antiquities of peoples there is no other document of inner life equivalent to speech in strength and directness: but also, none can entirely evade psychological interpretation. Consciousness has crystallized in innumerable shapes, and all that is needed is a clear eye in order to read in buildings, ornaments, and pictures the confirmation and the complement of the evidence which actions historically vouched for furnish about the character of their authors. Here there lies ready to hand such a mass of material as never yet was the property of any science, and we would be certain now already of the vastest knowledge, but that historians lack that psychological amazement which creates, whenever we are faced with any form, work, or kind of activity, the question what may be the forces which produce these. For the first time customs, sagas, and conceptions of gods, costumes, and household articles, languages and systems of writing are interrogated deliberately without any preconceived notion about their origins; there is here no pride in facts or hasty adjustment for the forge of metaphysical dogma; these data are to be understood, and, being understood, are to help in completing the picture of man.

The next success of these attempts will be a system, free of all moral prejudices, continuing all the genera and species of psychical and spiritual faculties; and this (as opposed to modern attempts, which are under the domination of time) will prove capable of penetrating the mentality of the most distant peoples and epochs, and to some extent of prehistoric man. Thence there arises immediately the question about the inner connection between qualities and the degree of their kinship. Some traits are always or frequently found together, and others seldom or never, and there is perhaps an inner necessity for each case. In some instances this is obvious, when, for example, we observe a closer connection between a sanguine temperament and euphoria as complementary dispositions. On the other hand, we do not immediately understand the curious but undoubted fact that psychological and mathematical aptitudes do not fit well together. The road to the understanding of such facts leads us far into the structure of the unconscious. But the foundation of a psychical morphology, if it is to be perfect, would be the doctrine of the driving forces which, as such, never enter into consciousness, and may vary to any degree whatever from the imagined motives of our actions.

Attempts in this direction have generally failed because of the inadequacy of the material, which was collected in the interest of a particular system rather than of psychology. We have in mind, for example, the continually recurrent attempt to reduce all psychical multiplicity to the one urge of self-preservation, which we find especially among the French moralists. The habit has grown up—not without justice—of mistrusting such precipitate and systematizing spirits, while at the same time it may be remembered that they often at least gave the impulse which led to the re-examination of prejudices which had become fossil, and, thence, to a deeper self-recollection. We shall certainly not refuse the guidance of popular proverbs and wise dicta of poets, however much we are bound not to take any saying without criticism. The untouched mines of knowledge in this respect which, for example, lie hidden in Goethe and Jean Paul, far exceed the entire production of a whole century of science.

We conclude by pointing to a fact which even now is hidden by a prejudice which commands almost universal assent. Even apart from the quality of indivisible originality, without the admixture of which no living individual occurs, it suffices to reflect on the innumerable genera of animals and plants to confirm the conviction that the ocean of life throws up, if not literally innumerable, still incalculably numerous species of Soul. Now if it be assumed that in the character of men the coupling of Spirit with vital cells having soul is continually proceeding afresh, then we may perhaps speak of the progressive penetration of Spirit into life during the succession of generations, and, to this extent, of "evolution" (which "evolution", incidentally, must end with the destruction of life), but cannot possibly outline a diagram which would allow us to anticipate in mind the multitude of species.

The greatest sage living among prehistoric man ten thousand years ago and passing through all its tribes could not have calculated that after so many centuries or millennia the historical process would begin in one or other of them; and in fact no sage among the ancients predicted the Christian process, which yet had in fact commenced with Socrates. If we were acquainted with western men only, then, however deeply we studied the conflict of Spirit and Soul in them, we could never derive the Indian variant of the same conflict, still less its manifestation as it occurs in Eastern Asia; for, without experience, we could not be acquainted with the *vitality* of Eastern Asia. Those who imagine that, following the fated way of mankind and more especially of its history they can *construe* the series of concrete manifestations, should foretell what will be the appearance of buildings, costumes, and languages three thousand years hence; or let them forecast the direction of change of these and other crystallizations of human nature no more than thirty years ahead; and, if they cannot, or miss the mark, let them admit to themselves that, misled by the faulty standard notions of an illusory belief in progress, they have undertaken the impossible.

We know of no "progress" except that towards complete dissolution and final destruction, in so far as things continue on the straight course down which "civilized" mankind has been racing since about 1790 at ever-increasing speed; and equally we know nothing of the capacity of life for new formations and of its emergency reserves. We know of no clearer manner of formulating the idea of plurality than by borrowing the phraseology of physics, and stating that it is necessary to become acquainted biologically with the notion that at certain stages of a living series new forces enter whose development cannot be forecast from past forms.

CHAPTER III NOTES

[10]   These sentences will meet with vigorous contradiction from those who, conversely, are convinced that love is the only key to the innermost secrets of another. This, too, might be true without necessarily being incompatible with our statements. Love may make Spirit visionary, and may enable it to reflect a foreign original: but the original of a personality is not the personality itself. If, then, in due course that keen sight of lovers develops, which is quite improperly called the keen sight of love, this is due to the fact that love has been disappointed by numerous discrepancies between the "original" and the person whom it inhabits. It is true that love was required for this. Thus here—as perhaps everywhere—we must look for the origin of knowledge in disappointment rather than in love. Two dicta of Goethe must here be quoted, apparently contradictory, but complementary in fact, since they do justice to both sides of the case. To Riemer he remarks: "Love is like a pair of glasses made to rest the eyes. ... Other glasses make sight keener and more clear; but with these, all deficiencies and faults disappear, and all kinds of things emerge now only which were invisible to the naked eye." But in *Ueber Falconet* he says: "What the artist has not loved and does not love, he should not and cannot describe."

[11]   Further details about the linguistic side of psychology will be found in *Ausdrucksbewegung und Gestaltungskraft*.

12   Numerous examples in A*usdrucksbewegung und Gestaltungskraft*, but especially in *Vom Wesen des Bewusstseins*.

CHAPTER IV

NATURE, STRUCTURE, AND MATERIAL OF CHARACTER

From the innumerable traits of character which have been fixed in language we take four at hazard:

Sense of gain;	Talent for music;
Sense of duty;	Memory.

However well or ill it may be possible to define them, it still is clear that in spite of the greatest differences there is a relation between the terms of the left side and between those of the right, but not between left and right. Talent for music comprehends (among other things) a particular kind of memory—namely, for notes and their combination: and a sense of gain will easily lead to acts which are at discord with the demands of a sense of duty; it thus is in a relation of contrariness to it. But the question whether it goes well or ill with a talent for music, or goes more or less frequently with a good memory, can no longer be decided from the meanings of the words, but only from a collection of relevant cases. The concepts of the left are incommensurable with those of the right.

But there is a general principle at the bottom of this which allows, if not all, still a very great number of terms to be divided into two groups which correspond exactly. The first manifests a different region or stratum or zone of the inner life from those of the second group; or the two serve to trace the foundations of two generically distinct functions of consciousness, as we have already proved by anticipation when contrasting character in the narrower sense with that side of personality which was called "talent" without closer definition. For the two concepts adduced on the right, and all kindred concepts, relate to some "talents", gifts, or, more generally, capacities; while those of the left without exception relate to strivings. The capacities in their totality are the material of personality, while in the strivings dispositions for the utilization of the material are realized, and these accordingly we classify under the nature (or quality) of personality.

Words like memory, talent for music, strength of will, and the like undoubtedly denote man's power to do. They relate to certain dispositions which bring it about that somebody excels in remembering, in apprehending a musical structure, or in manifesting strong and persistent volition; but these words leave it undecided whether these dispositions are utilized in fact. Memory, talent for music, and will-power may be practised or neglected, and, conversely, it is impossible to create them with the "best will" in the world, or to intensify them beyond the fixed personal limit: just as in the external world the weight of a material may be utilized for certain ends, but cannot be changed into another (that is, in a given place). The witty phrase (which reaches back from Heine, Amadeus Hoffman, and Brentano to Plutarch) about "good men and bad musicians" satirizes strivings after an end where the material needed to realize it is inadequate: conversely the frequent observation that in spite of great gifts the "proper drive" is lacking castigates a disuse of the material due to lack of interest. But the expression that somebody is "wasting" it looks at a talent as a capital which requires that conditions shall stimulate it before it will "work".

It might be objected that perhaps all degrees of performance in men are to be traced back to degrees of practice, in which case a comparison of performances will afford no criterion for the amount of the alleged talent. But we all know that if a man without musical gifts practises on the piano for so many hours in a year, his best performances will fall far short of the best performances of a musically gifted person who has practised for exactly the same time. Thus, where interest and practice are equal, different persons reach very different standards, and when the period of practice is unlimited there is, as has already been remarked, a characteristic maximum for each person which he cannot exceed. Indeed, this objection is nowadays raised more and more rarely; for it is a gradually mouldering heirloom from the school of "sensualism", and its heresy (taken over from the Stoics) of the *tabula rasa*. Goethe long ago said the decisive word: "Capacities are presupposed; their function is to become proficiencies" (*Elective Affinities*).

In fact, the school-practice of psychology nowadays puts investigation of talents in the first place. But it suffers from numerous disabilities which it has inherited from the above-mentioned school, of which the gravest in its consequences is the tacit assumption that talents are exclusively intellectual talents. To this we may object that every talent without exception (and therefore also an intellectual talent) is simultaneously a talent of expression or, as it has been called elsewhere, a form of formative power.[13] Thus, for example, there was never yet a remarkable talent of thinking without an uncommon capacity of "elucidating" speech; and those who insist on confining their investigations to intellectual components, overlook or neglect an important, if not the most important, aspect of the case, and consequently will produce at best mere caricatures of the conditions of talents. But further there are gifts of will and sentiment by the side of gifts of intellect—in so far as we employ this threefold division, which has reached popularity.

In the last chapter we analysed will-power and distinguished between the degree of energy and the degree of facility of will, and between these two and the degree of the will-capacity of the feelings. But whatever classification we adopt, we are always dealing with natural talents, and accordingly the contrast between strength and weakness of will is a contrast of innate faculties as much as that (for example) between good and bad memory. A man of strong and one of weak will can each alike practise or neglect his will: but with equal practice they will command very different degrees of will-power. Or let us compare a very sensitive with a very coarse or thick-skinned person, and we shall see at once why the coarser must always fall short of the more sensitive, for example in the apt apprehension of another's moods, because he lacks his talent of feeling.

Now already in the sphere of intellect almost innumerable variations appear. For example, not only degrees of strength of memory as such, but of memory for certain definite groups of objects. One man retains names, dates, and numbers easily and for long, another anecdotes, a third mental processes, a fourth his own experiences, a fifth impressions (images), and so on. Apart from the quality of the memory, whole series of other aptitudes operate, each, of which contributes to the quality of intellect, like a gift for apprehension, power to grasp, or to reflect, presence of mind, observation, alertness; a gift for inference, foresightedness, acumen, adroitness, power to observe, wealth of thought, logical thinking, critical power, wit, lucidity, profundity, and independence of judgment. Further, the conditions governing performance become innumerable as soon as we classify them according to the fields of their potential operation. There is a personal gift for the various arts and sciences, but also for every craft, business, technical knowledge, trade, and method of procedure. A man may show special fitness for carpentry, tailoring, and cobbling, and even for pointing pencils, cutting, and soling.[14] If, finally, we add all the attainable gifts of will and feeling, then the question arises what they all have in common that justifies us in comprehending them all under a single major concept, namely, that of the material of character.

It is just that which enables us to compare the most varied materials of the material world with regard to their weight: quantum. Aptitudes are quantitative properties. We have more or less energy than another, or more or less memory, lucidity, wit, delicacy of feeling, and so on. Any quality can, of course, be graded, and thus we can speak of more or less sense of gain, selfishness, unselfishness, and so on. But from this it merely follows that any quality may be considered among other points of view from that of a natural talent, and that in each the aspect of aptitude may be emphasized. But with respect to the aspect of talent only the more or less serves to distinguish characters, while the distinction into natures is based on a totally different state of facts which renders it possible to distinguish certain groups of qualities as having to do primarily with talent from other groups of qualities as having to do primarily with nature. We will adduce an example to prove this.

If I judge that somebody acts under the influence of a sense of gain, I have in mind no quantum of aptitude; and this is so true that there would be no contradiction in adding that he lacked practical disposition. Thus I am not characterizing his powers but his striving, and not his gifts but his driving forces. Driving force ("Triebfeder") is German for "interest". Characterologically both denote the same thing. On the other hand, interests (driving forces) are not identical with urges: the driving force of ambition may be called a certain direction of a man's interests, but the sexual urge of a bull cannot be called his sexual interest. Further details about this must, however, be postponed; now we confine ourselves to the driving forces (or interests).

By a driving force we mean the inner cause of a Striving in general and of an event of willing in particular. Now in order to designate the habitual object of a man's will, the strength, impetuosity, and pertinacity of his Strivings (for these are qualities of talents) do not serve at all: what is needed is to indicate his aims. Hence we must say more exactly that each driving force is the permanent condition governing a *direction* of his volition. Like "aim", the word "direction" is not used metaphorically, but in its real meaning (although there is an element of symbolism), whenever we assert that attention, striving, or will of somebody is directed to this or that. And, exactly as in the world of things directions may form angles, and, if they are directions of forces, may strengthen, hinder, or cancel each other, so the driving forces on which the directions of volition are based strengthen or hinder each other. The sense of gain in certain cases has a direction diametrically opposite to that of a sense of duty, and the resulting act may, in given circumstances, be at the expense of a defeat of conscience. If then we call the driving forces properties of direction (just as we have called the capacities quantitative properties), then we may hope that the following definition satisfies the most exacting claims for precision: quantitative distinctions of properties of character lead us to the concept of specific capacities, and distinctions of direction (or the resulting tendency) to the concept of specific driving forces.

There results a fundamental difference between the objects which we are here comparing. If I attribute to somebody an exceptionally powerful memory I am free to add that his power of inference is comparatively small; but if I refrain from adding this, those who hear me will not assume that the memory of the man in question is better developed than his other capacities, but that he has a better memory than the average of men. But if I attribute to him an exceptionally powerful sense of gain, then this implies that in case of conflict this sense is more likely to have the best of his sense of duty, and this fact would remain unchanged if the case were the same for the majority or even the totality of living mankind. Our immediate gauge for the capacity of one personality is another personality, our gauge for driving forces is another group of driving forces within the same personality. But we must examine the driving forces somewhat more closely in order to make it intelligible why we have described the totality of the directive qualities as the *nature* of character.

Every driving force or directive quality is at the same time a (specific) disposition of feeling, and every disposition of feeling is a driving force or directive quality. If anyone thinks it curious that the sense of gain, which he immediately recognizes and admits as a driving force, should further deserve the special name of disposition of feeling, let him reflect upon the following facts. If a sense of gain causes me to strive after the possession of material goods, then I have not only (what goes without saying) a knowledge of their significance, but further consider it an agreeable thing to possess them and most disagreeable to lose them. This may appear a platitude today, but it was not always so. The anchorites of the first centuries of the Christian era made a practice of giving away their earthly goods, and went in numbers to Egypt into the desert to wear shirts of camel hair and to live on locusts, and this conduct proves that the thought of earthly possessions was painful to them, and that to be rid of it was elevating. Consequently they clearly did not tend after property, because they experienced an objection to property: and it is doubtless a contrary receptiveness and nature of feelings which alone can cause modern man to desire violently and even passionately what those others disdained. The intensity of a desire varies with the receptivity of the feeling, whether the desire is one for possessions, or honours, power, revenge, and so on, or in short, whatever else may be the object of the impulse.

Conversely it is easy to see that the so-called sense of duty is far from being just an exceptional receptivity for the *concept* of duty: it is equally one of the conditions (impulses) of the execution of acts demanded by duty. The very considerable effort of will which a great many acts of duty demand removes all doubt on this point, and a glance at the results of a neglect of duty will finally convince us about the peculiarity of the "interest" which fulfilment of duty constitutes for the man who is possessed of a sense of duty: for neglect with him involves the so-called pangs of conscience, which he fears as much as the man who is possessed by a sense of gain fears loss of material wealth. Language emphasizes receptivity, as in *sense* of duty, or of gain, or again the element of impulse as in *lust* for power, or greed for possessions; and this varying emphasis is justified by the fact that it is the personal driving forces which primarily urge us to act, while the so-called moral driving forces urge us chiefly to refrain, both, of course, in relation to our other inclinations.[15] For essentially every commandment is a prohibition, and every action which is the result of such has essentially been effected at the cost of a personal inclination. Thus the relative driving forces may also be called inhibitive driving forces.

As has been shown elsewhere and will be further explained below, we can distinguish in every feeling, even in that of indifference, the aspect of impulse from the tone of mood. The feeling of fear is, besides a mental disposition which cannot further be described, an impulse to flight, whence it is immediately obvious why it can act as driving force, and can in men be the basis of such resolutions as tend to the evasion of occasions which arouse fear. The strength of fear can pass through many degrees, from slight apprehensiveness to terror, but its direction is always the same towards flight, and this property goes with the peculiar shade of mood which is the feeling of fear. Thus that which from one side appears as the peculiar nature of the feeling appears in its relation to will as a special driving force, and we say the same thing in two ways when we speak of a system of driving forces and of the nature of the personal dispositions of feelings.

The two zones which we have delimited against one another may be brought more vividly before the mind by a likeness. If his nature furnishes the material for the life-tune of the living man, then the material of character may be compared with the musical instrument which serves to translate the tune into sound. The results of Strivings, however similar, in two persons vary from each other, by reason of their different gifts, as much as the same tune by reason of the different quality of tone of two instruments. Conversely very different tunes may be played on one instrument, and similarly no degree of kinship in the faculties can guarantee a similarity in the Strivings. And the likeness would also fit the case of failure from lack of talent (or "poor music") in spite of the best will; we might here posit an improperly strung or otherwise damaged instrument.

A good simile always performs something more than the case demands for which it was devised, and this one may serve to lead us on to the fundamental concept of a third zone of personality. The same tune changes in the same instrument when the time is changed. We may play it more or less quickly, *andante* or *staccato*, and with varying emphasis. Similarly an event of the inner life, otherwise the same, may run more or less quickly, smoothly, or with interruptions, and may have the climax of its curve at the beginning, middle, or end. But if this happens regularly, that is, within a margin of fluctuation which is characteristic for each personality, then we must imagine as cause of this—and here the likeness fails us—certain dispositions, but no longer dispositions of material or quantity, nor of nature or direction, but of the inner mean (or medium) in which the experience takes its course: dispositions of the structure of the soul, or of the inner composition.

Of these the one which since earliest times has been the object of greatest discussion and debate is so-called "temperament". By attributing temperament to a man, we do not also attribute to him talent or a particular direction of his interests. For he might possess, or lack, temperament whether or not he had talents, whether he was meanly selfish or generous, self-sacrificing, and "self-less". Rather, the contrast between the presence and absence of temperament immediately evokes the idea of the contrast between liveliness and lack of liveliness, and especially that between rapidity and sluggishness of action. It is not a question of one's stock of force, or of directions in which forces develop, but of difference in the manner in which they run their course. We devote a separate chapter to the structure of character, and therefore here merely state without proof what is the differential characteristic of all properties of structure, without regard to the image of the psychical medium. They are not directional or quantitative properties, but properties of proportion and ratio, each of which may be represented as a quotient.

On looking back, we are satisfied that we have discovered three zones or regions of character, which though connected must at this point be distinguished in the clearest possible manner as being the spheres of action of three fundamentally distinct groups of properties; the material, or the totality of personal gifts (of mind, feeling, will): the structure or totality of dispositions of the personal medium, which determines in what form internal processes take their course: finally the nature, or totality of personal driving forces, which may also be called dispositions of feeling. The qualities of material are quantitative, those of structure relative, those of nature directive. Though in this book we intend to confine ourselves to the investigations of these three zones of character, we will briefly indicate what further qualities might repay research if we were to continue to follow the terms which language has handed down to us.

We are first met by at least one group of genuine qualities of character, namely that group which relates to the harmony or disharmony between the other qualities—the architectural qualities. To this group belong coherence, measure, harmoniousness, and incoherence, contradictoriness and disharmony; also firmness (stable nature) and infirmity (labile nature); clear and vague characterization; ripeness and immaturity, and similar qualities. But there is also a large number of names which, although deceptively similar to the genuine qualities of character, in fact class characters according to their consequences for social life, and, especially, according to their suitability in fulfilling the demands of the social spirit. Probity, righteousness, honesty, exactness, reliability, loyalty, trustworthiness, and many others together with their opposites are not properties of character, but permanent relations of the manifestations of character to the demands, claims, and rules of a human sphere of activity. These represent crystallized judgments about the use or harmfulness of a particular characteristic for our fellow-men, and it is clear that now the characteristic itself is denoted in a merely indirect manner. It is true that there are honest and dishonest persons, thieves and true men, and even (for example) peoples of thieves in opposition to other peoples among whom theft is so rare that it is punished as a crime deserving death. But it does not follow that there is a *sense* of theft, and the apparent truth of the opposite must not prevent us from first seeking out its causes, when it might (and in most cases does) appear that wholly different qualities produce the same result. If Paul, John, and Peter are "absolutely reliable", then more exact investigation might show us that Paul is so from the cause *a d f,* Peter from *a g m,* and John even from *w h n r.* This constitutes the transition to what above was called *pseudo-types,* which in exactly the same way are in need of characterological analysis and, so far as this is successful, will frequently reveal laws of association of true traits of character. Much virgin soil here awaits the plough. What insight we would obtain if we could succeed in exhausting the series of the possible conditions of no more than the following pseudotypes: the hotspur, quarreller, mystery-monger, boaster, pussyfoot, intriguer, climber, lover of children, pettifogger, tiger, "real" politician, and sound man of business!

Finally, though in practice the limits may be variable, still a logical distinction may be drawn between the real and apparent qualities of character and the properties of conduct, which latter stand midway between the two first in so far as they partly lead back to true traits of character and partly represent manifestations of changing traits of the kind in which pseudo-type is shown. To the former class it would seem that taciturnity, readiness, loquacity, rustic breadth, modesty, intrusiveness, boldness, hastiness, and carelessness belong: and to the latter calm, restlessness, indefatigability, clumsiness, *gaucherie,* smartness, servility, condescension, caprice. Their name, it may be remarked, is legion. However (with one restriction which will be mentioned immediately), this exhausts the possibilities. However difficult it may frequently prove to classify some traditional name, the meaning of whose content is clearly felt, under one of the groups here enumerated, it is equally certain that none will be found which would cause us to establish yet another group. It is true that the all but innumerable forms of self-esteem, and the forms of self-deception with their exceedingly numerous variants, which are due to steps taken unconsciously by personality to avoid and outwit feelings of inferiority, may demand separate treatment: nevertheless they can be divided without any remainder into qualities of material and into those of nature. One man may naturally have more *gifts* of energy, memory, or sensitiveness than another, as also greater capacity for self-esteem, pride, self-importance, and so on; one man is under the sway of driving forces like ambition, lust for power, utilitarianism; and another of driving forces like sense of honour, need of recognition, love of glory, vanity, self-admiration. Indeed, in the group of love of distinction (which will be discussed later) the interest of self-esteem acts immediately, as it acts in a mediated manner in all the driving forces.

The material, structure, and nature of character, its framework or architecture, the pseudo-typical action of character upon communal life, and the constant qualities of behaviour: this net of fundamental notions will serve to catch whatever may be advanced to characterize individual selves. One aspect only of the case appears to be wholly neglected: animal urges like those of hunger, thirst, sex, and innumerable others. It must be admitted immediately that we may and often indeed must assign them a place in our system of characterization, as, for example, when we have occasion to judge that one character has strong and another weak urges; that in one the sexual urge is over-emphasized, and in another gluttony; that one is the powerless slave of his urges, while another rules them in an uncommon degree. But in saying all this we would also have been speaking of the peculiarity of the interests, or, more exactly, we would have been laying stress on one aspect of their nature. As will appear, the urges are conditions and substrata of personal character, and especially of its nature, and in so far are already implicit in the driving forces. Urges in themselves belong to the character only of a vital entity and not of a personal ego, that is, of a vital entity *plus* spirit: but it is true that the personal ego would have ceased to exist if it were perfectly detached from its vital substratum. We shall therefore consider it an important task to pursue the nature of personality into the stratum of urge, and to investigate the forms which the nexus of life and spirit assumes. But these are the last and hardest questions of characterology, and we must here be on our guard lest we confuse them with answers. If, for example, we believe of somebody that he is capable of orgiasm, then this is no more than a problem until we also know what state of the personal ego is necessary and adequate to the existence of such states—a knowledge which to this hour nobody possesses.

CHAPTER IV NOTES

13   In *Ausdrucksbewegung und Gestaltungskraft* we have demonstrated that talent is simply a kind of formative power.

14   *Ausdrucksbewegung und Gestaltungskraft*, p. 167.

15   Language never operates *more geometrico*, and it must not, of course, be expected that "sense" or "feeling" on the one hand, and "urge", "desire", "greed", "passion", or "need" on the other, invariably form an element of expression in accordance with our classification. This would immediately be refuted by "sense of gain". But there is a distinct predominance in the sense indicated. It is to be noted that "spirit" here is used as meaning "interest"; "spirit of enterprise", of "business", of "contradiction", etc.

CHAPTER V

MEMORY AND THE CAPACITY FOR RECOLLECTION

In this chapter and the next we treat of the material of character, but observe a twofold restriction, first, in that we select only intellectual capacities, and next by occupying ourselves chiefly with such aspects of the facts as are unduly neglected by current psychology. The one procedure is adopted because, in qualities of will and feeling, the aspect of their *nature* is much more important than that of talent; the reason for the other procedure is obvious. Further, this chapter is rather prefatory of what is set out fully in the next chapter.

Modern investigation (and in part that of the ancient and mediaeval periods) considers memory as the most important condition of all intellectual functions, and it must be admitted that without it these could not take place at all. Deeper search, however, shows that without the remarkable arrangement which, in view of the purely human gift of recollecting, is called memory ("Gedächtnis"), even organic life would be impossible, and that we could never reach a clear understanding of said memory unless we began by making a distinction, foreign to current speech, between memory and capacity for recollection. Memory is a vital fact, capacity for recollection a spiritual, and the latter compared with the former represents one of its consequences under certain and new conditions.

In 1876 the ophthalmologist Hering gave a lecture, which later became famous, on memory as a property of organized matter, in which he sought to reduce all instinctive actions of animals to a memory of the living material. In the next year the lyrical poet Wilhelm Jordan published a grandiose didactic poem called *Andachten* ("Worship"), which among other things gave much greater profundity to the doctrine of "the memory of corporeal matter".[16] Since then several scientists have developed this idea and applied it, more especially, to the theory of cognition. But, as so often happens, what was thought to be a discovery had been known for years. Already in 1846, or thirty years before Hering, Carus, in his work, *Psyche, Zur Entwicklungsgeschichte der Seele* had demonstrated that the vital process simply demands the assumption that the living entity has the unconscious capacity of a kind of premonition of the future (which he calls the promethean element), and also of a kind of preservation of the past (which he called the epimethean). A single passage from his work should suffice to assure us that this greatest biologist of the late romantic period was far from the sensualistic doctrine of Traces, with its mechanistic failings, and had, once and for all, discovered and laid bare *vital* memory.[17]

"Thus the first divisions of the seed of a plant are prophetic of the nature and disposition of later leaves, and the leaves are prophetic of the nature and disposition of the corolla; and thus the very first plan of the blossom shows the definite structure of a form from which at the beginning of its life the whole plant emerged and which has remained so truly—though unconsciously—in its memory, that, at the height of its life, it wholly reproduces it; this form is the grain of seed. Indeed, if we observe life more closely, we see that in its tendency onward there must necessarily be a recollection of that which formerly existed; otherwise it is inexplicable why at the climax of development and after manifold phases have been passed through, something should recur of exactly the same kind as the germ from which the whole formation began. ... And again we recognize that a definite though unconscious premonition of the goal and direction of its evolutionary process must live within it, else the regular preparation of many phenomena which in themselves can be only periods of transition, and always subordinate themselves to higher ends, must remain quite inexplicable. ... The more we make these considerations ours, and the more clearly we understand that we have here an extremely definite unconscious expression of the after-sensation of the past and of the premonition of what is to come, the more we must be convinced that whatever we call in conscious life memory or recollection, and far more that whatever we call in this sphere fore-seeing and fore-knowledge, remain far behind the firmness and security with which, in the region of the unconscious life, the epimethean and promethean principle asserts itself before ever any present is known. ..." There are, however, other facts (which Carus in principle equally admitted), which deprive this brilliant exposition of any appearance of caprice.

If the chick which has only just left the egg immediately picks the grain, then beyond question it has recognized the significance of the grain in serving to satisfy its hunger; similarly the duckling discovers its true element in water into which—literally without reflection—it dives. The example is often cited of a species of wasps which brings to its larvae certain animals which it has paralysed but not killed with complicated stings, because they are destined later to serve as a living food for its young; it appears then to manifest the knowledge of a highly instructed anatomist, though in fact it cannot possibly have acquired it. A horse, which never before has met a beast of prey, is immediately seized by panic fear when it suddenly scents a lion, and gallops away in wild flight: thus, it recognizes the significance of the scent of lion, at least with reference to itself. Such examples might be multiplied to infinity and show irrefutably the error of the English sensualists when they spoke of the soul as of a "smooth tablet": for, though the soul brings no impressions with it into the world, it does bring a disposition for the interpretation of impressions, and it is these which are commonly called "innate instincts".

Reflective minds could not fail to see that the word "instinct" denoted a problem but not its solution, and it was natural to apprehend the condition of cognition not based on experience by analogy with memory, or (with Carus) to take it simply as the vital foundation of the capacity for recollection. In order to abbreviate future discussion we give here an outline of our own interpretation of the facts, although at this point it cannot be fully understood. The property of all living material—that it contemplates unconsciously—is the basis of vital cognitions. Thus in deep sleep the stream of life flows uninterrupted, and therefore nobody wakes in exactly the same humour in which he fell asleep. This kind of experience (where capacity to evoke dream-images would alone suffice to justify its name of "contemplation") accordingly does not require sensation, still less a co-ordinate consciousness: so that we must not be surprised if the disposition for this experience is inherited with the germ-cell.

If accordingly its condition is called memory then, first, it is evident that this vital memory must by no means be confused with the capacity for recollection. The chick which automatically picks grain and the baby that automatically sucks the breast do not recollect in the least that their parents did the same before them, as also their parents' parents: hereditary memory consists precisely in this that the impression of grains, or of the breast, is accompanied by an experience of a certain significance which makes the cause of the impression to be sometimes sought and sometimes avoided. We would be involved too deeply in investigations connected with the theory of consciousness if we were to explain what other conditions must be added in order that images may become impressions, and contemplations so-called experiences; but our examples will make it immediately clear to what degree the effect of impression upon living substance belongs to vital memory, and therefore must likewise be held distinct from the capacity of recollection. Now men and animals receive, and plants do not receive, impressions, and therefore the following list of the chief kinds of important functions which vital memory enables the living entity to perform refers exclusively to the former two.

I. *Recognition.*—Any given impression effects a change in the living substance which receives it; not only generally, but, with reference to the image which it mediates, in such a manner that subsequently a similar impression is experienced in a different manner from that in which it would have been experienced if it had not had the first impression for precursor. Consequently to every essentially prior image there corresponds the experience of a deeper impression, whose most universal characteristic is called "the quality of novelty", and to every essentially subsequent image, the experience of a more shallow impression, whose most universal characteristic is called "the quality of being familiar". The process of becoming shallower grows roughly with the frequency of repetitions. Now at this point, this kind of experience has nothing whatever to do with recollection. If I meet a friend in the street I do not in so far recollect anything but simply recognize him. Similarly the dog knows his master (by scent), the horse its stable, and the bird its nest. As acquaintance and familiarity grow, the experience becomes so shallow that in the vital entity which is capable of consciousness (that is, in man) it is no longer capable of evoking any consciousness: in that case no impression corresponds to the occasion of stimulus, but only an unconscious attitude.

II. *The Habit of Attitude.*—Every day we go through innumerable motions unconsciously and through others at any rate without reflection, and the sequence of these actions, which often is very complicated, not only serves to realize an end, but at some previous time was practised for that purpose. "Unintentionally we grip a body which looks like iron more firmly than a piece of wood of the same size: but we could not do this unless we had learned at some previous time to distinguish iron and wood by their concomitant properties of density, weight, and surface texture. A mountaineer utilizes, from moment to moment, with the greatest aptness an enormous mass of experience about the recovery of a lost equilibrium, while perhaps his consciousness is busy with the various kinds of rock which surround him."[18] If I learn a language I am forced continually to think of the meanings of words: but when I have done this many times over I am finally capable of speaking the language as a matter of habit, and make use of my capacity of recollection only as a makeshift—that is, whenever I am at a loss for a word. The process of inducing habit, under the influence either of necessity or of choice, is called practice. The process of practising leaves no doubt that, to impress something into the Soul is also an incorporation, and that vital memory, as memory of material, is that property of vital substance by virtue of which its capacity of calculable motions is seen to be the presence of its motional past. It suffices to have considered this a single time to prevent any future confusion of vital with mechanical motion. The training of animals is based upon the development of habits of attitude.

III. *Expectation of Impression.*—Although the function of vital memory which is to be mentioned is implicit in recognition, it is good to emphasize it especially; we mean expectation of an impression. If "a child once burnt is shy of the fire", this expresses that in the Soul of the child the view of the flame is connected with the expectation of painful heat, because on some occasion he put his finger in the flame and was hurt by it. A dog that runs away at an uplifted stick expects to be beaten because on some previous occasion it was given a blow. At this point we venture to interpose a remark relating to the theory of cognition.

It is true that among series of impressions there are some where the underlying facts are related as cause and effect; but the great majority is of a different kind, and the connection between the impressions is never the reason which forces us to consider a series of objects as causally connected. If we see lightning we expect to hear thunder, and in fact lightning is the immediate cause of thunder; but we also expect to hear the "c" of the octave after we have heard the first three notes of the common chord: but these are not the cause of the "c" which we expect. We do not here inquire after the origin of the concept of causality: all we intend is to guard against a confusion which not only has occurred, but also has been the occasion of fundamentally erroneous interpretation of causality (like Hume's).

Expectations arise the more promptly and decisively the more the original connection of images was accompanied by powerful emotions. A cat that has once been hurt by a man will always run away from him, and if that man was a workman in somewhat rough clothes, then it will always run away from a man wearing a workman's dress. We have now effected the transition to a fourth function of memory.

IV. *Acquired Character of Impressions.*—Except in a newborn baby there is no present impression which is not coloured and changed somehow by former impressions: thus each man's personal history has a share in forming the character of his impressions. For a man who, when he was young, fell violently in love while hearing a waltz, this same tune will have a higher exciting power after many years; it will therefore have acquired a character which other people do not discover in it. The colours which our own feelings imprint upon the character of images have been called "projections", and it is true that these take place continually, and are entirely avoided by nobody. Now the occasion of the impression also has its own character which offers resistance to characters which are thrust upon it, and therefore we suspect that there is a difference and even an oppositeness of persons, in so far as in one group the receptivity to the character of the images is such that it never allows real play to merely "projected" character, while in the other groups the original colours are buried in a sense under the reflected light of personal feelings. Hence there result two types of apprehension of which we treat in the next chapter. For the capacity to judge we repeat that "projection" is a source of error and not, as has been thought, of knowledge. Insight into the nature of things and of men is reached by the man who, undeceived by the false colour emanating from personal moods, has the power to extract this nature by feeling, and knows to distinguish the proper colour of images from that which is due to the light in which they are seen, of which he is himself the source.

But not only past events mask the images due to impressions to such a degree as to distort their character, but also those permanent moods in which the fundamental constitution of the living entity is manifested. The student who "has taken it to heart" that he has just failed in his examination sees everything in a gloomy light; the student who has just passed brilliantly sees everything in a rosy light; but also the constitutional pessimist "sees black", and the constitutional optimist (the euphoric type), "sees white", if we may say so. But the conditions of permanent moods also condition the relation of, and the distribution of emphasis over, the material of memory; and consequently "psychogenetic" feelings and vital memory always co-operate to render fast one and the same illuminating colour.

When the experience of an impression has been the cause of exceptionally severe mental agitation, it may be the origin of fairly stubborn psychical disturbances, which are called traumata. For example a child, who was very close to a withered Christmas tree which caught fire, may fall for years into paroxysms of crying whenever so much as a match is struck before his eyes. A person who was involuntarily involved in a railway accident is prevented by the terrible shock for a long time from entering a railway train, and, if he insists on doing so, may suffer from sickness and giddiness.[19]

V. *Phantasms.*—Among other secondary conditions, which need not here be discussed in full detail, there is the change effected in the living substance by a powerful impression which brings it about that similar impressions bring before the inner eye images which are riveted to the original impression by means of powerful feelings: these are called phantasms. For example, if I hear the waltz-tune which I heard in my youth when I fell in love, then there may be before my inner eye the phantasm of a girl's figure, and there may ensue the images of whole series of processes which were connected with that figure. Thus my soul is diverted from the present impression: from the space of perception I have been transported into the space of phantasms, and am in the condition of day-dreaming. In principle the same thing happens in night dreams, only there the play of phantasms is caused by other stimuli than day-impressions, and in its development is no longer impeded by these. At times this happens to everyone, but to some more often than to others, whence it is possible to distinguish the phantasy-type from the perception-type. This will be dealt with in the next chapter.

This exhausts the chief kinds of vital functions which cannot take place without vital memory. As has been observed, they are common to men and animals. Apart from original "instinctive" cognition, animals and men alike have recognition, habits of attitude, expectation of impression, distortion of the character of an impression by its past, and action of phantasy, at least during sleep. But the capacity to recollect is peculiar to man. The dying dog of Ulysses recognizes his master after twenty years, and we may imagine that in the interval he dreamed of hunting expeditions which they made together: but he cannot recollect these. Animals have an extraordinary memory, but man alone has recollection. The latter cannot arise without vital memory, but in order to arise it further requires Spirit coupled with vitality. The details of the process have been set out elsewhere, and therefore we here confine ourselves to essentials.

Consciousness in its most proper sense is Ego-consciousness. Ego-consciousness is confined to man, and the world which corresponds to it is far different from the world of non-Ego-conscious experience. The vital state of an animal is preponderantly one of sensation (and urge), and there corresponds to it a world of bodies different as images are different; the vital state of original man is preponderantly one of contemplation (or action), and as yet without Ego-consciousness; there corresponds to it a world of corporeal images: to the vital state of self-conscious man of history there corresponds a world of things having properties. The Ego finds itself only in the reflection of *things* having temporal persistence; and it is only in the reflection of a pondering of the temporally persistent self that bare happening changes into a non-reversible series of distinguishable events, or, more briefly, into the line of time which stretches between present and past. If we were to raise into consciousness the process which in grown man goes on unconsciously, and whose result is recollection, then it would have the following appearance.

Through the operation of vital memory, and occasioned by certain impressions, a phantasm arises or is about to arise, but comes into conflict with those impressions which have their origin in the world of objects of perception. It is the conflict between the occasion of perception and completed (or only incipient) phantasm which leads to Ego-recollection, or more exactly to the reflection "I am now here", and, thence inevitably to reflection on the nature of the phantasm; not I who *am receive* the impression to which the phantasm corresponds, but I who *was received* it, and the phantasm is an image of recollection. According to the witness of the German language at least recollection is self-recollection [Sich-erinnern], and thus contains a consciousness of the uniformity of the Ego at various instants of time. The derivation is incomplete because it does not decide why the occasion of the phantasm is placed in the past, but it suffices for our purpose.

If then memory and capacity for recollection must be kept apart, even where one is meant with reference to the functions of the other, then we are right in distinguishing between power of memory and facility in the capacity to recollect. It is true that the latter has an insuperable barrier in the total store of memories, because nobody can recollect what does not belong to this store; but the capacity to recollect at will often shows very different degrees in person who may be supposed to have equal memories. There are men of strong memory and difficult capacity to recollect, men of comparatively weak memory and facile capacity to recollect, and finally men in whom memory and capacity to recollect largely correspond. The failure of our power to recollect is often the cause why we search painfully for a datum (a name, street, date), but in vain, while it is in our store of memory all the time; for later it occurs to us by itself. In persons of difficult capacity to recollect the strong memory which they nevertheless possess is revealed by the fact that length of time steals far less from their store of memory than from others who have more facile powers of recollection, but are weaker in memory. As everybody knows, the contents of memory fade, other things being equal, proportionally to the time which has elapsed since their acquisition; a fact which, as we may remark in passing, is quite compatible with the other fact that everybody without exception recollects many impressions from earliest youth until (say) his fifteenth year far more vividly and thoroughly than impressions of later life; for the early impressions took place under circumstances of much greater emotional emphasis, and therefore "other things" were not equal. Personal capacity to recollect may serve to fix one's eye on its own nature, but also on its origin. We first turn to the process of memorizing.

I. *The Process of Memorizing.*—It is the acquisition of some school task which is important for scholastic business, and therefore investigation of the process of memorizing (degree of facility in learning, durability of retention) has been almost the only object of professional psychology; hence what is relevant may be read up in any manual. The results of exhaustive investigation have not been very fruitful, and the output as far as characterology is concerned has been next to nothing. We therefore confine ourselves to indicating a few main points.

It requires no experiment to prove that a content having meaning is more easily memorized, and is retained longer than, for example, a series of meaningless syllables; and verse, especially rhymed verse, is better retained than prose. Further, we all know that repetition facilitates learning. If at one time I have studied physics and, as I think, have forgotten everything in course of time, then if I once more take up the laws of physics I shall nevertheless learn them more quickly than when I first studied this subject. Numerous experiments have shown that a distribution of repetitions over several days is more favourable to the process of memorizing than their immediate accumulation.

Further, it has appeared that a coherent whole is more easily mastered if it is learned in one piece than if it is divided into parts to be learned severally: finally, that relatively quick learning is preferable to relatively slow learning. In these respects all persons are more or less alike, but there are very notable differences in respect to the absolute speed of learning and the length of retention under equal conditions of memorizing; and it should be emphasized that typically quick learners are by no means also quick to forget. Thus it is certain that some men have a stronger innate memory than others.

Now "innate memory" is a vital fact which like every other vital fact can be trained to the limit of its efficacity, but cannot be intensified beyond that. What have been proclaimed on occasions as methods for strengthening the memory are at best methods to make recollection easier: the memory is not strengthened. If I hear that matches were invented in 1832, I shall soon forget it again: but if somebody tells me that this was the year in which Goethe died, and that his dying words were "More light", then I shall probably not forget the year in which matches were invented for the rest of my life, although my memory is no more efficient than before. So-called mnemotechnics aid recollection by devices which in principle are always of this kind. Persons to whom helping ideas from outside are always occurring while they learn have been called "ingenious" learners, the others "mechanical" learners. (The terminology is based on Kant.)

II. *Recollection of Experiences and Recollection of Objects.*— The personal nature of the capacity for recollection is, for characterology, of infinitely greater importance than the technique of memorizing; for the former points back to the personal properties of the nature of the memory. What interests us impresses us, and what impresses us is more easily apprehended and longer retained than what was indifferent. The nature of the personal memory is related to the driving forces (= interests) in such a manner that in similar circumstances the capacity to recollect increases with the interest in the subject. If A is fond of mathematics and dislikes languages, and B likes languages and dislikes mathematics, then an erroneous view would be reached about the difference in strength between their memories if both were to be examined on their power to remember mathematical propositions, and the opposite erroneous view would be reached if both were examined on their power to remember words. However, the efficiency of power to recollect does not correspond immediately to the degree of liking. Of two scholars who equally like mathematics, one will be better than the other at remembering mathematical propositions. Gifts (and consequently memory) are rooted in one stratum of personality, and the driving forces in another; and the two may either aid or hamper each other, as is the case, for example, if somebody's main interests do not extend to those facts to which he could bring the greatest natural talent. We now proceed to the two most important specific properties of memory.

Observation is usually confined to memory of objects, and to illustrate its power some great scholar is perhaps cited. But the memory which is required if a man is to write stories like those, for example, of Gottfried Keller, is not necessarily less, and may be much more powerful than that of a distinguished scholar; only it does not relate so much to things absolutely as to objects whose apprehension is based on personal experience. The same is true of the memory, which often is enormous, of great statesmen like Frederick the Great, for the place in life, fate, and qualities of innumerable individuals. In the memory of experiences, again, the prevalent memory for feeling or mood is distinguished from prevalent memory for sensuous, perceptive, or intuitive data. This does not mean that one man chiefly remembers moods and another images of intuition: it means that the apprehension and selection of that which is most easily and longest retained is determined in one man by the sentimental character of objects, and in another by their intuitional image. A painter, for example, on seeing a landscape, immediately memorizes the exact distribution of its colours and forms, and can draw by heart a great part of it, after a fashion, even years later. If a poet had perceived the same landscape, he would later have a much less clear recollection of colours and forms, but would retain the character of the landscape for many years with the utmost exactness, and would be able consequently to make a description of it which, in a receptive hearer or reader, would evoke a *phantasm* of the landscape—often containing numerous individual traits.

Now a preponderant memory for moods does not denote the man of a subjective direction of apprehension, who will occupy us in the next chapter. If a landscape of gloomy character appears gloomy to me, then I have correctly reflected it, so to speak; and if it appears cheerful just because I happen to be in a cheerful mood, then I have falsified its proper character by a subjective addition. My memory of moods is something different from my tendency to falsify moods, and there is a faithfulness in recollecting moods as there is one in recollecting facts. Of course, it is further possible to distinguish persons who have a good memory especially for their own moods, and others who have an equally or even preponderantly good memory for the character of images of impressions; but, though such divisions may be important, we must here confine ourselves to the main outlines. The often discussed question whether feelings are recollected immediately or only through the mediation of intuitional elements is without object for us, since it is our conviction that in real experience imageless characters and images of intuition without any mood-character are alike never found.

The characteristic of a strong intuitional memory is the "sensuous liveliness" of the images of recollection, or, more exactly, the accuracy, clearness, and definition with which details which can be distinguished by intuition are brought before the mind, and the capacity for this is one aspect of the vivacity of recollection, but is not identical with it. The thing of perception can be composed neither of its intuitional nor of its non-intuitional properties, but rather, in relation to these, is a unit of significance which with a minimum of intuitional force is apprehended and impressed upon the memory in such a way that it can feed, for example, the richest capacity for combination ; and, if it is true that a poor store of sensuous data among one's memories does involve a fading of its contents, still an excessive wealth contains the danger that the object may fall apart into a mosaic of details which are threatened by final dilapidation.

Some people better remember tonal and other visual properties. For example, one learns better what is recited to him because he chiefly uses auditional impressions to help recollection; another learns better what he absorbs by reading because he requires images of the pages. A musician excels the layman in retaining auditional, and a painter and draughtsman in retaining visual impressions. Hence the popular distinction between an auditive and a visual type, which, however, must not allow us to overlook that man as such—that is, compared with all animals—is a creature of eyes whose visual impressions have undoubted supremacy over all other sense-impressions, with the sole exception of the blind. It is only under this supremacy that sometimes auditional and sometimes visual memory has the higher emphasis.[20]

Things are one genus of objects. Correctness of recollection for thing-processes is manifested (among other things) by the exactitude with which they can be described later; a careful description gives an account also of numerous details of sensuous appearance: and therefore, seen from *this* side, there is a closer connection between intuitional memory and object-memory than between object-memory and mood-memory; and it is proved once more that the degree of clearness in the process of sensuous presentation (called imagination by many) must not be confused with the attractive force of phantasms, and still less with these images themselves which (for example in the true artist) are born of a creative mood. The conceptual relations between processes or, more briefly, concepts, are yet another genus of objects. At bottom these are based upon vital units of significance which are supported by mood-memory, frequently in spite of an extremely meagre supply of images: hence, seen from this side, mood-memory stands nearer to object-memory.

We have thus already thrown light upon object-memory itself. On the one hand it is thing-memory (in the widest sense), on the other memory of word-meanings, and, finally, of concepts. Both species admit of numerous distinctions: there is an especially developed memory for names and numbers, anecdotes, family affairs and personalities, for every particular science and even for each province of such a science. But an investigation of this matter would not advance us in principle; here therefore we make a stop.

CHAPTER V NOTES

[16] We give a few of his most important lines:

"It is recollection of her own cradle when the red stinging fly glues grains of sand into a pointed arch as soon as she feels that her eggs have ripened to maturity.

It is recollection of her own food during the maggot-state when the anxious mother straddles over the caterpillar and drags it long distances, lays her eggs in it, and locks it in that prison.

The larva of the male stag-beetle feels and knows by recollection the length of his antlers, and in the old oak carves out in double dimensions the space in which he will undergo metamorphosis.

What teaches the fisher of the air to weave the exact angles of her net by delicate law, and to suspend it from branch to branch with strings, as firm as they are light, according to her seat?

Does she instruct her young in this art? No; she takes her mother's duties more lightly. The young are expelled uncared for from the sac in which the eggs have been laid.

But three or four days later the young spider spreads its little net with equal skill on the fronds of a fern, although it never saw the net in which its mother caught flies.

The caterpillar has no eye to see how others knit the silken coffins from which they shall rise again. Where have they all the skill to spin so? Wholly from inherited recollection.

In man, what he learned during life puts into the shade the harvest of his ancestors' labour: this alone blinds him, made stupid by a learner's pride, to his own wealth of inherited recollections.

The recollection of what has been done a thousand times before by all his ancestors teaches a new-born child to suck aptly, though still blind.

Recollection it is which allows man in his mother's womb to fly, within the course of a few months, through all the phases of existence through which his ancestors slowly rose long ago.

Inherited recollection, and no brute compulsion, leads the habitual path to the goal which has many times been attained; it makes profoundest secrets plain and open, and worthy of admiration what was a mere miracle.

Nature makes no free gifts. Her commandment is to gain strength to struggle, and the conqueror's right is to pass it on to his descendants: her means by which the acquired skill is handed down is the memory of corporeal matter."

[17] *Psyche: Contributions to the evolutionary history of the soul* by Carl Gustav Carus. New edition published by Eugen Diederich, with introduction and commentary by Klages. Part One has been translated into English by Renata Welch as *Psyche: On the Development of the Soul – Part 1: The Unconscious.*

[18] *Ausdrucksbewegung und Gestaltungskraft*, p. 57.

[19] Even where "hysterical mechanism" is not pronounced (cp. Chapter VIII), such events are a welcome occasion to the organism for fixing the disturbance. Thus it is almost certain that the famous "accident-neurosis" underwent a certain increase after the legislation about accidents, both with regard to frequency and gravity of the cases. Indeed, "compensation-hysteria" has become a regular term.

[20] A motor type must on no account be co-ordinated to the visual and auditive type. There is a motor type, and we shall soon see in what it consists: but its opposite is the sensor type. A man can thus be a visual type and a motor type, *or* a sensor type: or, again, he may be an auditive and motor type, *or* sensor type. If visual, auditive and motor are all co-ordinated: this is a glaring proof that the unhappy "sensualism" is still active to blind us to the polar character of movement-experience and impression-experience. We revert to this in the text. In order to understand the motor type, we first must know that impression-experiences lead to perception only with the help of movement-phantasms or of "virtual movement", as Palágyi prefers to call them. (Compare especially his *Naturphilosophische Vorlesungen*, also his posthumous *Wahrnehmungslehre*; both published by Barth, Leipzig.) Some movement-phantasms are connected with every impression, and with the movement-phantasms slight impulses are connected, i.e. impulses towards the actual execution of the movement. A man can read a letter without speaking, only because he is continually in a state of virtual speech, and this process is accompanied by a desire (generally unnoticed, but in principle noticeable) to pronounce what is being read, which frequently leads to soundless movements of the tongue and lips. Similarly we do not see a tall pine without a slight impulse to stretch upright, or a flying bird without a mute desire to fly (however feeble), etc. In this respect all men agree; but they differ considerably in what follows.

The desire is more or less pronounced—sometimes because it is abnormally strong and sometimes because it is abnormally uninhibited. The latter case is exemplified in very old people who cannot read a letter without whispering. The abnormal strength of desire is one condition at least (or better, one component) of the motor type; but to this must be added something else, which is decisive. In some people the impression-pole predominates over the movement-pole: these constitute the sensor type; and in others the movement-pole: over the impression-pole: these constitute the motor type. In the former the impulses which lead to movements are determined by already existent stresses upon impressions; in the latter, the impression receives its stress only in accordance with movement-impulses which it succeeded in stimulating. We give an example of this from the special province of the psychology of handwriting.

Many exceedingly talented interpreters of handwriting reach their remarkable results only after they have imitated some words out of the document which they wish to interpret; they belong to the motor type. Others of equal talent must be particularly on their guard against copying in this manner, because this confuses the impulses towards interpretation which they derive from mere inspection of the document. They belong to the sensor type. If these "imitations" of the motor type are carefully examined, they turn out to be exaggerations of certain striking and "characteristic" details of the form which they copy. Thus the view which they take of the character of the objects which are under contemplation is stressed and completed only by the realization of movement-impulses which were stimulated by contemplation, and, so to speak, through them. Conversely in the sensor type, delicacy of apprehension of character is adversely influenced by actual attempts at imitation, for now the expression of movement has become independent and distracts them from stresses of impressions; and it was the predominance of these over the experience-movement which, for this type, was essential to the apprehension of their character. One has but to bring to mind a group of painters, artists, or composers, in order to feel clearly that the pictures or pieces of music manifest sometimes a sensor type and sometimes a motor type.

CHAPTER VI

FACULTIES FOR IMPRESSIONS AND DIRECTIONS
OF APPREHENSION

In every act of perception a distinction must be made between the content of the impression and the act of apprehension which is added to it, although usually bare recollection does not suffice to separate the two, whose separation resembles the chemical analysis of a structure whose compositeness is no more obvious than is that of cooking salt. It is true that we are on exceptional occasions aware of this. For example, if a few minutes ago the clock had struck three, and we had not noticed it, and if in spite of this we could now remember it, then the act of apprehension and the experience of the impression would be demonstrably non-coincident. But even without reference to such events, which after all are not quite common, the distinctness of the two may easily be proved.

The immediate visual impression is far from containing what we believe ourselves to perceive under the stimulus of every visual, datum—the depth of space. This we imagine that we see in a painted landscape, the colours of which lie on one plane; and on the other hand a blind man on whom a successful operation has been undertaken at first sees things which are at different distances around him essentially as though they were mere patches of colour on a plane at a terrifying proximity to the eye. The visual impression does contain data which permit the development of the seeing of depth, but it is only their highly complex connection with a wholly different sphere of experience—that of self-motion—which permits of the act of spatial perception which is thus not related merely to something present, but also to something which is past, but also (by virtue of vital memory) merged in the present impression. Other examples will make this abundantly clear. If the moon rising on a distant horizon appears of impressive magnitude, then we have unconsciously compared its present image with the absent image of the moon at its zenith—that is, we have compared the impression-content of the moon with the recollection-phantasm of the moon.

Not only the impressions which we have experienced, but also the judgments which we have passed are part of our memory. The lowing of a cow and the roar of a lion are different acoustically: but this would never serve to explain why in open country the one would fill us with pleasure and the other with apprehension. Rather, with the roar of the lion we perceive the lion himself, and it is the echo of all the lion's properties, whether learned by proper experience or from conversation, which strikes us with that roar and brings to our act of perception a material compared with which the acoustic impression sinks into a stimulus containing an almost negligible portion of content. Thus in every human perception the whole past of his experiences takes part, and therefore we cannot investigate his manner of perceiving without having investigated his memory, nor his memory without searching after the source of its peculiarities in his manner of perceiving. Both form an indissoluble whole— manner of perceiving and nature of memory—and demand to be investigated with regard to their mutual relation; and if we now lay emphasis on manner of perception, we presuppose what we have already adduced in the last chapter about memory and capacity for recollection. Once more we must distinguish the vital conditions of the manner of perception from its spiritual conditions, giving to the former the name of Faculties for Impressions, and to the latter that of Directions of Apprehension. We first turn to the Faculties for Impressions.

I. *Personal Receptivity for Impressions.*——Primarily men differ according to their degree of receptivity for impressions: some are absolutely more receptive than others. Each individual is more receptive when rested than when tired, in early youth than in old age, and more receptive for objects which please than for those which are indifferent to him: but in spite of all this there is an average freshness, breadth, and strength of receptivity, and this varies extremely from person to person, whence there naturally follow certain differences in the nature of the memory, which may be used as fitting examples to demonstrate that those properties which may be classed as talents appear usually, if not always, as dispositions of sentiment as well as of intellect.

The fact that great poets employ ten thousand different words or more, while the current language of mediocre intelligence requires two hundred to five hundred, might lead us to assume that the poet stands in a special relation to the world; but in any case we would have to take into account not only his greater grasp of the linguistic element, but also his greater sensitiveness, by virtue of which he is continually absorbing fresher, richer, and stronger linguistic impressions than the owner of a mere habitual speech: so that he owns a store of words which excels the equal or even greater apparatus of a non-poet by virtue of superior significance. (We observe, but only in passing, that our example must not be inverted, because the characteristic and essential relation of the poet to the word cannot be exhausted by any analysis, however exact, of his powers of receptivity. For almost identical faculties for receptivity might belong to an eminent student of languages, philology, or phonetics.)[21]

The personal degree of receptivity in general crosses with the personal modifications of receptivity, on which subject the essentials have already been stated. Thus if, for example, somebody has a strongly over-emphasized receptivity for visual impressions and another for auditional impressions, then the two could be compared only if their particular talents were made the basis of the comparison, or if facts common to the spheres of both senses were used, like language.

II. *Personal Fullness.*—If the capacity for impressions were taken metaphorically as a body, then it would offer us two contrary surfaces, the outer surface which might be distinguished by the degree of receptivity which has just been discussed, and the inner surface according to which each impression would receive a peculiar stamp, because as soon as it has arisen, or rather, while still in the process of arising, it would fall under the domination of some particular vital nexus. The Greek philosopher Protagoras is supposed to have claimed for psychology the Heraclitean doctrine of the perpetual flux of reality by asserting that the content of perception from moment to moment is the result of the fusion of an external event (the world) with an inner event (the experiencing soul). If we disregard the sceptical side-issues and conclusions which played their part, we need not hesitate to call Protagoras, by virtue of his epoch-making work, the father of European psychology and the pioneer of epistemology in particular. But the essential meaning of the case is made clear most quickly if we begin once more from vital memory.

It is certain that the content of every impression effects *some* change in the living organism; and it is equally certain that the "trace" left by this impression is undergoing continual change through the growth or decay of the organism which, while alive, is undoubtedly an entity which changes in the Heraclitean sense. If then two individuals have simultaneously received identical or very similar impressions, then after a considerable interval the effects of these will vary very largely in accordance with the nature, age, and growing force of the organism, which unceasingly seeks literally to assimilate all physical *and* psychical elements, and also, for example, rejects some psychically indigestible element, or else drags it along as a foreign body. But, further, it is obvious now that this so-called trace of the impression turns into something different in a rich and in a meagre soul. In the former it will become a vital part of a full-blooded fancy, and as such will bloom of itself; in the latter, as a part of an anemic circulation it will itself turn grey, sere, and withered. Hence we must conclude, in a Protagorean manner, that at the very moment when an impression begins, the same stimulus necessarily creates two generically different images in two different vital entities, for in each of them the recipient mind participates, sometimes charging it with significance, and sometimes drawing its own significance from it.

Thus looked at, the individual capacity for impressions may appear to depend on the individual memory: but we can equally well imagine the individual memory as depending on the individual capacity for impressions. For ultimately the fact that the individual is capable at all of impressions is based on its most fundamental nature, and this is also true of its particular direction, of its nutritive force, and of its creative force to transmute the sensuous material. Indeed, it is part of the peculiar atmosphere of many people that with each word which they pronounce, or even by their mute presence, they are drawing from a full vessel, while others, even when they make preparations for a broad demonstration, seem to be dragging a meagre equipment painfully into the light. We imagine the series of differences which belong to this sphere as stretching between fullness and emptiness, and call the opposition between the extremes that between the full and the empty.

What we have just described is certainly an important aspect of personal experience; still, we are not here concerned with the fullness of experience as such, but only in so far as its foundations offer a contribution to personal talent. The manifestation of this contribution in the individual case depends upon the other capacities of the person in question; according to secondary circumstances it might be able to increase gifts of reasoning, or fancy, or "intuition", in artistically gifted individuals creative force, and in those with more practical gifts, address, and promptness. These remain open possibilities, for fullness and emptiness are of far too general a nature to be able to guarantee more definite consequences even in the one field of talents. The various talents which now remain to be defined are related to so comprehensive a characterization as species to genus, but they justify separate treatment, since in fullness and emptiness alike now one and now the other side preponderates and gives the colour.

III. *Personal Warmth of the Material of Intuition.*—We saw already in the previous chapter that the enormous individual variations with regard to the sensuous freshness of the images of intuition must not be allowed to count simply as measures of the degree of vitality; we can add that sensuous freshness will easily fade more or less in such personalities as (in accordance with their talent) make their impressions the occasion of thought and abstraction instead of dwelling upon them. Their relative incapacity to bring before the mind past images with any degree of sensuous exactness is therefore no immediate index of internal poverty: it *may* be an index of the fact that intellectual vitality predominates over sensuous vitality. We call the extremes coldness and warmth; which is to indicate that the total state of definitely sensuous natures (and hence each single content of consciousness) appears plunged in a mood of warmth, and that of definitely non-sensuous natures in a mood of coldness. The popular antithesis between so-called warm and cold temperament of course denotes something different, and at best can be rendered more acute by the co-ordination of types of sensuousness bearing the same name; but on this matter experience decides. Thus, in Schiller's works, we meet a "fiery" temperament, but this is composed of enthusiasm, sympathy, and an impulsive desire for expression, which are by no means incompatible with sensuous coldness: while in Stifter's works we meet sensuous warmth, while the passion which co-exists with this lacks an impulsive desire for expression, and therefore makes a far less "fiery" impression.

This disposition for impressions is more particular, and accordingly its effects upon personal gifts can be more closely defined. The extremes which are here before us are the foundation, as has already been observed, of the distinction between a sensual and a spiritual mind; they often (though not invariably) are associated with the distinction—which will later be touched upon—between preponderantly abstract and preponderantly concrete thought, and form part of the basis of the psychic distinction between youth and age. We only recall the preponderance of an abundance of coloured images, and of fancy, in youth, and the incomparably greater vividness and magnificance of its dreams. In short, among thinkers and scholars and men of action, there is more coldness in the nature of the impressions, and among poets and artists more warmth.

IV. *Personal Motility of the Material of Intuition.*—If (for example) Hölderlin is compared with Jean Paul, or Kleist with Stifter, then the differences between them cannot easily be understood without the fundamental assumption that the first member of each pair belongs to the roaming type, and the second to the staying type. Particularly if we compare the language of Hölderlin's *Odes* (where sentences which end with the line are exceeded a hundred times by those which run beyond), or the unarrested flow of Kleist's prose in *Michael Kohlhaas* with that of Stifter's *Nachsommer*, which continually appears to be coming to rest, then we can hardly avoid the conclusion that, apart from differences of temperament, a fundamental difference in the motility of the material of intuition is here in action which, on the one hand causes the spirit to pass from image to image, and to have its strength in speeding over the world, and on the other causes it to be arrested by the image, and to manifest its truest nature in comprehending, or in attaining profundity. When they go with an analogous structure of character, the former might grow into the "flight of ideas" and the latter into the "fixed idea". We call the extremes the opposition between lightness and heaviness of the material of intuition.

V. *Personal Depth of the Capacity for Impressions.*—Degrees of motility add something essentially anew to the opposition between fullness and emptiness; but the opposition between profundity and shallowness, which must now be mentioned, coincides with the former opposition in so far as profundity is one aspect of fullness, and shallowness one side of emptiness, but one aspect only, which for that reason deserves special emphasis. We compared above the capacity for impression to a body having two surfaces, in order to derive from the existence of the inner surface the participation of the proper life of the Soul in this sensuous process; and now we wish to point out that with the growth of the fullness of the Soul a growing over-emphasis of the inner front, as compared with the outer, must take place. The richer the Soul, the more does it take consciousness captive, and the poorer it is the more will consciousness need supplies from outside. This is the foundation of two widely divergent types of spirit, the introverted and the extroverted, to each of which again there belongs a characteristic particular colour of each content of impression. For the introverted spirit the impression has a weight of meaning which it wholly lacks for the extroverted spirit, and the latter on its side will seek ceaselessly to make good what it lacks by accumulating impressions. But these facts also have their obverse side.

Where the capacity for impressions has reached the extreme of shallowness, the impressions finally appear without exception under the aspect of banality; while the extreme depth of the capacity for impression has the consequence that innumerable stimuli, which remain without significance for the recipient, never come to have action at all; hence adaptability often goes with shallowness, and a diminished gift for adaptation with profundity. In northern Germany the word "Tiefsinn" [literally "deep-mindedness"] is used for profundity of thought the result of psychical conditions, as well as for spiritual benightedness.[22]

Our characterization of the faculty for impressions will be seen to include a characterization of the directions of apprehension which would fit these; but still it remains a characterization of the vital side of these manners of apprehension. If now we make the spiritual side of character responsible for a different classification of the capacity for apprehending and judging, then the objection that finally it too must still be based on differences in the nature of vitality would appear to be all the more valid because we intend ourselves to bring forward certain connections (which in fact have already been mentioned) between these and the faculty for impressions. But from now onwards, even the connections which belong thither pass through the intermediate link of the driving forces (= interests) in which, apart from vitality, Spirit always takes a part. Such dependence, however, is not here our immediate concern: our investigation is aimed at the faculties for apprehension themselves, although we shall not neglect to throw an occasional glance on their relations to the stratum of interests.

I. *Degree of the Activity of Apprehension.*—We found ourselves compelled to distinguish degrees of receptivity for impressions, and similarly we must now imagine that there are degrees in the conditions for the apprehension and spiritual appropriation of the contents of impressions. This process immediately causes it to emerge that we are here on wholly new ground. A man who is very receptive of impressions, but has ill-developed powers of spiritual appropriation, stands, to a man who may be supposed to have an equal receptivity for impressions, but well-developed powers of spiritual appropriation, in the relation (other things being equal) of a dreamer to a man of action. This has no immediate connection with the contrast between fullness and emptiness. There too, indeed, the difference in the capacity for impressions, and also, of course, in vital memory, is based on a difference of the internal surfaces; but this difference is now accounted for by the fact that the internal side is preponderantly occupied by Vitality in the one case, and by Spirit in the other. In the owner of the former nature an invariably passive experience of the Soul preponderates over manifestations of the Spirit, and in the owner of the latter the ever active Spirit preponderates over the world of events of experience. Accordingly one tends to surrender more or less to his impressions, while the other subordinates them to that direction of his apprehension which is the natural resultant of his interests. Where there are considerable talents, the latter will effect great achievements, the former, in similar circumstances, will have great experiences; and when talents fail, the one is in danger of a shallow life and heartless formalism, the other, in similar circumstances, of stagnation and animal narrowness.

II. *The Vital and the Spiritual Direction of Apprehension.*—A sharp distinction must be made between oppositions in degree of the apprehensive activity, and the opposition between the preponderantly vital and the preponderantly spiritual direction of apprehension, which for its part manifests the influence of the opposition between fullness and emptiness upon the spiritual nature of men. Fullness in general is vital fullness, and emptiness in general is vital emptiness, and therefore both manifest themselves immediately in the fullness or meagreness of experience, which includes those qualities of receptivity of impressions, together with its consequences, which were treated above, and further manifest themselves, as goes without saying, in the manner of spiritual apprehension and digestion. If we look upon the history of spiritual development in man, it is easy to fix two extreme groups, apart from a wide intermediate group of ambiguous cases; one of these groups can be understood only if there is a preponderance of a mode of apprehension which depends on Life, and the other only if there is such a mode which depends on Spirit. For, just as there are vital compulsions, so there are spiritual demands, and the perception, apprehension, and even the entire thought of many persons are sometimes governed by the former, while those of others are mainly governed by the latter. This is not the last word about fullness and emptiness; it is possible to bring forward differences of spiritual assimilation of emptiness, or again, of fullness. It is hardly necessary to say that the dependence of thought on Life has its strength in discovery, and that the dependence on Spirit equally often in distinguishing and demonstrating. We will, however, make this plainer in examples.

If we compare Goethe and Schiller, it might prove difficult to discover any difference in the depth of their apprehensive activity. Both are eminently creative natures, and, as such, have the keenest and swiftest gift of apprehension, as well as a mighty intellect. But Goethe's apprehension and thought are *relatively* more dependent on Life, Schiller's on Spirit; hence the former draws his best discoveries, so to speak, from the depth of his vitality, and always first requires to have experienced personally (or, more exactly, to have had an intuitive experience of visual character) in order to reach certainty about a matter; while the latter is forced to bring to bear on every impression the powerfully active demand of Spirit, which often hurts the content of the intuition, although sometimes the gain is that the marrow is pressed out of the very poorest impression, so that the yield is such as Goethe would have been able to extract only from much richer material. Schiller has expressed this opposition with the clarity and analytic force which were his, in a letter to Goethe, dated August 23, 1794. He calls it the opposition between "intuitive" and "speculative" Spirit, and thus has made a pertinent observation, if not upon the matter itself, still on one of its commonest and most important consequences. We quote some sentences from this letter, since they form an unintentional contribution to characterology. (The italics are Schiller's.)

"*Your observing eye, which rests so calmly and clearly upon things,* never exposes you to the danger of entering on the wrong path upon which speculation, as well as capricious and uncontrolled imagination, so easily stray. Your true intuition contains everything—and that much more completely—which analysis pursues with toil: and your own riches are hidden from you only because they lie within you as a whole: for, unfortunately, we know only what we analyse (!) Hence Spirits of your kind rarely know how far they have advanced, and how little cause they have to borrow of philosophy, which, indeed, can do no more than learn from them. *Philosophy can only analyse* its data, but the art of giving is not the business of the analyst, but of that genius which, under the obscure but certain guidance of its reason, follows objective laws in its combinations. ... A just and truly heroic idea, which sufficiently shows how thoroughly your Spirit binds together in a harmonious unity the rich totality of its imaginations. ... At first it might indeed appear that no two terms could be more thoroughly opposite than speculative

Spirit, which starts from unity, and intuitive, which starts from multiplicity (!) But if the former seeks experience in a pure and honest Spirit, and the latter seeks laws with free and independent intellectual power, then the two cannot fail of meeting half-way. ..." From Goethe's splendid answer (August 27, 1794) two sentences at least deserve to be quoted, in which he clearly defines the vital dependence of his method of investigation. "You will soon see how great an advantage your sympathy for me will prove as you discover, on closer acquaintance, a kind of obscurity and hesitancy in me, which I cannot master although I am fully aware of it. But there are several such phenomena in our nature, by which we still are gladly ruled (!) so long as it is not too tyrannical."

If now we compare these two men with the greatest thinkers of the Romantic period, they both fall short of these in the vital dependence of thought; while at the same time we confess that the exceedingly vitalistic attitude of the Romantics also conceals certain dangers, and especially that (at which Goethe hints) of obscurity and ultimately of faulty formulation due to neglect of the commands of reason. If it is desired to see the distinction widened into a gulf, Goethe need but be contrasted with Kant, or, better still, romantic metaphysics with Kantian criticism.

Another example which will repeatedly be taken up would be that of the intellectual difference between typically masculine and typically feminine characters. The view excogitated by males that the typical woman has less intellect than the typical man is thoroughly false. The typical woman has a *different* intellect from the typical man, the chief cause of which is that women's comprehension and thought are essentially based upon Life, while men's are essentially based upon Spirit. Hence again it follows partly (but only partly) that universal thoughts, notions, laws, maxims, and programmes sway the masculine type of apprehension far more strongly than the feminine. Here the converse, too, may be defended: Goethe's spiritual nature is more feminine than Schiller's, but that of both is more masculine than that of the Romantic period.

III. *The Subjective and the Objective Direction of Apprehension*—When Schiller characterizes the vitally dependent direction of apprehension as objective in the truest sense, he is undoubtedly correct. We stated already in the last chapter than an emphasized recollection of experiences must not upon any account be confused with a subjective falsification of the facts; now, however, we must state more exactly what we intend to mean by the opposition between subjective and objective direction of apprehension. In making this contrast we follow popular usage, according to which any apprehension which is biased and therefore inadequate to the facts, would be subjective, while every unbiased and therefore adequate apprehension would be objective. But, for once, we prefer the two foreign words, because we desire to save up for another subject the distinction (soon to be discussed) between a personal and a factual manner of apprehension, and because subjectivism cannot in every case be explained from the point of view of bias. If now we expressly premise that we are concerned only secondarily with apprehension of facts and primarily with that of values, then the question immediately arises wherein the correctness of these estimations consists. The quickest road to the answer is to make clear where they fail, from a few examples.

A merchant who has just made an unexpectedly successful stroke of business, and therefore sees the world in a rosy light, inclines to think his fellow-men better and more amiable than they are. A lover is in danger of being blind to the faults of his beloved, and an envious man to the good points of the object of his envy. Those who consider cats' "treacherous" are, without knowing it, under the influence of early Christian belief, which saw in the sacred beast of Isis the incarnation of the devil. It is immediately clear that all these persons reached incorrect estimations, because they either did not apprehend at all the facts about which they were to pass judgment, or else apprehended them through the dim and distorting medium of their own nature which has nothing to do with the facts. "We may be deceived by an intention which unconsciously distorts, from sentimental or intellectual prejudice, from emotional relation to the object (love, hatred, envy, etc.), from a mood which lends its own colour (projection), from lack of sensitiveness, from self-exaltation of reason which blinds the soul, and from many other causes besides."[23] But for our present purpose, all causes of deception may be subordinated to the one and most important cause, which is revealed by the proverb which says that the wish is father of the thought, that is, of our judgment that something is true; and we recognize easily that, if we would assign correct values, an essential condition is that we shall accept the content which is to be valued with the completest possible absence of desires. Nobody can completely cast off his wishes and interests; but one man can do so better than another, and in any case his peculiar sense of actuality will operate only in so far as he can. Thus, then, the foundation of right valuation is seen to reside in the sense of actuality.

If it be recollected that we called sentimental dispositions driving forces, and conversely, it might be objected that, if thus the condition for erroneous attribution of values is based upon personal interest (whether temporary or lasting), then the theory of subjectivity and objectivity of apprehension falls under the doctrine of driving forces, and not under that of talents. We do not deny that there is here one of those close relationships which, on principle, we pointed out in advance; but it appears that, even when driving forces are equal in strength and in direction, there are enormous differences in the capacity of men to keep their estimations independent of their driving forces. Some have the gift of apprehending facts and of judging values almost irrespectively of their personal desires: these are characters whose apprehensions have an objective direction: whereas, when others judge values and apprehend facts, this is largely a mere function of their interests: in these characters apprehensions have a subjective direction. Both may have a strong sense of actuality: but in subjective natures this is complicated with their wishes and inclinations, while in the objective natures it preserves itself by the side of these. Thus objective natures must be considered as having a more independent sense of actuality.

In opposition to a very common prejudice, women—at least in their judgment of persons—are universally more objective than men. The typical man, when in love, invariably exalts the object of his love and debases the object of his hatred, and consequently in this sphere tends strongly towards the formation of "illusions". A typical woman, on the other hand, may be passionately in love with a man, and yet have a keen eye for his faults; but she does not love him the less. And she may detest a rival, and yet fully recognize her mental and bodily superiority; but she detests her none the less. It may be objected: but surely man as judge is universally fairer than woman, and, if women had to administer the office of judges, would we not have to fear innumerable subjective judgments? This would indeed be the case; but the reasons lie elsewhere, and not where they usually were sought. And so we pass to a third opposition in the directions of apprehension.

IV. *Direction of Apprehension towards Persons and towards Facts.*—We call personal that direction of apprehension by virtue of which the subject finds himself unconsciously referred to the personal aspect of every possible case, and unpersonal, or directed towards facts, one by virtue of which he finds himself referred to the unpersonal or factual side of objects. The contrast is clearest when we compare a preponderant interest for persons with a preponderant interest for facts like State, church, law, profession, sciences (applied and pure), arts, politics, etc. If the former reaches a very great intensity it is called a passionate interest, whereas the latter in the same case is generally called enthusiasm. To personal interest, however, there belongs, apart from the person as such, everything which concerns it; the clothes which somebody wears, his manner of life, birth, and death, christening, marriage, and finally the content of every possible kind of gossip. Conversely, the same facts can become the objects of an impersonal interest. Thus if I investigate the marriage customs of various peoples, then my interest is turned upon facts and not on persons. But we must add especially that the (unconscious) direction of apprehension generally goes with the correlative direction of interests, but at the same time must be judged as an independent quality of that talent which the direction of interest which bears the same name is designed merely to serve.[24]

It has often been said, and might be demonstrated from evolutionary history, that the preponderantly personal direction of apprehension is feminine, and that which looks on facts, masculine. It was shown above that women not infrequently excel men in objectivity when the apprehension of personal data is concerned; we now investigate the question whether the preponderance of a personal direction of apprehension may lead to false judgments, and, consequently, what may be the final expectation of impartiality in either of the sexes. A young man runs a greater risk of over-esteeming the singing of the girl he loves than would a loving girl in a converse and similar case; but the girl, if, for example, she is a student, is more likely to prefer one lecturer among others, because she is interested in *him* and not in his lectures. But then we would have to assume that a female judge would be likely to have far more cause than a male to judge *not* "without respect of person" because she feels sympathy or antipathy for the accused; for the non-personal fact of the law might, though its content were valued adequately, become negligible in comparison with the personal fact of "accused". We will spend a moment on investigating the probable substratum of this difference in talent.

In a character where apprehension is chiefly directed upon facts, universal (or general) feelings—for example, a feeling for truth, justice, political society, etc.—have a primary influence upon thought, and even upon the manner of perception; while in a character where apprehension has a preponderantly personal direction, personal feelings—that is, feelings of personal inclination, admiration, and love, personal repugnance and disgust—have primary influence. Thus if a man possesses convictions, sentiments, or maxims, this also always means that he must seek to bring them into equilibrium with his personal feelings, since otherwise he would infallibly undergo a conflict of feelings. If, for example, he loves a girl, then there is something in him which seeks to find the girl beautiful or interesting or good, or, in short, excellent in some respect. Edward in the *Elective Affinities* furnishes a typical example. He is not yet conscious of his budding affection for Ottilie, since whose arrival only a single day has passed; but already the affection is operating in him and causes him to assume certain good qualities of which he could know nothing whatever, even if they did exist. "Next morning Edward said to Charlotte: 'She is an agreeable, entertaining girl.' 'Entertaining?' replied Charlotte with a smile. 'Why, she has not yet opened her mouth.' 'Really!' said Edward, while he seemed to reflect. 'That would be strange.' " If, on the other hand, maxims and convictions having hardly any sentimental colouring are peculiar to women, then their desire to harmonize them with personal feelings will be much weaker than with men. A woman can love a man without discovering in him any extraordinary beauty, or interest, or goodness; for her his value consists of the fact that she loves him. Thus the potential injustice of man consists especially in a distortion of his estimates of value in favour of his personal feelings, while that of women consists in an unconscious refusal to attribute significance and binding force to universal values, personal feeling being made the sole criterion. It is incorrect to say that feeling rules women, and reason men; the fact rather is that with typical woman, personal feeling, and with typical man, general feeling, is decisive. But this does not prevent his estimations of value from being corrupted by his personal feelings. This brief exposition of the connection between certain ways of feeling and certain ways of apprehending throws perhaps a full light upon the meaning of the contrasted talents which have here been treated.

V. *Concrete and Abstract Direction of Apprehension.*—In order to understand the opposition between concrete and abstract direction of apprehension, we will bestow a moment upon the logical opposition after which it is named. Literally, concrete means "grown together", and abstract "taken off". All concepts, the objects of which cannot exist independently, are thus abstract, as redness, sound, motion, light, virtue, number, multiplicity, equality, anger, government, and so on. For in fact and in itself there is no such thing, but only red, sounding, moving, shining objects, and virtuous, angry, governing beings. In order to reach this concept certain properties have then been taken off from the existing facts (hence "abstract") and have been made independent. Akin at least to this distinction is that between generic and individual concepts. If I speak of table, tree, or Swiss, then it is not that which corresponds to such a concept which exists, but only a definite table, tree, or Swiss. Then, again, the generic concept is abstracted from the individual case to which it is applied. Nevertheless, we shall count these units of significance among the concrete, because they can be represented by something which exists independently. And this already tells us where the peculiarity of concrete concepts must be looked for. Redness does not exist independently, but there is a red ball, rose, or table-cloth, and thus the concepts of these are concrete concepts. Relative to these, abstracts are concepts of properties. If we start from them, the thing appears to be put together out of its properties, and therefore grown together (hence "concrete"), whereas in fact it denotes the permanent substratum which causes the properties (accidents) to form a whole.

If there were not one kind of talent for the apprehension of the concrete side of objects, and an opposite talent for the apprehension of their abstract side, then of course the logical distinction would not justify a characterological one. But we need not look far around us in order to see that some people operate better throughout with concrete concepts, and others with abstract concepts, and we have already touched upon one cause of this fact. For concrete apprehension demands that the individual case be dwelt upon in some degree, while abstract apprehension demands a capacity for movement from case to case—a contrast which has various vital reasons, one at least of which we already know in the contrast between the staying and the roaming type of sense. This again reminds us of spiritual differences between the sexes; at the same time we might point to the fact, never probably disputed, that among men there are more abstract intelligences and among women more concrete intelligences—a fact which vouches for the aptness of the distinction. But the two polar opposites have certain foundations of feeling in common, a consideration of which will definitely assure us of the existence of the former.

If, on seeing a wicker chair, I feel tempted to sit down on it, then I have treated it as a concrete entity; but, if it affords the occasion of a conversation about wicker chairs in general, their comfort, extent, and mode of fabrication, then I have treated it as a representative of its genus, and hence as abstract entity. Now this is no longer possible if I am in an individual relation to an object, and especially if I am in a personal relation to it. My individual relation makes the related entity something individual for me, that is, unique; and my personal relation finally makes it quite incommensurable with other entities. Of this nature are, for example, all the relations which subsist between a man and some person in his personal dealings, but also his relations to his dog or his cat, his home, his house, and garden, to a memory, and finally his relations to some place where at a given time some event which was of importance to him took place. The individual person of my surroundings, the dog, memory, house, or place where first I met my beloved or a dangerous enemy, are unique facts, which resist equally stubbornly classification within a genus and analysis into mere properties. Peculiar nuances of feelings here always play a notable part, and, to this extent, it may be asserted that concreteness of thought grows with the participation of the mind (its sentimental part). Woman is more devoted to personal interests, and man to interests in facts, which is the decisive reason why concrete intelligence preponderates among women, and abstract, among men; and although in principle it is possible that a more abstract direction of apprehension may co-exist with preponderantly personal interests, and a more concrete direction of apprehension with interests directed preponderantly upon facts, still there exists one sentimental basis which is served by the concrete direction of apprehension, and another which is served by the abstract; hence there can no longer be any doubt about the existence of these directions of apprehension themselves.

VI. *Close-Focused and Far-Focused Direction of Apprehension.* —The opposition between the concrete and the abstract direction of apprehension must not be confused with a difference of the direction of apprehension based upon oppositions of degree of the gift of seeing. A man may bring a suit against somebody whom he has never seen and is then related, point for point to a mass of details of which only a small minority are actually seen. But even the relation to the individual visible case may be more or less close. A painter who proceeds to make a sketch in colour of the forest before his eyes is in an intensely visual relation to the forest; a speculator in land who intends to cut down the trees and sell the land is in a visual relation to the forest which may have any degree of weakness. Oppositions in visible intensity are thus not simply interchangeable with the opposition between concrete and abstract, although these two circles do intersect.

If we consider the ends of the series, the opposition between typical representatives of visual and of non-visual apprehension is even greater than that between minds operating in a typically concrete and in a typically abstract manner. Here, however, a reference to differences between the intelligences of the sexes would no longer be helpful. For, among women, an overemphasis of concrete thought

112

generally goes with an overemphasis of intuitive force of thought only with respect to definite objects like dress, arranging of flowers, furnishing of rooms, and domestic arrangements generally, perhaps also to dancing and gymnastics, while in the sphere of the decorative and still more of the independent arts, it usually falls short of the intuitive force of masculine thought. Rather, it is clearly the opposition between definitely artistic and definitely inartistic natures which rests (among other things) upon oppositions of degree of the intuitive force of apprehension; that is, if by "artistic natures" we understand not poets but personalities who, if they have not the power to practise the so-called plastic arts, at least have more than the average understanding for them.

Further, the type of thought which is relatively rich in images may be concrete or abstract within its peculiar range and as a true faculty of apprehension stands out clear from the vital warmth of the object of intuition. A man who draws a landscape in crayon has no less close a visual relation to his object than when he paints it in oils, but in the former case the relation is more abstract and in the latter more concrete, and although he is related even more abstractly to similar objects within the range of his studies of the arts, still he has not left the close-focused direction of apprehension. We have but to remember that many abstract objects of thought, like redness, sweetness, and cold can be represented visually, and that many concrete objects, like an individual character, cannot so be represented, and we shall agree in principle to the following double classification: both the concrete and the abstract manner of apprehension can be close-focused and far-focused, and, conversely, both the close-focused and the far-focused manner of apprehension may be predominantly concrete, or abstract. At the same time we do not wish to deny that in fact intuitional closeness goes with concrete thought, and abstract thought with intuitional distance.

The case is similar with the theoretical and actual relation between thought which is full of images and "warmth of the material of intuition". It is true that complete absence of images in the soul is incompatible with the visual imagination of objects which are absent from the senses; but, as we found occasion to remark repeatedly in the last chapter, it is an act of spiritual caprice when the intuitive content of objects is called up arbitrarily. It is compatible with a moderate degree of imagination, whereas a gift for day-dreaming (phantasy) is always passive, and even when it is of abnormal strength, need not necessarily accompany a capacity for exact mental representation. Nevertheless, a spirit which is turned in that direction will in fact find support in this vital disposition; and in the end there will result a very peculiar formation of thought, co-existing with a dependence of understanding upon the vital element. In order to give a correct idea of the importance of the contrast, we trespass for a moment upon the field of primitive intelligence, the investigation of which does not form part of the plan of this book.

Originally there are no concepts, but only units of significance, and accordingly the peculiarity of primitive results of reflection is missed if we imagine the differentia to consist in abnormal concreteness, or in an actual incapacity for generalization. This leads into difficulties at every step. The criteria which we have produced enable us to name the peculiarities of the primitive intellectual attitude without risk of confusion or contradiction, whether the selected examples are known or unknown facts: these are, its dependence on vitality and its visual element—both these qualities being at their greatest intensity. One example in place of innumerable ones may serve to explain this. The Eskimo have three distinct names for a seal: one for seals in general, one for seals lying in the sun, and the third for a seal drifting on an ice-floe.[25] The explanation is this: the visible image of a seal lying in the sun on the beach is thoroughly different from that of a seal drifting on an ice-floe, and therefore in a pictorial language the terms for the two may also be different: and in every case there is a similar explanation. In very many cases we may describe this as though primitive thought were more concrete; in other cases this is impossible. The example which we have quoted offers a pretty proof that this is not so. For the Eskimo have a word for "seal in general", and what they describe in opposition to this as "seal lying in the sun" and "seal drifting on an ice-floe", is not a subordinate species but a visible situation very characteristic of the life of a seal.[26] It is clear that this may tempt us to all kinds of considerations about our meaning of the principle of identity, and, at times, it has even given rise to the erroneous idea that the principle of uniformity is not valid for primitive intelligence. Here we have confined ourselves to using a typical individual case in order to show how important a part can be played in the formation of elemental units of significance by the fact that apprehension is close-focused, whence may be inferred how far the world-picture of conceptual minds may differ from that of definitely sensuous minds.

VII. *The Formalistic Direction of Apprehension.*—A combination of extreme abstractness and an extremely close-focused thought allowed the Greeks to create Geometry and Philosophy, of which the whole of Western science is the younger sister. A combination of close-focused thought with extreme concreteness allowed the Latins to create a service of religious ceremony (which reaches as far as Roman Catholicism) and the enormous structure of Roman Law. On the other hand, the classical period shows only traces of that which determines the spiritual state of the West more and more completely, partly in the Middle Ages, and especially after the so-called Renaissance: namely, the formalistic direction of apprehension. If we are asked for an opposite of this, too, we must comprehend all the manners of apprehension enumerated hitherto as substantial, whence the formalistic direction itself would become a direction of thought lacking substance, and, ultimately substratum. And in fact it merges more and more, in process of time, with a doubt of truth which (in a manner essentially different from that of the ancient forms of scepticism) makes it its principle to assign to actuality the same value as to the products of human caprice. We shall touch upon the metaphysics of the case at a later point: here we confine ourselves to a sketch of the actual facts.

Classical (or, as we may boldly say, Greek) thought to which every psychological work (including the author's works) owes its origin, is unmistakably moribund. In its place we see four other modes of thought flourishing at the moment: and the fundamental concepts which we have expounded do not suffice to explain this at the decisive point: financial, mathematical, technical, and sporting thought. In the last two types parts of the new (as has been hinted) mingle with the old:[27] and only in financial and mathematical thought the new has wholly mastered the old —to such a degree that it is possible to be a great philosopher, and yet to be wholly ignorant of modern finance, or a great financier and yet to be perfectly blind to philosophy. But modern mathematics—if its nature is inferred from the spiritual structure of modern mathematicians—is the theoretical aspect of the same fact of which finance is the practical aspect: and this is the formalistic method of apprehension (together with the sentimental direction which belongs to it). Like some invisible ray, it long ago succeeded in forcing a way through the finest pores to the heart of intelligence, decomposing it internally and assimilating to itself the attitude of understanding even in the most distant fields. If its victory should be completed, as can hardly be doubted, then the old races of mankind have run their course, even if there were no deeper causes for their fate: and the reason would be an inability to adapt themselves to the formalistic method of apprehension. But where is their essentially distinctive trait?

In the earliest ages, and also at the first stage of primitive development, trade consisted in the barter of goods, or of one man's overplus against another's, sometimes under the shelter of arms, and more often by way of present. A last survival of this practice is the custom, almost universal among peasants and common elsewhere, of making specific presents in return for presents. There was a need for universalizing the means of barter whence there developed among the most diverse tribes a tendency to set up a standard of value, and to take for this purpose an object which appeared desirable to a maximum number of tribes, either because it was useful or because it was ornamental, or because it was rare. In this manner, payment has been effected by a great variety of objects in the past; and in part this is still the case in distant lands: beans, dates, nuts, pepper, rice, cheese, tea, tobacco, salt, fishes; also feathers, shells, tortoise-shell, pearls, linen, beaver-skins, sable. The Latin word for money—*pecunia*—is derived from *pecus* = cattle. The case is the same in principle when bars of metal are preferred (iron, copper, bronze, tin, silver, and occasionally gold), as much being broken off, roughly, or after weighing, as the value of the goods demands: for metals can be worked up in many ways. Again the case is much the same when metal is used in the practical form of spearheads, rings, or rods. Meanwhile, we need but recall the passion for stores of gold among Celts and Teutons, and the facts that peasants invariably prefer to pay in kind rather than in cash, in order to notice that the standard of exchange-value is beginning to become independent. We think that in possessing money we possess all because it has universal validity (the two words* have the same root) although without food a man must starve between his bags of money.

We need not explain further how the means of exchange underwent the first increase of abstractness when coin came into use; ethnologists assume that it was invented once only —by the Greeks of Asia Minor; a second and abrupt increase took place when the idea was formed of substituting for this materially valuable means of payment (which naturally is subject only to slight fluctuations in value) mere assignments of the equivalent of money in the shape of *assignets*, bills, bank-notes, paper money, cheques, etc. In a note of worldly wisdom Goethe tells us about the magic of the introduction of paper money and credit in Part II of *Faust*:—

---

* Namely, "geld" (money) and "gilt" (has validity).

117

Such a piece of paper in place of gold and pearls
Is so convenient—we know what we have.

The other side of the picture has been seen by many of our contemporaries in all its terror during the period of inflation, when it was common to hear "notes are an illusion".* If while watching the shrill confusion of the Stock Exchange we were struck by the quaint thought that here figures—mere figures— were being fought for with feverish heat, this thought might be followed by a feeling of horror when we reflect that these battles of figures can decide the fate of millions in a second. The figure here has a meaning— land, petrol, machinery, railways, labour, etc., but what lives in the battling heads is not its meaning but its own absolute self: the symbol has gone beyond that which it symbolized and thought, operating by symbols, has taken the place of thought operating by units of meaning, or even by concepts. But this is the essence of formalism.

We cannot here attempt to follow the analogies between the development of finance and mathematics: all we can do is to point out that the first great development of modern mathematics was inspired by the study of natural history, but nevertheless coincided with the first great development of modern capitalism during the sixteenth and seventeenth centuries. But it suffices to reflect upon the action of calculation in order to reveal once more where we must look for the essence of the formalistic method of apprehension. First, it is peculiar to number as such that it has no content. Five does not mean five fingers, five apples, or five pounds of sugar, but the relation of any given amount to another which has arbitrarily been taken as unit. And not this only: the same applies to "equal", "plus", "minus", "times", "divided by", etc. We could not immediately solve problems like 3 plus 4, 12 minus 5, 7 times 9, 42 divided by 6, if we first wanted to reflect on the meaning of the connecting word or symbol, and on the origin of its magic power which allows us to find the solution without the trouble of reflecting. Five may be

---

* German, "Scheine sind Schein".

multiplied by 7, but not virtue by government; and no method of procedure which will allow us to learn something about virtue or government can be compared in the least with the procedure which we use in order to form the product of two factors. In principle the same applies to the process of raising to a power, of extracting roots, to calculation with negative, irrational and imaginary numbers, and to the use of logarithms, and of the differential and the integral calculus. It is not power of abstractive force, and still less a talent for (Greek) logic[28] which guarantees an understanding of "higher" or of "lower" mathematics, but the wholly different capacity for using mere symbols as though they were units of significance having a content. "Mathematics is ... an art, like Rhetoric. In both the form alone has value and the content is indifferent. Neither cares —Mathematics whether it calculates farthings or guineas, or Rhetoric whether it defends truth or lies" (Goethe in the *Sprüche in Prosa*).

If we take in a very wide sense the saying of the famous mathematician Hilbert—"in the beginning was the symbol"—then it must be admitted that non-symbolic thought does not exist: but if it is taken in a narrower sense, it seems to us to be very apt to describe, not thought, but formalistic thought: for the latter does not merely rely upon symbols, but *consists* of the permutation and combination of symbols—as is proved by any calculating machine. We do not, of course, deny that genius of no common kind was required in order to invent symbols which can be used without losing their validity, as vehicles of and even as substitutes for intellectual movements, while at the same time acquiring the independence which mathematical symbols have acquired. But there must be no illusion as to the fact that if such a symbolic language is invented, and perfected from day to day, the symbol begins to become all-powerful and threatens to swallow facts, as money, by a different kind of omnipotence, swallows values. The aims of formalistic thought are these: the results of thought without the labour of thought, answers without any previous search, and domination of the Spirit without using as a medium and instrument consciousness, which still is in parts dependent on vitality. It is certain that the perfect formalist would be an unconscious machine having an uncanny faculty for infinitely variable reactions, in which case it might be constructed in a factory, or like the Homunculus, in a retort.

The manner of apprehension which is dependent on Life and close-focused took us, so to speak, close to the lower limit of thought—the point where thought has only just begun; on the other hand, the formalistic manner of apprehension approaches its upper limit, where it is on the point of ceasing. At the "lower limit" thought threatens to change into images: at the "upper", to vanish into numerals, whose connection with actuality is so tenuous that it finds expression only in the symbol, which is always sensuous in some way. Observing this, we must assume that there is a formalistic manner of apprehension and gift of thinking where unsubstantial symbols are mainly or exclusively used: especially where calculating power is great, a power which may be taken as the very image of formalism, whether it is found in a mathematician or in a financier; or in a chess master for whom figures and squares represent only conventional rules, or finally (at least to some extent) in a skilled general, for whom, men, according to the expressive phrase, are primarily "material", that is, numbers and figures. The reader will have no difficulty in divining for himself what kinds of human creations must die as a consequence of the growth of formalism, and which, on the other hand, will only then reach their full development; we will draw his attention to one symptom only, which, although apparently superficial, applies to every kind of intelligent activity and indicates that a formalistic talent is at work—namely, rapidity of execution. Wherever we find it present in abnormal strength (that is, we repeat, in functions of the intelligence), we may conclude that the process of intellectual mechanization is beginning or in an advanced state, that the peculiar "calculating" intelligence is present, and hence that the decline of conscious thought is beginning. In his highest functions the formalist is anything rather than a thinker, but he is very closely related to the man of action whose intellect from the typological point of view always has a predominantly formalistic appearance. The vital reason which renders possible this direction of apprehension is almost identical with that of the predominance of the will, of which more will be said in Chapters IX and X.

If we were to continue our investigations we would be able to distinguish many more directions of apprehension, and in the end we would set up a whole system of figures, intersecting, so to speak, at many points. But it is not likely that we would discover many of equally fundamental importance with those which we have mentioned, and it is probable that most of them would turn out to be merely subordinate species.

CHAPTER VI NOTES

[21] If talent is simply one kind of formative force, then what makes a poet is not any particular kind of receptivity for language, but the capacity to express in language his essential experience. This applies in principle to every talent, for example, that of the thinker, the engineer, or the arithmetician. We shall revert to this in Chapters VII and VIII, and here merely wish to mention that on these lines the contrast between presence and absence of talent does in fact coincide with presence and absence of formative force; but not with the contrast between motor type and sensor type, with which we dealt in the previous observation. The expressive power of the *sensor type* is not necessarily less in degree or value than that of the motor type merely because it moulds itself (so to speak) according to the impression-stresses, instead of forming them, as does the other type; while, with respect to formative force, it has no immediate relation at all to this contrast of types. For by it we mean that side of the capacity for expression which enables its bearer *not* to deflect every stimulus into motor-effects, but to form a material so that it shall be the image of the inner life of the personality, or (to put it with reference only to artistic work) of its soul. The essentials about this matter, however, will easily be discovered in Chapter VIII.

[22] A trained psychologist will not imagine that he is a doctor, but unfortunately many doctors think that they are trained psychologists. It is certainly true that the State examination in medicine requires a far greater sum of individual pieces of knowledge and of skill than a degree with psychology as main subject, but psychology requires training in a manner of thought which nobody—literally nobody—will command who does not devote a lifetime to it. The psychological fairytales of doctors are throughout so poor that one regrets the time spent in reading them. Naturally there are exceptions—most honourable exceptions; but they are too few to make monstrosities like the following unfashionable.

In the first edition of this work (1910) we introduced into the study of individual talents the distinction between the outward and inward-looking mind: whereupon two foreign words, extraverted and introverted, were employed by medical men, and an attempt was made to make this a supreme principle for classifying all characters in general. The result, to put it most politely, was nil. Thus the matter would be of no importance but that it was connected with an utterly wrong view about certain mental diseases. In the body of this work we began from depth and shallowness, and this in fact only touches one special case of the spiritual dispositions for directing the view. It is possible to begin from these too, but in that case we shall have to consider whether a shallow or a deep inner life by choice turns outwards, and whether it is a deep or a shallow life of the Soul which by choice turns inwards. If, further, we distinguish between the possibility of an excessive predominance of one or of the other direction, then the consequence (as anybody can see for himself) will vary greatly in these two different cases.

We show by an example what distortions result when this principle is entirely neglected.

The poet Hebbel—according to a newspaper report of a lecture by a certain psychiatrist—is supposed to have been an introvert, or, as others express it, an "autist", or, as still others probably will say, a "schizoid" character. (We make bold henceforward to use in place of "schizophreny", a term which wholly misses the mark, the more popular term of "madness", although in the therapeutics of lunacy it is reserved for a more special condition). If we assume that the poet Hebbel was mentally in the main introverted, we must ask if this condition went with a rich or poor inner life. In the former case it would simply be the appropriate mental state, although at the same time it would involve all kinds of oddities and eccentricities, as well as diminished adaptability: whereas, if it accompanied shallowness and sterility, it would be the basis of excessive self-importance, self-reference, and Ego-centricity. But we may remark at once that it could in no case be so much as a preliminary to madness. If to be "melancholy" or "mazed" (as it is sometimes called) is popularly taken in the same ambiguous sense in which evidently many doctors take this "introvertedness", this is a last echo of the belief which is widely spread among primitive races that madmen have a sort of sacredness as being persons elected as the habitation of some demon: it thus offers no occasion to the psychiatrist for holding a similar view. Now observance of the distinction between depth and shallowness naturally leads (a) to a confusion of profound spiritual life with introvertedness and of introvertedness with profound spiritual life, and (b) to the view that introvertedness is a neurotic symptom or even a mild form of insanity. Such views were at one time the particular hobby of Lombroso. But meanwhile the ruling tendency had changed considerably. The "pathographs" were at pains to comfort the Philistines by showing that men of genius are madmen: the modern wisdom prefers to instruct us that madmen are geniuses. Both schools are of equal value—that is, of none. Behind all this there lies the wish (not uninteresting to the student of the psychology of the times) to confuse the boundary between sick and sound, and to whittle down a profound contrast of kind into a mere difference in degree. But in the end even this is a matter of fashion which might be passed over in silence but for the fact that it tends to block the path to the simplest truths. If we take the system of symptoms of so-called "schizophreny" (erroneously named after the image of schism, which is valuable in the doctrine of neurosis and psychopathy, but wrong as applied to insanity), as applicable to the characterization of insanity in general, we shall be unable to understand the facts in the least so long as we cling blindly to such phrases as "introvertedness", "autism", etc. However "introverted" a man may be, this will not cause him to suffer from ideas of reference, or fixed ideas or hallucinations, etc. And conversely he may so suffer, whether for the rest he is introverted or extraverted. It is amazing what things men can fail to see once they have put on the blinkers of wrong concepts. If we consider for one moment that the lunatic—that every lunatic—is blind to ordinary methods of conviction (whether by way of the senses or of judgment) in *some* respect, then no great acumen is required to show us what is the most universal characteristic of the fact of lunacy—of any kind of lunacy: it is that the vitality of the patient is cut off relatively from the common life of the world. Already Herbart had rightly anticipated this in his own manner: "Those are bereft of reason whose thoughts can no longer be disturbed in their flow by inner or outer contradiction" *(Lehrbuch zur Psychologie*, 1816, p. 22). It is not the condition which determines the direction of the spiritual view, or schisms in process or perfected, but solely isolation of vitality which can, and must, serve to explain insanity. A sane vitality demands a living contact and interchange with the life of the world. This contact cannot wholly cease, else the man would die of starvation; but what may be called the side of the soul, or, more briefly, the soul-contact may, from whatever causes, be largely interrupted, and this finally to such a degree that we may say that practically it has been removed. This weakness and final lack of contact is the essential condition of any kind of insanity. (We remark merely in passing that this will explain to those trained in biological thought why persons severely affected by schizophreny are so exceedingly insensitive to vegetable and mineral poisons. A "madman" may require as much as three times the fatal strength of a sleeping draught in order to obtain adequate sleep.) Once this is known, a good many other things which are fruitlessly discussed today become clear.

Thus, for example, it is probable in a way that a lunatic will more often be introvert than extravert; but nothing prevents us from assuming an extraverted kind of insanity. Indeed, this is certain to occur where the inner life is very shallow. For that severance of which we spoke does not mean that the patient is incapable of further perceptions or is not even, perhaps, greedily set upon fresh objects of perception, but that the connections with the *Life* of the world are interrupted. We need not further explain ourselves on this matter, because whoever reads this book to the end will know our meaning. Further, the schisms, of which we shall also have occasion to speak in Chapter VIII, may or may not exist by the side of this separation, and this may complicate the manifestation of the disease in several respects; but insanity never consists in schisms. Further, it is obvious from this that a lunatic may have a rich or an extremely poor internal life. For although a rich soul may be kept from its normal food by reason of extensive severance, still it is far safer than an equally rich soul, having many contacts, from the danger of spending or wasting itself. Paranoiac types (to resuscitate the old term) when full of life are natures which revolve about themselves and often preserve themselves in an astonishing manner. Hence it may be seen (*a*) that in principle there is no connection between so-called genius and lunacy, and (*b*) that it is no longer difficult to find a key to certain abnormal traits in genius, as well as to certain traces of "genius" in madmen. Finally, we may say that the poet as poet, whether he be Hebbel, Kleist, or Hölderlin, is always a man whose contacts with the Life of the world are much above the average and that therefore, from the typological point of view, he is furthest of all from madmen. But in spite of all this, the contact need not necessarily be affected by the senses as in Goethe, but may also take place through the agency of magnetism, electro-dynamic forces or fluids which as yet are unknown to physics, and have a more powerful influence over the sleeping than over the waking organism. The poet may dream revealing dreams—

dreams, that is, which reveal the world. If now we still see the poet as man not so very rarely suffering from mental disease, we must not look for the reason in the fact that he is a poet, but must ask what dangers for the person are involved when the Soul lies open to Life to an exceptional degree. But we must call a halt. It is enough if we have made it plain to the unprejudiced reader how the crude confusions and speculations of incapable writers have obscured obvious facts, to the loss both of psychology and psychiatry.

23 *Ausdrucksbewegung und Gestaltungskraft*, p. 123.

24 At this moment woman is developing a process of becoming masculine, for reasons which remain to be touched upon: it may be assumed that in time it will have some considerable influence upon her talents, and in parts this process has already begun; but this influence has not yet penetrated into the strata which we have discussed. We offer an event negligible in itself, but significant as a symptom, to prove that we are here not dealing with directions of interests but with genuine talents. Persons: three highly educated ladies, two married and one still unmarried, a young man (about twenty-five years old), also highly educated and unmarried, and, fifthly, the author. The subject of conversation is marriage, married life, etc. The author maintains the view that marriage is essentially an economic union, so-called love not being indispensable, while any marriage with an inadequate economic foundation has trouble in store. The unmarried lady contradicts. The other man agrees with the author, pointing to advertisements inserted by women with a view to marriage, which always end with the remark (or its equivalent) "assured position essential". Immediately the three ladies react as one: "Ah, he reads that kind of advertisement." The young man—somewhat embarrassed—hastens to assure us that he does so from psychological reasons. Possibly the assumption of the ladies, in the other sense, was correct, possibly he really did act from psychological reasons, but in any case the remark of the ladies reveals a characteristic predominance of the personal direction of apprehension, and that evidently in the manner of a talent. There could be no question of any interest in any possible desire of the young man to marry (an interest due to love certainly did not exist in one); the interest provoked by the course of the conversation was directed on the one side upon the proof of a general proposition, and on the other upon its refutation. Only a special gift and aptness can explain that, from the remark of the young man, a conclusion should be drawn suddenly and quick as lightning which, quite apart from the subject, deals with his personal inclinations and wishes.

25 Cf. Abegg, *Die Sprachen der Naturvölker als Ausdrucksformen des primitiven Bewusstseins,* in *Mitteilungen der Geograph-Ethnograph Gesellschaft,* Zürich, vol. 23, 1922-3, pp. 41-60.

26 From vol. i of our *Geist und Seele.*

[27] At present there is a complete lack of characterological investigations of mechanical talent. Talent for mechanical invention certainly requires a direction of apprehension which is dependent on Spirit (or, more exactly, on will), extreme concreteness, and a portion of near-sightedness. But this is a mere frame, which would be filled only by the analysis of the mechanical manner of manifestation.

[28] Those who wish to be convinced by elementary examples that arithmetical and logical thought do not harmonize are referred to *Ist Arithmetik ein logisch korrektes Lehrgebäude?* an excellent dissertation by W. Koppelmann in *Annalen der Philosophie*, vol. vi, fasc. Annalen 1-3.

CHAPTER VII

THE STRUCTURE OF CHARACTER

All properties of talent in character are quantitative since each of them can be measured only by a scale: all the properties of the structure of character are relative properties, each being represented by the proportion between magnitudes. It is also true that every property which must be taken as a quotient is part of the structure of character. We have discovered three properties of structure: the personal capacity for stimulation of feelings (noted by alienists as "affectivity", but by no means understood): that for stimulation of the will—which at least approximately corresponds to the valid part of the meaning of "temperament"; and the personal capacity for expression, which was suspected by earlier psychology and vaguely designated by "humour".

Personal Capacity for Stimulation of Feelings.—If any given feeling, like hope, fear, content, moroseness, joy, grief, love, hatred, admiration, envy, is considered externally, so to speak, then it is usual first to distinguish its nature (colour or quality) and its strength (intensity). Further, numerous forms of development are observed which allow us to distinguish between temporary and enduring feelings, and between many different ways of waxing and waning. A more exact investigation reveals that each colour or nature or quality of the feeling (which again show degrees, especially of depth) is partnered by its own definite impulse which in turn, apart from its strength, possesses peculiarities of direction. We shall revert to this. But, however carefully the analysis might be made and its results described, certain essential differences among characters would be overlooked so long as feelings were considered in and for themselves and their relation to other sides of personal experience, and especially to the contents of consciousness, were neglected. Thus for any given feeling there is a regular and hence normal manner of origin; and there *can* also be odd and even abnormal manners of origin. If somebody showed evident signs of being flattered at an obvious insult, then our surprise would be a certain sign that we are accustomed to a different event, and thus consider insulting or offensive remarks as stimuli for very definite feelings; and if somebody were brought to weep and sob whenever he received good tidings, and to rejoice wildly whenever he received bad tidings, we would doubt his sanity.

Such examples instruct us that among other things we must also consider the *origin* of feelings if we wish to become acquainted with personal peculiarities of feeling. If we follow this indication, we soon observe that in some persons normal feelings are produced by very slight stimuli, whereas in others far stronger stimuli are required in order to excite them: the capacity for stimulation of feelings is a constant which, between the extremes of utmost ease and utmost hardness, passes through a pretty lengthy series of magnitudes.

Before we adduce examples to illustrate the two poles, we would state emphatically what is *not* meant by capacity for stimulation of feelings. First, we do not mean a particular receptivity in a person for certain classes of stimuli. If without further explanation "irritability" is attributed to a person, we mean to say by this that he is generally easily annoyed. Such properties do exist; there is angry irritability, or extreme capacity for joy, a temper easily spoiled, exaggerated trustfulness, melancholy fear, suspicious caution, abnormal timidity, etc. These, however, are specific dispositions of feelings which are part of the peculiar nature of a character, and these we must neglect if we wish to discover a personal constant for the origin of feelings in themselves. Nor is this difficult, for, of two relatively morose persons one will experience an increase in his moroseness from slighter occasions than the other, and of two relatively cheerful persons one will experience an increase in his cheerfulness from slighter occasions than the other, and this means that any given feeling occurs, within the range of his specific receptivities, more easily for one person than for the other.

Secondly, we do not mean the difference in the actual strength of the feelings. The degrees in absolute intensity which can be reached by human feelings vary extremely, and certainly do not coincide with the degrees of ease with which the feelings arise. Insignificant occasions may serve to arouse a passion, but this passion need not necessarily reach that strength which it reaches in another person whose passion is aroused with much greater difficulty. We do not at the same time dispute that the converse too may occasionally be the case. For example, children normally change from laughter to tears incomparably more easily than do grown-ups even between the corresponding moods; but nobody will assert that the passions of a grown man of violent disposition are less powerful than those of children. We now turn to an example.

If we imagine any cause of surprise, if possible without any tinge of fright, like the unexpected arrival of a very dear friend, the unexpected cancellation of a theatrical performance which had long and eagerly been looked for, the sudden news that a big factory is on fire at the other end of the town—then surely it cannot be denied that the normal feelings of joy, disappointment, and curiosity seize with much greater ease and lack of inhibition upon some persons than on others who yet can certainly not be counted as more devoid of passion. The former are characters whose feelings have a capacity for easy stimulation, the latter are stimulated with difficulty.

It might appear at first sight as though here (as with the properties of talent) we were concerned with a disposition which could simply be graduated. But a more exact investigation reveals a double front at each stage of excitability. If, in considering a case where feeling is easily stimulated, we refrain from any glance at the condition which made its existence possible, then we remain ignorant whether the person of whom it is a characteristic is to be called sensitive, impressionable, and *open*, or rather excitable, restless, uncontrolled, easily upset, and *irritable*; and if we do the same when we meet with feelings not easily excited, then we do not know if the person in question is to be called serene, "harmonious", contemplative, and *deep,* or rather unresponsive, passionless, and *dull.* Thus we may possess a disposition which is easily excited because it is more open to the surrounding world, or again from exaggerated irritability; or a man may possess one which is not easily excited because of a particular depth in experience, or again because he is dull or thick-skinned. A capacity for easy or difficult stimulation of feelings appears sometimes as an advantage to be explained by the presence of a certain "force", sometimes as a disadvantage which bears witness to the absence of a contrary force. Hence it results that we must derive the personal constant of capacity for stimulation of feelings from two conditions which conflict with each other.

We can construe dispositions only from the properties of their manifestations, and therefore we now ask ourselves whether there is a characteristic of the feelings themselves in which the reason why they are easily stimulated manifests itself, and an opposite characteristic which would reveal to us the reason why they are not easily stimulated. But we have already given a name to the latter—we have called it "deep". For the depth of experience (which may be graduated like strength) which may be recalled by anyone if he compares moments of deep experience in his past with moments of shallow experience—is that property of a feeling which never arises from causes of slight value, a condition, therefore, which opposes the stimulation of this feeling. An immediately intelligible contrast to this is found in liveliness of feeling, which recollection can equally lay hold of; a condition required by the slightest stimulus to set free feelings. Capacity for stimulation (C) thus grows with the growing liveliness of feelings (L) and diminishes as their depth (D) grows; which may be expressed by the formula $C = L / D$. If we give the value of 1 to the numerator and the denominator then the value of the quotient too will be 1. Thus a capacity for stimulation of feelings three times as great could be reached in two fundamentally different manners: by multiplying L by 3, or by dividing D by 3. The former we call the plus type, and the latter the minus type.

$$\overset{+}{C = \frac{L}{D} = \frac{3}{1} = 3} \qquad\qquad \overset{-}{C = \frac{L}{D} = \frac{1}{\frac{1}{3}} = 3}$$

The plus type exemplifies increased capacity for stimulation of feelings due to increased openness, and the minus type the same from abnormal shallowness. The converse results when the capacity for stimulation of feelings is reduced to one-third of normal.

$$\overset{+}{C = \frac{L}{D} = \frac{1}{3} = \frac{1}{3}} \qquad\qquad \overset{-}{C = \frac{L}{D} = \frac{\frac{1}{3}}{1} = \frac{1}{3}}$$

Here the plus type corresponds to less easy capacity for stimulation of feelings from more than ordinary profundity, and the minus type to the same from abnormal shallowness.

Personal Capacity for Stimulation of Will.—The structural peculiarity which is now to be discussed touches the doctrine of Temperament, and, indeed, seeks to transplant its sole valid kernel into a more rigid science; and further, the notion of the Four Temperaments (sanguine, phlegmatic, choleric, melancholy) haunts minds not all of which are uninstructed; accordingly, we take our course for once by way of mental history. We need only to mention names like those of Kant or Wundt in order to demonstrate, by examples of varying modernity, that the learning of professors of the theory of cognition and of "psychophysics" is no safeguard against an uncritical acceptance of archaic articles of faith, although an unbiased look at life suffices to show us that for many persons we would remain at a loss about the temperament to be selected, while for not a few we would have to make combinations and posit, for example, a melancholic-sanguine type or a choleric-phlegmatic. Bahnsen, perhaps, throws even more light on the matter, who, in his lively tract *Beiträge zur Characterologie* (1867) recognized that the concept of melancholy at any rate, in the modern sense, does not fit into the series; he retained, however, the fourfold classification and evolved, besides four main species—choleric, sanguine, phlegmatic, and anaematous—three subordinate species for each, or altogether sixteen temperaments.

There is hardly a more instructive example of the tough vitality of a custom whose meaning and origin have been forgotten, and particularly of the almost daemonic vitality of a number, than this fourfold division of temperaments. We may, indeed, preface our further account with what every psychologist might suspect even without historical data, namely, that the attempts, spread over twenty-five centuries, to divide into four regions, first the human body and then the soul, were inspired by the sacred nature of that number, which was selected by the Pythagoreans from the symbolism of numbers (which in turn is older still) and was clothed with the show of metaphysical significance. We are far from casting suspicion upon any view merely because it can be proved to have its roots in mythical images and symbolical numbers. However, we are not here concerned with the Four and its possible original meaning, but with the Four as stimulus of certain philosophic and metaphysical speculations which cannot be considered successful.

The (female) Four was first enthroned by the Pythagoreans and surrounded with apotropaeic insignia of partly real significance and partly childish imagery; next the Greek Hippocratic medical school (about 400 B.C.) imagined man as composed of the four "elements" (or, in modern parlance, four aggregate states) of earthy (firm), watery (fluid), airy (gaseous), and fiery (flame-natured), and his health as conditioned by their equipoise (later: temperare = to regulate, hence temperament). The seat of hot and dry fire was supposed to be the yellow gall (χολή), that of cold and wet water the phlegm (φλέγμα), that of moist and warm air the blood (lat., *sanguis*), and that of cold and dry earth the black gall (μέλαινα χολή), which was specially invented for the purpose. If one of the four preponderated, temporary or permanent disturbances resulted. Thus, for example, an excess of gall was supposed to create hot fevers and ulcers, and an excess of water chilly fevers and catarrhs. This is the famous "doctrine of humours" to explain the origin of diseases (pathology of humours) in which so far no psychological intentions can be discerned.

But fundamentally these "elements" rest upon a method of turning properties (the hot and the cold, the dry and the wet) into things, and thus unconsciously they were taken as having a psychic element, and that in the sense of a symbolism which is still current in language: burning love, blazing anger, the fire of enthusiasm, hot desire, cool behaviour, chill contempt, a flowing delivery, dry speech, and so on: and inevitably a psychical classification attached itself to the physical classification. This first was done in the "Problems" of Aristotle (or pseudo-Aristotle, for, even if they are not mainly spurious, they were certainly subjected to a recension in the Alexandrine period). The black-galled, or melancholy, type is here treated as a psychological type, but in a sense which has now become strange, in which, together with the choleric (or gallish) type it constitutes one total type. For the Aristotelian writer begins from the fiery nature of the gall, which, for him, naturally, is the vessel of excitement and passion, and is supposed to give power of poetic enthusiasm or heroic activity. But, being a Greek, he is well acquainted with all the phenomena of intoxication, and knows also that excess at the beginning is followed often by moodiness and exhaustion, and therefore makes the exciting element to mingle with blood, on its way from the gall, in a twofold manner—the hot and the cold. Those "whose gall is cold and black often become gloomy and idle; those who have much gall and hot, become excited and brilliant, tending to every kind of passion and desire, and often are loquacious. Others reach madness or ecstasy, whence arise Sibyls and Bacchantes, and all those who are credited with divine inspirations". This point is further developed, and there results what would now be called a psychology of genius. The close relation to ecstasy remained peculiar to melancholy into the Middle Ages, and occasionally as late as the eighteenth century; we recall Goethe's lines, which can be fully understood only if this is remembered:—

> Hence the poetic genius
> Is at home in the element of melancholy.

The doctrine of Temperament was later developed in every direction by Galenus (about A.D. 200), whose medical views held almost undisputed sway until the Renaissance. In course of time innumerable analogies crystallized around his fourfold division. The colour of hair, pigmentation, ossification, facial types, bodily habit, circulation of the blood, peculiarities of digestion, and disposition for disease were all classified by Temperaments, and the most diverse urges and other traits of character were connected with them.

It will be seen from this historical outline that name and number of Four have remained, but that the meaning of the thing has changed very considerably in the course of time. In view of this, attempts at definition are useless: indeed, all the authors who since Kant have occupied themselves with the Temperaments, use different criteria to distinguish them. However, by the aid of our feelings for meanings we can roughly describe what these four names generally convey to us today. We find that in the connotations of melancholy a disposition for gloominess preponderates, whence, for example, mental therapeutics treats "melancholy" as essentially synonymous with "depressive"; in those of choleric, a readiness for sudden passions, more particularly that of anger; in that of sanguine, speed and haste of all vital processes together with rapid exhaustion; in that of phlegmatic, their slowness. Thus the so-called four Temperaments could not be upheld even if they could be defined in the exactest manner, and even if their meaning at least, as denoting types, could be exemplified by perfectly appropriate facts: for in them there is a conflict of wholly diverse principles of classification.

Modern melancholy—a specific disposition of feeling, and as such part of the nature of character—would demand, as counterpart, a serene temperament, and this is not found in the series; so that mental therapeutics, to be consistent, had to add exaltation or euphoria. The choleric type turns out to be a mixture of the specific disposition of feeling which is called angry irritability (nature) and an abnormal capacity for stimulation of the feelings or "affectivity" (structure). As counterpart this would have (a) a meek type, and (b) difficult stimulation of feelings. Hence both must be segregated as pseudo-temperaments, in so far as we intend to look for the foundation of the modern view of Temperament in the characteristics which experiences show in their *development*.

Two facts permit, or rather compel, us to do this, of which the most important is the fact that a second usage of the word Temperament has grown up. For *the* temperament of a man is spoken of nowadays far more frequently than the four Temperaments; as when it is said that somebody has much or little temperament, is full of temperament, or without it, or shows no trace of it. If then it were desired to count melancholy as a true Temperament, this would involve giving two distinct meanings to the word; for it would be impossible to substitute "a great deal of melancholy" for "a great deal of temperament", or to mean a very melancholy person by a person having a great deal of temperament. Rather, temperament obviously is a single disposition which may be graduated indefinitely, or, more briefly, it is a personal constant of temperament, which of course can be arranged upon a series (like capacity for stimulation of feelings) between two terminal points which are relatively opposed and should serve particularly to elucidate its nature. And here we are helped by a second circumstance—namely, that according to its modern meaning the undoubted opposition between the sanguine and the phlegmatic type is essentially an opposition of degree, the contrast which is before the mind being that between abnormal rapidity and abnormal slowness of the vital processes. But such a classification would then be based upon properties relating to the course taken by processes, the reason of which must be looked for in the structure of character, and in that alone.

Of course such vague indications as rapidity and slowness will not serve. For we soon feel, on a little reflection, that many phlegmatic persons excel many sanguine persons in rapidity of grasp and of recollection, and even in intellectual adroitness. We accordingly ask the course of what processes is here intended if not exactly defined, or in regard to what processes of experience the extreme differences in the ease with which they arise has furnished the ground for the development of the opposition between natures full and barren of temperament and natures sanguine and phlegmatic.

Eros, according to Plato, is compounded of riches and poverty, fullness and emptiness, possession and lack: this definition in truth defines the bases of a theory of Striving. For this applies to any desire or craving, to every impulse, yearning, or wish. Whether we are planning a journey or only feel a vague impulse to roam, our striving is always turned upon something which we want, and vanishes if we have it. We *have* our goal (in imagination), and we have it *not* (in reality), since we lack it. Thus the process of Striving can exist only in so far as these two, the force of the goal which draws us and the resistance of that which still severs us from it, are together active in us. Two forces of opposite nature lie at the bottom of the process of striving (in its widest meaning): the force which is turned upon the goal (the driving force) and the retentive force which supports the consciousness of its absence, or, the mental resistance. The former corresponds to the platonic fullness, the latter to emptiness, and only when both are together does there arise that for which wish, impulse, striving, desire, craving, yearning, and want are names which emphasize accidental traits.

When we spoke above of the opposition in the ease with which feelings arise, we already indicated that in every feeling the qualitative side (colour, mood) must be distinguished from the impulsive side. The feeling of lack which goes with hunger is different in kind from that of thirst, the feeling of joy different in kind from anger: but violent hunger and violent thirst, violent joy and violent anger have in common the *strength* of the emotions, and form pairs of contrasted terms with slight hunger and slight thirst, slight joy and slight anger. But generally it is insufficiently understood that the quality of being capable of gradations with regard to strength or intensity applies only to impulses, is manifested in emotions, and appears to belong to moods or colours only, and that no mood, of whatsoever nature, occurs quite without some co-ordinated emotion. Otherwise obviously it would be impossible to make a scale of intensities of one and the same feeling, for example, that of joy, for then a new mood would correspond to each new stage, differing from its predecessors no less than does joy from anger. Easily as this may be understood, there were numerous reasons which withstood its acceptance, the most important of which is that, while each feeling can pass through various degrees of intensity, yet feelings which lie extremely ready to impulses (like joy, anger, zeal, expectation, hope) are a distinct class from such as do not lie ready to impulses (like grief, sadness, sorrow, disappointment, resignation). Thus if slight joy in relation to intense joy is a state of more intensive impulse, then intense grief in relation to slight grief is a state of more inhibited impulse. The usage of language, confused in appearance, but in fact consistent, became suddenly clear when it was understood that the emotive part of a mood always consisted of two components, an impulsive and an inhibitive, which might preponderate in turn; and now the differences in strength always, and in the same sense, fall into the emotive part if only it is remembered that, according to the nature of the mood of the feeling, the intensification is habitually applied now to the impulsive force, and now to the inhibitive force of the co-ordinated emotion. But it is permissible and even necessary to take into account personal differences in the ease with which feelings arise, and it is equally permissible to scrutinize the emotional aspect for itself, and, accordingly, to form a series of degrees of capacity for stimulation of impulse. With regard to the aspect of impulse feelings which are qualitatively different are always distinguished from one another by the relation between the impelling and the inhibiting component, and similarly differences in the personal capacity for stimulation of impulse can be developed only from the habitual relation of the two components. Thus we have once more reached the quotient of impulse and resistance.

The feeling of impulse is distinct from that of willing by the act of will, which effects a fundamental change in the former. But, among the immense number of feelings of impulse which fills the waking life of modern man, there is only a negligible number to which no event of willing is added, consuming part of the intensity of the feeling of impulse by transforming it into energies. But in order that resolutions, impulses of will, and acts may follow on mere impulses of feeling, it is necessary that the force of the urge shall overcome inhibition at least momentarily.[29] If accordingly we substitute capacity for stimulation of will for capacity of stimulation of impulse (and in any case the former is inevitably a visible index of the latter), we have thus reached the conclusion that the personal constant of temperament is the personal capacity for stimulation of will (W), which, in turn, results from the habitual relation between the urge-force (U) and the inhibitive emotion (E).

$$W = \frac{U}{E}$$

It is to be noted that U here is urge-force, and not urge.

We proceed to ascertain, step by step, what the formula can yield us. First, it saves us from confusing a lively temperament with a passionate nature. Whom do we call passionate? The man whose actions are guided by feelings which are at once strong, deep, and lasting. Such bases of will, referred to persons, are called passions in the narrower sense, referred to general facts, enthusiasms, and, finally, to objects which are considered ethically base, lusts (lust for drink, for gambling, etc.). If now we consider that every passion implies for its victim the danger of excess, against which instinct raises the bulwark moderation, then, in future, we shall no longer confuse rapidity governed by temperament with passionateness, nor expect that passionateness will accompany a capacity for easy stimulation of will. The proverb says as briefly as truly: "Still waters run deep." Our formula renders so crude a confusion impossible, for its preponderance of urge-force over the inhibition does not even coincide with the strength of feelings, and shows no connection with their lasting nature, and is actually in conflict with their depth.

Above we took the urge-force as the attractive power of the goal; we will now consider somewhat more exactly what is its significance for the will in this form. A poor man is attracted by the idea of money and wealth, an energetic official by that of promotion, an artist, perhaps, by that of fame; an envious man is fascinated while he is tormented by the idea of another's happiness, an ambitious man by that of distinction, and one who loves rule, by the glittering image of power; and obviously it is the attractive force of the imagination of the goal which lends urge-force to will in order that it shall force its way through the consciousness of obstacles. Unconsciously we measure it against this consciousness when we estimate another's efficiency. A "lively interest" in a cause is credited with inflaming the will to the removal even of heavy obstacles, and we fear that there may be rapid exhaustion where the real "driving impulse" is lacking. But it is generally forgotten that it is precisely the consciousness of obstacles (before which it is true that lack of interest will surrender) which is equally essential to the origin and progress of volition. For if we allow a growing preponderance to the attraction of the idea of the goal until finally it wholly dominates us, then there follows first an underestimation of the obstacles, then a forgetfulness of their persistence, and finally a state of desireless content, realization being anticipated in bare thought. Sunk in the dream of the pleasant things which we desire, we skip, so to speak, the barrier which separates us, and in the end experience no further impulse of desire. It is certain that the attraction of the idea of the goal is the lever of the effort of volition, but it ceases to exert its leverage as the feeling of the resistance of facts vanishes against which it first could measure itself as a driving force. Seen from this point of view, certain typical events become clear which perhaps have served more particularly to guide the origin of the modern idea of temperament.

Popular legend knows and delights to invent variations upon the theme of bad luck due to excess of zeal and lack of retarding power. We recall the famous milkmaid who, carrying the full jug on her head, works out what it will fetch and what she will buy with the further resulting profits— eggs, fowl, pig, calf, cow—until she jumps for joy and buries the fair prospect under the broken pieces of the jug. Or, again, there is the busy glass-blower on the haunted summit of the Riesengebirge, who, halting with his heavy basket of glassware, considers the profit which his heavy load will yield him. First, a donkey to carry his load; and then, "once I have a donkey", he goes on to think, "I soon shall make it into a horse, and once I have a horse in stable I soon shall have a field to grow his oats. One field soon turns into two, and two into four, in time into broad acres, and at length into a farmer's estate". At this moment the wicked spirit of the mountain, Rübezahl, disguised as a gust of wind, upsets the basket with its load of glass, and every piece is smashed.

But surely the attitude of the sanguine type will here be recognized. It is true that both the milkmaid and the glass-blower are also dreamers who, while imagining as present the beatific goal, quite lose sight of a less friendly reality. But we must not forget that nobody would ever strive after a goal which he could not imagine present at least for a moment. Every man who strives has moments, at intervals, when he dreams of the accomplished realization—although he soon remembers again the actual present moment. Without the capacity for dreaming ahead there would be no more striving, although it is true that, conversely, its excess (as it has just been presented) may dissipate the wish. Before that point is reached it only makes the striving more volatile, causing it to pursue the goal more blindly or else more hurriedly, and always with a comparative neglect of obstacles which stand in the way: striving which is full of temperament is uninhibited or easy striving. The perfect contrast to this is the type of Fabius Cunctator, the eternal hesitater, the prudent and cautious, who looks so much that he never leaps at all, and sometimes fulfils the poet's profound words

> He would go to sea, but will not go on board,
> And always remains fast in the idea.

Accordingly, striving without temperament would be striving internally inhibited, or difficult.

Our formula allows us to derive these extremely typical cases immediately from the personal relation between I and E, and at the same time it is confirmed by them, and also points out to us that, for the easier as well as for the more difficult stimulation of the will, we must again distinguish between a plus and a minus type. If once more we call the quotient 1, then we reach a threefold capacity for stimulation of the will (*a*) by multiplying the urge-force by 3 (plus type) and (*b*) by dividing the resistance by 3 (minus type); and we reach a capacity for stimulation of one-third magnitude (*a*) by multiplying the resistance by 3 (plus type), and (*b*) by dividing the urge-force by 3 (minus type).

$$+ \qquad\qquad -$$

$$W = \frac{U}{E} = \frac{3}{1} = 3 \qquad\qquad W = \frac{U}{E} = \frac{1}{\frac{1}{3}} = 3$$

$$W = \frac{U}{E} = \frac{1}{3} = \frac{1}{3} \qquad\qquad W = \frac{U}{E} = \frac{\frac{1}{3}}{1} = \frac{1}{3}$$

Experience is in accord with this and among natures which are definitely full of temperament shows us partly such as are quickly fatigued, like schemers, promoters, faddists, "kite-fliers" and "windbags", whose fire of straw is soon extinct, as it quickly flared up; and partly characters of unwearying activity, pursuing their aim with unchanged and burning eagerness, whose undiminished resilient powers into old age are strikingly illustrated by the proverb about the rolling stone which gathers no moss. Conversely, there are phlegmatic types who are really sluggish, whose indifference is shaken only with difficulty, but also such as are capable of a penetrating activity and steadfast endurance once they are "on fire". Further, we remark at once why the increased capacity for stimulation of will generally (but not necessarily) goes with specific receptivity for those feelings which are emphatically impulsive like eagerness, hope, cheeriness, and so on, while a diminished capacity goes better with specific receptivity for feelings in which the emphasis is on the inhibitive element, like gravity, suspicion, and a tendency to look backwards; whence there results of itself the not uncommon combination of a sanguine temperament with carelessness and some euphoria, and of the phlegmatic with moroseness and hesitancy.

Finally we shall not go wrong if, even in the plus case at each extreme of temperament, we count upon the possibility of those foibles which would constitute the exact obverse to these good qualities. Among the good qualities which attend a capacity for easy stimulation of the will are high spirits, initiative, flexibility, carelessness, speculative thought; among its dangers or weak points, lack of concentration, of method, distraction, a flighty and superficial nature. The advantages, on the other hand, of an extreme difficulty in stimulation of the will are steadfastness, a sense of realities, thoroughness, endurance, conscientiousness; and disadvantages or weak points, moroseness, clumsiness, obstinacy, lack of resolution, obsession with single ideas.

A cursory glance at so-called manic-depressive insanity instructs us that, for its opposite and limiting states, among others, the contrasts between the capacity for the stimulation of the will must be adduced, and that the particular manifestations of manic excitability, as well as of depressive (and even stuporose) difficulty in admitting excitement, are intelligible only as minus types, but, as such, are completely intelligible. Kraepelin repeatedly emphasizes of mania (his excellent description of the facts may be perused in his world-famous *Lehrbuch der Psychiatrie*) that in spite of an impulse to movement intensified to the stage of mania, "the process of association is in fact notably slower". Only if we derive manic excitability, not from an increase of U in relation to E, but from an abnormal reduction of E in relation to U, do we immediately understand the sudden change which sometimes occurs in the accompanying mood, so that it becomes a mood of similar tempo, but essentially different colouring—a furious joy, for example, changing into furious anger. And we also understand why the apparent vehemence with which interest is manifested from moment to moment is accompanied by a capacity for being distracted by the mere "exhibition of objects or calling out of words" which suffice to change the direction of attention so that the activity of thought by reason of its incapacity of steadily retaining the idea of any goal, soon offers the familiar picture of "idea-flying confusion". Similarly the analogous traits of depressive difficulty in responding to excitation result, one and all, from abnormally diminished impulsive force. In the one case it is the lack of inhibition, and in the other the paralysis of Strivings which offers the sole (structural) explanation of the morbid contrasts.[30]

Only when it is clearly understood that there is such a thing as a specific capacity for stimulation of the will do we get sight of several problems and complications which were invisible before. Although it is probably clear from our exposition, we still expressly emphasize that we have not been speaking of the will as such, and still less of its strength (which was touched upon in Chapter III), but only of the differences in the ease with which it can be excited. A great capacity for stimulation of the will does not coincide with great will power, although it does not, on the other hand, preclude it. The examples of a sanguine anticipation of the goal, described above, have shown us that the realization of success is hindered when it is imagined in a lively fashion; and we saw the reason. Also, a methodical pursuit of the goal demands that no heed be paid to distracting stimuli, and for this some inhibitive force is required. The extremely sanguine type, childlike in the volatile nature of its striving, has a temperament which is a less useful instrument for a volition tending towards its goal than the type which is not easily excited: as has been observed, it sometimes shows a lack of thoroughness and perseverance. But strength of will is a thing for itself which may be influenced adversely or favourably by the form of temperament, but is not produced by it, so that it may also accompany easy striving, or may be lacking where striving is difficult; hence there exist sanguine types which yet are persevering.

Those, further, who have learned to distinguish a capacity for stimulation of feelings and of will must no longer expect that both must be found in the same person under the same sign, and will foresee that various combinations may exist. Where there is increased capacity for stimulation of feeling combined with great impressionability, and strong capacity for stimulation of will is based on these, then there will result the classical sanguine type, a character which is easily inflamed, always mobile, shaking off ill temper by action, lively and flexible; never a spoilsport, always ready for amusement and (because he never bears the weight of undigested recollection) generally appearing serene, merry, and even jolly. There is a less pleasant result where a capacity for easy stimulation of will is coupled with feeble capacity for stimulation of feeling, since it is favourable to restlessness, hurry, empty zeal, a restless craving for activity, aimless readiness for undertaking schemes, a shallow impulse after change, and a stale craving for amusement; and there is a complete change in the picture when a high capacity for stimulation of feelings goes without the gift of easy reaction. Then there result natures which are excited without need, take everything too seriously, easily feel injured—whence the double meaning of the word "sensitive"—and not infrequently tend to excessive conscientiousness and self-reproach.

The above theory of temperament was first made public in lectures on characterology during the years 1905-7 at Munich, and at the same time we published its outlines in the *Graphologische Monatshefte* (1906), which we were editing at that time. Later, we embodied them (although in a very compressed form) in the first edition of this book (1910); we treated it on several occasions in periodicals, daily newspapers, and numerous single lectures; and the result of all this was at least so far to arouse the attention of scientific circles as to produce the lively assent of some scientists and the no less lively dissent of others. We do not doubt that some day it will be part of the axioms of the study of character, although it is probable that until that moment a good deal of water will flow into the sea. We will here consider one objection only, partly because it seems to be particularly attractive to some, and partly because it allows us to throw light upon a fresh characteristic of the facts.

Let it be objected that the capacity for stimulation of the will does, after all, vary from case to case, and consequently quite different qualities are affected by the changes both of U and of E. A schoolboy who is greatly interested in mathematics, but has no talent for languages, appears incapable of stimulation while languages are being taught, and conversely: thus the necessary driving force is lacking from lack of interest. A character capable of great self-control increases the resistance to impulses by the force of his will; and finally, quite extraordinary displacements are caused by the interplay of driving forces. A man who is fond of pleasure and at the same time troubled with a strong sense of conscience will suffer from internal conflicts: and the resulting inhibitions have nothing to do with his temperament. How then can we *find* a personal capacity for stimulation of the will, apart from the nexus of driving forces? But if we cannot discover these, then the assumption of their existence is utterly baseless.

To this we may reply that, if we had not found it, then such terms as a strong and a weak temperament (terms which speculation has not furnished in advance) would have died out long ago as being meaningless. It thus remains only to obtain a notion as to how they were discovered, and why at bottom nobody doubts that some people have much and others little temperament. For this purpose it must evidently be possible to neglect the driving forces. But now in fact, apart from the field of "interested" actions, there is another field, of almost equal size, of neutral attitudes of men, where the participation of their inclinations is negligible; it comprises the manner of knocking at a door, of calling "come in", of saluting in the street, of passing a dish; the manner of shaking hands, of jumping off a car, patience or impatience in waiting, and much else of the same kind. If our friend, whom we meet on a rainy day on an ill-paved road, is a sanguine type, he will cross the road diagonally without caring whether he soils his shoes and trousers; whereas a phlegmatic person calmly uses the dry passage which connects the two sidewalks at right angles. If we ask our sanguine neighbour at table to pass a dish he will put out his hand in the directest way, and is frequently in danger of knocking over an intervening bottle, whereas a phlegmatic person often seems to be rather hard of hearing, though really no less polite—so slowly does he comply with our request. The one never "has the time" because he is always afraid of missing something, the other always has ample, for the simple reason that he always allows himself the time. The one often misses his connection because he arrives too late, the other because he over-hurries and arrives too early.

Our whole life is full of this kind of event; and especially there is hardly a better standard for the degree of personal capacity for stimulation of the will than the degree of our disposition for patience. If one observes the behaviour of people on a Sunday at the station, where they are assembled in numbers for an excursion, and the train happens to be rather late, then, although certainly there will be very few whose interests are affected by the delay in leaving, it will still be easy to discover that there are the widest differences in their behaviour. Some will soon become restless and finally furious, and find it necessary to vent their annoyance about the scandalous delay in loud exclamations, while others evince perfect equanimity and rather tend towards a humorous contemplation of the impatient ones. The former are those whose will is easily stimulated, the latter those whose will is stimulated with difficulty.

It is further to be remarked that the constant of temperament is one of the least variable properties of character; and, although in every person with growing age a certain decline in the degree of excitability takes place, it still is true that no pure sanguine type ever became phlegmatic, while those qualities which we generally consider more deeply rooted, like a youthful tendency after perfection, and an "idealistic" point of view, vanish completely in the course of a lifetime. Accordingly, the capacity for stimulation of the will is a permanent index of the differences in peoples and races. Speaking comprehensively, we may say that (for example) Asiatics are characterized by a far more difficult excitability of the will than Europeans.[31]

Personal Capacity for Expression.—So far we have been speaking of the stimulation of impulse, that is, of a purely internal process. Now we know that every vital process is accompanied by its bodily process which, in relation to the former, we call its expression or manifestation; but many such bodily processes are not even noticed by the person in whom they occur, and the great majority remain invisible to the observer as, for example, slight variations in the motion of the heart, in respiration, in electric tension, in the activity of the bowels, in the innumerable chemical transformations in the blood, the glands, the nerves, and so forth. Hence we distinguish between the manifestation of life in the wider sense and that which becomes visible—which we call the expression of life. If we assume (what is probable to begin with) that there is a personal capacity for expression (E), then we must consider this too to be a capacity which depends upon the ratio between two dispositions, growing necessarily with growing excitement (Ex) and diminishing as the resistance to expression (R) grows:

$$E = \frac{Ex}{R}$$

The stimulation of the impulse was seen above to be the sign either of the strength of the urge-force or again of the weakness of the resistance, and similarly the strength of the expression is sometimes evidence of the strength of the stimulation of the impulse, and sometimes of the weakness of the resistance to expression; and (once more) the converse is true.

We have dealt exhaustively with the constant of Temperament: here we speak more briefly, only complementing our exposition by a word-for-word copy of parts of a work which we devoted to this subject twenty years ago. It cannot be doubted, according to the principle of expression, that movement grows as the stimulation of impulse grows, and that the inhibitions of movement grow as the impulses are blunted. But it will be asked, what is a resistance to expression, and what forces us to form such a curious concept. For once we answer by bringing in a consideration based upon evolutionary history.

Every animal being, and man in particular, has an interest in not showing certain mental processes. A man in love seeks to hide his love in public, a timid person his timidity, the ambitious man his ambition, the envious his envy, the jealous his jealousy, and so on. Many will do more than to hide their inclination, they will seek to simulate the opposite, as we all do a thousand times semi-automatically when we treat a person, our sentiments towards whom are anything but friendly, with conventional acts of courtesy. Originally all self-control serves as self-protection. If now we consider that man has been forced during innumerable centuries to practise self-control in order to preserve his life and well-being, then we would have to consider it a miracle if no organic resistance to expression had developed within him.

We can discover numerous prototypes of this in the animal world. When many animals feign death at moments when they imagine themselves in danger, this is no action, but a reaction which takes place necessarily, and is due to the instinct for self-preservation; and it takes place at the cost of the fear which no doubt possesses the animal, and for its part would manifest itself in flight. But the technique of deception and the drill in maintaining a countenance received an intensification far beyond all similar cases in animals from the fact that man's communal life already in prehistoric times came under the power of cult-customs whose sphere, diminishing progressively in historical times, was replaced by the no milder power of ethical rules. An infraction of customs, and, later, of ethical standard and sense of right, resulted at the least in temporary or permanent exclusion from the community, and hence, among primitive peoples, in almost certain destruction, and among civilized races in an ostracism which in severe cases seems hardly less terrible: to say nothing of the bloody side of criminal justice, which goes beyond anything that the individual may have dreamed of hell. If it could be determined with dynamometrical accuracy whether men fear more the loss of life or the loss of reputation, we would discover no small percentage of slaves of their honour, who would be ready, if necessary, to risk their life for it. Many soldiers have attained the courage to face a storm of bullets only through fear of the reputation of cowardice which otherwise would attach to them.

We grasp the root of the matter if we consider that the need for self-esteem, which is all-powerful in man, necessarily was fused with the demands of the community, and thus in prehistoric ages led to the cultivation of the peculiar sense of honour which fundamentally distinguishes men from the whole of the animal creation. If now we retain that the contents of the sense of honour may vary in the most diverse manner with ages, peoples, and groups, and that (for example) there is honour among thieves as well as among true men, then we may say that, beside the various considerations which forbid expression, there stands in man (apart from the instinct for self-preservation in general) the powerful driving force of the sense of honour, which finds an expression exactly like every other direction of interests; but this means, in relation to the expressions generally, an organic resistance to expression.[32] Now the magnitude of this resistant component is part of personality, and therefore it must be possible to evaluate it in order to estimate the strength of excitement; hence we must no longer expect that equal strengths of expression in different persons are necessarily evidence of equal strengths of excitement. Are we really to draw this ticklish conclusion; and would facts confirm it?

This question has an interest from the point of view of the history of science, and also what has just been adduced still agrees with our convictions, and therefore we proceed to answer the above question with the help of an extract from earlier writings, which was alluded to above. "Anger certainly has its signs, which become more acute and powerful as it grows; but, if we compare several men with one another, then we soon observe that, where intensities may be supposed to be equal, the expressions may be very unequal. Some natures manifest a high degree of expression of excitement when the excitement itself is slight, while there are others whose demonstrably powerful emotions are manifested in slight and almost invisible symptoms. But here conscious exaggeration, dissimulation, or self-control do not come into question. Nobody likes to show signs of fear, and nearly everyone of love. But a person of the first class will appear more timid, and one of the second class less fond, than he is in reality, although each wishes to show the opposite. And the deceptions which may arise thence grow further when in the same individual the 'incongruity' varies for different mental states, or for different expressions of one and the same state. Thus the reflex action of blushing occurs with almost morbid ease in precisely those persons whose vital pulsations otherwise hesitate to enter on the path of expression."

After this reference to personal differences in the ease of expression there follows, for the first time, an attempt to interpret as a part of the category of expression the fact that there is specific talent, and, by confining formative force to particular personal spheres, to obtain a further proof for the existence of differential resistances to expressions. "We have long been familiar with analogous phenomena in the sensitiveness and sensibility of the senses. A blind man makes more delicate his feeling of touch, and for temperature; a deaf man almost finds a substitute for the lost power of hearing by greater attention of sight. Compared with certain 'natural races', we 'civilized' men are almost in the case of deaf and blind. By refining speech and writing into a means of expression of almost magical perfection, we have not only lost the eagle keenness of the two chief senses, but also and especially the gift of unconscious observation which enables the savage without apparatus to apprehend almost imperceptible traces of events, or to compress many sentences into a single call and gesture. Apparatus and books have incomparably more perfect efficiency with us; thus we were able to neglect as superfluous the art of sensuous interpretation. We were naive students of the physiognomy of things, we have become calculating controllers and detectives. ... It was one of the inconsistencies of a psychology of which one half was paralysed to pay attention in the analysis of talents only to peculiarities of apprehension, although the differentiation of the capacities for expression surely may claim equal attention. A born teacher—the orator or poet, for example—have, each in his own manner, to concentrate the totality of expression into the sole vehicle of speech. One might say that they suffer from an excess of expression by speech, and it may happen that their whole capacity for expression is paralysed, while the wealth of sound of their language is far beyond the normal. ... The more frequently and intensely we make use of an organ the more powerfully it develops, but in doing so it appropriates the totality of available energy: this is true of the body and, equally, of the soul. Those who, like the typical lecturer, have formed the habit of continually explaining facts, will finally form, not only a tendency to extract from every content of experience that fact which may be taught logically, but will also acquire the gift of deriving it more particularly by the method of expressing it in speech. They thus acquire the excess of capacity for thought-expression at the expense of the sensuous immediacy of their inner life. Professional one-sidedness, rooted in one-sidedness of expression, in turn brings the latter with it, and produces it only in so far as the undivided and universal gift of expression still is available. And, indeed, nothing can break more thoroughly the capricious impulsiveness of the savage than the compulsion of a profession. This, once understood, implies the law of practice in general. A loss in expressiveness of the whole is the necessary price of perfection in expression of the parts. Whatever may be the nature of "self-control", and however certain it may be that it alone enables us to act methodically, it is certain that it diminishes our capacity for surrendering the body to the dim security of its own motions, and for 'letting ourselves go' unrestrainedly under the incorruptible promptings of our blood. Schiller judges quite correctly that it is no small step towards humanity 'to practise pure will by breaking natural necessity in oneself, even in indifferent things'. But, again, it is just this ideal man of Kant and Schiller to whom Nietzsche objects *per contra*: 'He has destroyed and lost his instinct, he can no longer trust in the "divine beast", and surrender the reins when his reason sways and his path leads through deserts.' "33 Here the exposition enters upon the same thought with which on this occasion we began.

It is in perfect harmony with this that current language is acquainted with the distinctions which our theory demands. A powerful capacity for expression is at least *part* of the meaning of such words as "abundant", "overflowing", "extravagant"; and a feeble capacity of "quiet", "measured", "introspective". In view of the supreme importance of linguistic expression, we might expect similar contrasts in this sphere too, and in fact the communicative, loquacious, and talkative person has for opposite the man of few words, the taciturn and the monosyllabic. It is here particularly clear that ease in expression need not necessarily coincide with more than usual strength of emotion. Experience shows that intense emotion does not by any means correspond to loquacity, and conversely a taciturn person may be exceedingly excitable—as may be inferred from his burning eyes.

Different ages of men, the sexes, and peoples vary even more with respect to ease of expression than with respect to excitability. That of children is always greater than that of grown-ups, that of women (at least on the average) greater than that of men (except in matters of social decorum), and that of Latin races, greater than that of the Germanic (maximum contrast: Italian and Englishman). A high capacity for expression is treated as part of the concept of *spirits*, and therefore it is usual to speak of the bright, jolly, and merry spirits of children, but hardly of the spirits of a man of sixty. But all the words here adduced contain something further, namely, an *urge* for expression which sometimes is overemphasized and sometimes remains below the average: this is of an importance which could hardly be exaggerated for the health of the mind, and this, we think, justifies the next chapter, which is in the nature of an interlude.

CHAPTER VII NOTES

29   This is as true of the resolution to refrain from an action as of the resolution to act. In each case there is a command of the Spirit, occasioned by an impulse; for without impulse no resolution could be reached. But if an action (for example) is left undone from lack of resolution, this is, of course, genetically a wholly different matter from its nonexecution when this has been resolved upon. Conversely, a command is a command whether it orders forward or halt, and in each case an impulse is required.

30   Above, we called our formulae schematic. Possibly mathematics possesses a more appropriate term for what we mean. In any case we will take the manic-depressive change of state as the occasion for defining our meaning somewhat more closely. Such formulae are modelled upon those employed in physics and are, of course, formulae determining measures. The numbers (or, rather, amounts) which occur in them state what multiple of an arbitrary, but very exactly determinable unit of measure is found in each case. (The numbers thus vary with the unit of measure.) Now it would be difficult already in itself to give units of measurement for vital processes which could be not merely estimated, but defined with such accuracy that they could be taken as genuine measures; and as a rule the best procedure is to rely solely on estimates. But even if we assume that this difficulty might be overcome (Fechner, for example, tried to overcome it), still every person would in strictness require a fresh standard of measure. Thus in one and the same person it is easy to distinguish by estimation inhibited from non-inhibited states (or attitudes), and we have every right to explain the less inhibited state by a diminution of his R in relation to his U; and also we may judge the average attitude of one person to be less inhibited than that of another, and may accordingly form the opinion that the resistance of the former, in relation to his own urge-force, is less than the resistance of the latter in relation to *his* urge-force; but we can no longer form even a rough estimate of the relation of the R of the one to the R of the other, and of the U of the one to the U of the other. Thus it is quite possible that in the state of manic excitement U is greater than in the states of excitement of sane persons, and further that it is greater than it is in the same person once the manic phase has passed off. But what we may not but must assume is that in relation to the U of the manic person (whether the U is of average force or above) his R is exceptionally small. Our equations served to mean that in one case U is to R as is 3 to 1, and in the other as 1 to 1/3, but in fact we mean that in one case it is as $3x$ to x, and in the other as y to $\frac{1}{3} y$, where the unknown terms x and y can never be found because we lack a unit of measure applicable to all persons alike. It was this which we tried to express by the adjective ''schematic''. The equations, however, do not become any the less valuable as means for making it easier to find a path. In each case we have only to set up the so-called formula of efficiency (by multiplying the right-hand side by the numerator of the fraction) in order to understand immediately why one case deserves to be called the plus type and the other the minus type.

If I write the plus type thus: $\dfrac{U}{R} = \dfrac{3}{1} = 3$, then the formula of efficiency is 3 X 3 = 9.

If I write the minus type thus: $\dfrac{U}{R} = \dfrac{1}{\frac{1}{3}} = 3$, then the formula of efficiency is 3 X 1 = 3, which shows clearly how the plus type is a real *plus* as against the minus type.

[31] Consider, for example, buying and selling as practised in an Oriental bazaar. An Oriental will bargain for the same article with perfect equanimity for days, while a European loses patience after an hour, and often much sooner. Gobineau makes a fine artistic use of these differences of character in his *Nouvelles Asiatiques.*

[32] If we speak of the expression of a sense of honour we do not, of course, mean any acts of self-control due to such a sense, for such would be *acts* inspired by a sense of honour: we mean the effects of a present state of a sense of honour, which act quite automatically; and these, without exception, consist in inhibitions of impulses.

[33] The sentences quoted at the beginning by themselves come from our *Probleme der Graphologie* (1910), which has long been out of print, pp. 50-1; this also applies to the last two sentences of the main quotation, pp. 52-3. All the rest comes from our *Graphologische Principienlehre* in the *Graphologische Monatshefte*, 1904, pp. 34-5.

CHAPTER VIII

OF THE NATURE OF HYSTERIA

Capacity for Expression and Impulse towards Expression.—We must here anticipate and digress into the field of the driving forces. Besides the *capacity* for expression, there is, as has been said, an *urge* towards expression. It appears already in infancy, manifests itself during childhood as the urge to play (or as the moulding or formative urge), and at a later stage shares in the urge after activity in sport, or the equally widespread creative urge. The motor-aspect (which may be derived biologically) is emphasized by the French with their expression *plaisir de mouvement.* For, if we examine the most universal side of the impulse-movements which are common to men and animals, namely, the faculty of self-motion, it is only proper to understand it as the expression or realization of an urge towards motion, which, for its part, is the most prominent aspect of the urge towards expression.

An equilibrium between capacity for and urge towards expression is obviously the natural state, and this in fact generally exists in a healthy child, but, as the resistance to expression grows as the child reaches maturity, the equilibrium gives way to a certain disproportion, the capacity falling short, more or less, of the urge; this is sometimes accompanied by an increase of some of the capacities of expression at the expense of others: this, as has already been mentioned, is a chief source of specific talent. The consequences vary accordingly as the urge after expression is strong or weak. Where the desire after expression is weak, there is an inhibition of expression which leads to the development of a dislike of expression which, like every disturbing factor, reacts upon the general attitude of the person, and especially upon the self-esteem. The person who suffers from such an inhibition makes a virtue of necessity, and credits only those with truly deep feelings who do not express them, while he attributes shallow and feeble

156

feelings to those who, as the expression is, wear their heart upon their tongue. This is correct in some cases, and completely false in others. Such a person also tends from lack of openness to more self-analysis than is expedient; he loses ease of conduct and ceases to be naive. This quality (and this alone) he shares with members of that class whose expression is inhibited in a second manner, which alone we intend now to consider.

If the lack of capacity for spontaneous expression is accompanied by a powerful desire after expression, a conflict would arise which would be unendurable in the long run, and especially would prove destructive of the self-esteem of the person in question, were it not that the troubled organism found a substitute in an impulse (of progressively increasing independence) towards representation of states of feeling, which in turn brings with it as an inevitable consequence that the feelings themselves are exhausted in the service of the interest which is taken in manifestations of feelings, and become more and more atrophied. The more harmless forms of this disturbance are known as states of exaggerated feeling, of exaltation, and faddishness; the graver forms are the main characteristics of what is nowadays called the hysterical character. Our views on the hysterical character have been published in several places,[34] but we intentionally neglected acute hysteria. We here take the opposite road, and open an approach to the hysterical character by minute analysis of the character of hysteria. But three remarks must first be made.

The formula which governed the theme of our former exposition, and also guides us here, was: "reaction of the impulse after representation against the feeling of vital impotence". It makes clear that we consider the disproportion between urge and capacity as merely secondary, and as essential the fact of vital impoverishment, where the patient, under the influence of the enduring feeling of his own existence, will not let go the illusion "that he is sharing in the banquet of life with all his senses and vitality". But it would be hard to obtain a deeper insight precisely into the nature of this defect without an appreciation of the defects in the manifestation of expression. Our second remark deals with the name of hysteria (from ὑστέρα = womb). It is based on the notion, which has long been recognized to be false, that hysteria is an affection of the female creature only, and that it is centred at the organ of sex. In fact, hysteria is a variety of biological parasitism, but we retain the name which has gained currency, the more so since many have forgotten its origin. Thirdly, however much exact acquaintance with the mechanism of hysteria may be demanded of the student of character, this would not have been a sufficient occasion to introduce a separate chapter, but for the fact that it offered a welcome occasion for discovering one side of the life of the feelings which, being once understood, will make it easier to understand the system of the driving forces.

Hysteria.—There are certain manifestations of hysteria which are known to us under the name of "imaginary illness"—a name due to the views of an earlier period. If we wish to make use of this expression once again, then we must reject the idea that the patient merely simulates the disease, and bring to the surface again the ancient but not quite extinct notion which makes the image of the disease a real entity capable of impressing itself upon the organism like a seal upon the warm wax. If then the sufferer from hysterical neurosis appears more generally as the more or less defenceless victim of the transforming influence of the most various images, we could hardly escape confusions as dangerous in their consequences as they are difficult to avoid, unless we thoroughly go into the meaning of the "images" here before the mind.

Our doctrine of the actuality of images—which will become clear only step by step as we proceed—teaches that by the sway of images in the living material we are to understand vital processes which *can* produce phantasms, but by no means must do so necessarily and, least of all, may be compared with the intellectual activities of bringing before the mind, called by some "imagining". The legitimate question whether there are in fact such processes, and why we should see in them a manifestation of images when in fact they do not necessarily cause us to experience even a phantasm, may properly be answered by a few examples.

If we consider that after fertilization the urge or desire is stimulated in the germ-cell of the maternal organism to add cell to cell by millionfold repetition, until a new organism has been built up of analogous form to the maternal organism, then we could hardly find a better description for this process of growth than by remembering that in the fertilized cell there act, as moulding power, the images of the growing body. But those who think it too bold to let the process of growth and ripening (which certainly is profoundly unconscious) take place by virtue of the power of images which came into appearance only by virtue of this process, will no longer fail to recognize this power and its unconscious sway if they consider the relations of the finished organism to the surrounding world. For the nature of the so-called instinct of brutes (touched upon above) means that, by virtue of such relations, they make a selection from among the world-images, seeking what they require in order to live, what is wholesome and pleasant, and avoiding what is harmful and hostile.

An attraction of vital magnetism connects a thirsty horse with the sight of water, a hungry cow with the impression of grass, the eagle at prey with the image of fowls, kids, or hares; and it connects each one of them with that side of the images, and that section of the world which it has the gift of choosing, and recognizing unconsciously as its element and home. A duckling, scarcely capable of motion, runs into the pond, while the hen which has just hatched it flutters and warns it: it has recognized the water for its element, not from the very slightest reflection, but because of the peculiar attraction which makes its soul receptive of the impression of water. The impression *is* not the attraction, but only stimulates it. An animal in need of food *seeks* food when there is none, its habitation and element when it lacks these, and the flights of migratory birds which start upon their journey in autumn are separated by thousands of miles from the impressions—of ambient atmosphere, climate, and habitat—after which they strive, driven by vital magnetism, somnambulant.

One talks of urge, and rightly emphasizes in it the aspect of requirement, of lack. But a glance at any given example suffices to make it clear that a need could never lead to the satisfaction of that need without the unconscious presence of the attractive power of the image which promises satisfaction. However we analyse the sensation of thirst, whether physiologically or psychologically, we shall find nothing in it that in the least resembles the appearance of water (whatever organ of sense reports it to the sentient being); and we would be for ever unable to make any statement whatever about the experience of thirst unless we decided with Aristotle to call it an impulse after union with the liquid; but then we would have introduced into the state of need called thirst unconscious attractive power in the shape of the *image* of the liquid.

The distinction just discussed between the aspect of impulse and the aspect of mood in feelings, applies also, of course, to animal feelings. In feelings peculiar to man, driving forces are observed; in animal feelings, urges. Urges are vital causes of movement, and vital movement (as opposed to purely mechanical movement) is directed upon a goal which can be determined genetically. The impulsive strength of the urge manifests the strength of the need or lack, and its direction, the attractive power (which has already been discussed) of the image. This it is which already at the animal stage gives its peculiar quality to the various urges of hunger, thirst, migration, play, sexual intercourse, care, attack, defence, flight; and it plays at least a part in the element of mood which is part of every human feeling. Accordingly, if the element of mood in feeling testifies to the connection (now close, now loose) between the soul and the actuality of the images—and, in testifying, it also postulates —then we may properly speak of an image-content. Feelings in which the mood-element is notably weaker than the impulse-element must be called weak of image, and those where the mood-element preponderates strong of image.[35] If this is once seen, we hold the key which will enable us to understand the fact that images may be experienced, and may guide vital processes without the help of phantasms, and even more without any consciousness of these.

Original man won his way out of the animal state by a change in the weight of the poles, when the vital process of sensation (both of his own and of foreign bodies) which had governed hitherto, became dependent upon the vital processes of contemplation (of images) which had hitherto been governed by it: thus the emotional or corporeal side of feeling became dependent upon the spiritual mood; hence from this point on, fancy, or the gift of day-dreaming, had power to strike off the bonds of here and now. The attractive force of images, which hitherto had been realized only in the change of bodily states, now came to light autonomously, determining the body henceforward differently, and to different activity from that which the mere impulse of urge could ever have determined. A stag when thirsty is forced to look for water, and lacks it until he finds it; but thirsty man had and has the power to dream, waking, of water and of drinking—to picture to himself water and drinking, and, finally, to objectify their image materially; more generally, the images, which hitherto have acted only in the directive attraction-force of urges, and so to speak, blindly, awake in him; and simultaneously there awake, relinquishing their animal emotions and overcoming them, innumerable new desires—as innumerable as the potential images of those elements which gave him birth: the world awakens and becomes revealed for what it is: an actuality itself of the images, in relation to which now all vital processes appear as means and approaches to the contemplation of actuality. Here lies the deepest root of myth, symbol, and art, and here too the deepest root of every kind of magic.

Our derivation of the psychical birth of images from the so-called instincts has shown us how and why the living material decides for itself what images of perceptions attract it, which shall be capable of repelling it, and to which phantasms it surrenders itself. If all the processes which affect corporeal and spiritual selection and formation are comprehended together under the name of formative processes of the widest meaning, and if we give to the reason of their existence the name of the image-creating capacity of life, then we must consider two fundamentally different consequences which follow if we grow poor in this quality: immediate over-emphasis of will and the apparently (but only apparently) opposite property of vital capacity for being influenced by accidental events (suggestibility). In order to understand the former fact we must be acquainted with what follows. First vitality (or Soul) is coupled in man with Spirit, whence results the Ego (this will be considered later), and only now Spirit can seek to seize upon experiences of impulses (and upon these alone)—which experiences may become subservient to will, while at the same time the mood-element of feeling (that is, the image) is excluded. The monstrous growth in power of the element of will in historical man had for essential condition his impoverishment in image-creating capacity. The man of will and the hysterical person are both inhabited by Ego-sensations which have become weak of image—and, as such, they are closely related. Many men whose actions have influenced the history of the world were hysterical, and all without exception were skilled artists in stage-management; and many hysterical persons again go far beyond the average in the effective power of their will. The "hysterical mechanism", too, is incompatible with no degree of willpower, but is incompatible with the slightest degree of imagination. At this point, however, we will confine ourselves to the latter.

If for the moment we neglect the fact that impulses of urge are convertible into impulses of will, then it is clear that the organism will lack direction more and more as its formative faculty declines: it will be able to oppose less and less selective affinity, and imprinting faculty of its own to the vital influence which accompanies every perceived image.

162

This explains three peculiarities of hysterical suggestibility: the fundamental indifference of the events which exert influence; the frequent fact that the causes are unobserved, as also are the channels along which their influence is directed; and the corporeality (which is almost without exception overemphasized) of their action. Any given seal can be imprinted upon the wax, and in each case will give an image, and similarly the hysterical organism responds with fundamental changes in the functions of its body to causes of perception whose significance for the organism has never entered the consciousness of the percipient entity. And, as the wax imprint can easily be changed by the application of a fresh impression, so the hysterical organism *can* at least offer the most incalculable variety of "symptoms" arising in this manner. But we will not confine ourselves to concepts, however obvious their validity, but will attempt to share the experience of living through the process up to the point where the line needs to be produced only a little in order that we may understand what we cannot ourselves experience.

Our so-called imaginations are the creations of the activity of our Spirit (that is, processes of thought tending to make present to the mind conditions of affairs capable of being intuited), and must on no account (as has already been observed) be confused with images, which have a capacity for vital activity. The activity of imagining is of course always connected with some life-processes, but even when, as sometimes occurs, these relate to exactly the same state of affairs, the activity must be rigorously distinguished from these. The following example easily explains this. A doctor, who during a cholera epidemic "imagines" this sinister disease in the greatest detail, analysing its causes, the course it takes, and symptoms, does not for this reason catch the disease. But if anybody is forced to concern himself with it in his "imagination", from violent fear of contagion, he is, in fact (other things being equal), in greater danger of infection than those who are indifferent and fearless; but not because he indulges in imagination, but because in his state of fear the image of the disease (or rather, the image of becoming diseased) *acts* organically, inhibiting and paralysing the protective instincts of the organism.

In such a case (which is quite normal) the work of imagination manifests itself in feelings of an emotional kind which cannot possibly escape the consciousness of the patient; but in others, the feeling of fear (which in a manner is symptomatic) is so feeble as to allow itself to be screened from consciousness by the impulse of self-esteem; but this by no means affects the process of imagination; only, consciousness is barred from the feelings which announce it. Thus a man may go to the hypnotizer on the stage, after energetically rebuking a slight tremor of fear which he has silenced, with the bold words, "*I* cannot be hypnotized". And behold, he is one of the first to lie in an unresisting trance, because (if one may so put it for the sake of brevity) his It was of quite different opinion from his ambitious *I*, which intentionally was deaf to the warnings of the former. This, too, is a perfectly normal case which is, perhaps, thought curious by some only because they do not yet understand that body and spirit are two inseparable poles of one and the same living entity.

In this and similar cases we may observe the action of imagination by the help of recollection. But an abnormally unstable equilibrium of the organism, due to a morbid decay of the independent force of its formative processes, must be assumed when a hysterical maid-servant, who has been in service for some weeks with a family, a member of which is suffering from lung trouble, suddenly begins to cough in a distressing manner without being infected *and* also without having been afraid of the disease. Indeed, she may well shine in her devotion to the patient and know absolutely nothing of the origin of her own indisposition. We, as spectators, will have no doubts about the state of affairs (assuming that the doctor has been unable to discover any organic cause of the trouble), although we dimly feel that an argument by analogy alone does not suffice, and that something else is at work (which for the moment must remain obscure) to enable the operation of imagination to succeed—by what may be called the spiritual road—and yet to be unobserved. The patient all the while has observed nothing at all.

But even this comparatively simple case is not normal. For the process of imagination can take place without the feelings habitual in us, and may evade consciousness altogether; and the imagination which has taken place may in its natural course belong to the history of the patient exactly as consciously known events which effect the greatest emotional change and bring about a fundamental alteration in the mode of life, belong to the history of non-patients. This being so, we should not be too greatly surprised if the cause of the imagination can be discovered only as the last link in a long chain of intermediate terms, and often eludes discovery altogether. Nor does this greatly matter, for the cause of its action *qua* imagination must never be looked for in the peculiarity of the cause, but solely in the fact that the hysterical organism is fundamentally at the mercy of any imagination, although in different cases there may be indications of different strength pointing to a selective action which leads us back to peculiar traits of the character.

The functional disturbances thus caused are mostly of a predominantly bodily nature, but in part also of a predominantly mental nature: they are of almost infinite variety, though it is true that certain groups are especially favoured. Perhaps the commonest cases are, among bodily disturbances, hoarseness, asthma, stomach troubles, disturbances of the circulation, of the activity of the heart, of the functions of the bowels; in women, disturbances of menstruation, partial paralysis, writer's cramp. Among cases which are half-way to mental disturbances there are hysterical deafness, dumbness, blindness, lack of sensation (various kinds of anaesthesia, and also of analgesia); and among disturbances which are predominantly mental, there are disturbances of memory (various kinds of hysterical anamnesia), innumerable idiosyncrasies, apparently meaningless abnormalities of behaviour, and so on. Certain functional disturbances *may* pass over into "organic" disturbances, and in any case it must be remarked that theoretically we have no means of measuring the limits of the power of imagination. It is possible to die of imagination, as it is possible by imagination to recover from severe illness. In any case those only who have made themselves at home in the doctrine of the reality of images will no longer find it strange, and in the end will find it quite reasonable, that in deep hypnosis a haemorrhage will stop on command, that a drop of distilled water on the hand of a somnambulist (to whom it has been suggested that it is vitriol) will cause a blister, that a dervish will lick red-hot iron without hurting his tongue, that a fakir can pierce his arm with a dirty needle without blood-poisoning, and that a nun will show genuine stigmata as the result of imagination.

Janet has attempted to explain hysterical symptoms with the assumption of an inner cleavage, primary or subsidiary— an explanation based on psychological tact rather than on analytic thoroughness, and all the more useful for that reason. The primary notion here is that vital processes of which consciousness is fundamentally capable are cloven off from consciousness, and this notion is based on the fact (among others) that effective causes of imagination must be equated with external interferences to which the organism could not oppose the selection of an elective affinity, their usurped influence thus being related to the patient as is the infectious cause of disease to the living body. Its symptoms are not due to the proper life-feeling of the hysterical character so much as to the life-feelings of alien entities (= undigested images) which have bought their vital effectiveness at the cost of complete, or nearly complete, incapacity of consciousness: that is, from the non-critical point of view, because reflection upon them would mean their incorporation in the sphere of the Ego, and hence the loss of their absolute, if not of all their power; but, in fact, precisely because this loss would immediately admit the act of reflection and the activity of conscious incorporation. Finally, however, we shall be forced to see in the light of a cleavage or schism the reason which renders possible so curious a receptivity, and this reason, above all, we must further describe. We may, however, remark parenthetically that contents of imagination *may* come into consciousness as alien entities (whether the patient does or does not believe in their independent actuality), and that this is the basis of those phenomena of daemoniacal possession for the introspective description of which we are indebted to Professor Staudenmaier, who presented them as "parts of his subconsciousness which had reached independence".[36] The popular view, on the other hand, goes widely wrong when it seeks the key to the hysterical formation of life in the violence of the repugnance from which the self-esteem of the patient can save itself only by the "repression" from consciousness of the events which cause shame and disgust.[37] Self-esteem certainly plays an essential part in the character of hysteria, but in another place.

But it is time to return to the capacity for expression, and now to keep carefully distinct two fundamental forms of its weakening, the vague outlines of which already appear dimly from our previous consideration of the image-content of feelings. Feeling (with its foundation) may be divided into the side of impulse (which is devoid of images) and that of mood (which is guided by images): and similarly the capacity for expression may be divided, since to the former *alone* the mere capacity of self-motion would correspond (or briefly, motility), and to the latter alone the capacity for shaping of forms (or briefly, formativeness). In the animal urge of impulse the two are connected in such a manner that each impulse after movement is given its direction by the attraction of the images which operates in it: in original man visible images govern the impulses toward movement, and consequently forces capable of forming a given material govern the locomotor forces; in the historical living entity formed by Ego-sensations which are weak in images, the capacity of movement has grown at the expense of the capacity of formation. As the mood-side of feeling (which is saturated with images) fades, it is accompanied not by a weakening of the capacity for movement, but by the impotence of formative power.

Now if we assume that it is precisely with this that the central feeling of impotence connects itself, that is, that the urge which is directed upon formation is in conflict, for reasons of self-esteem, with formative impotence, and if further we imagine that, for whatever reason, there is no question of any compensation from over-emphasis of volition, then vital receptivity for comparatively indifferent impacts of impressions appears as a protective adaptation of the individual to the chief conditions of its self-affirmation by means of organic imitations of formative processes. A "failure of the health-conscience" in hysterical persons has sometimes been mentioned, but it must be remarked that their vitality rather shows a welcome and a readiness for impacts of imagination, and that, indeed, they are interested in them—in which case their interest has a chance of satisfaction, if at all, on this side of consciousness, or if consciousness is excluded altogether. In other words, histrionics are required, the guiding power of which remains unknown to the consciousness of the "principal actor" as much as to that of the spectator. Nevertheless, the mimicry and the origin of the performance are still recognized by their entire lack of originality. The hysterical organism in its logical perfection and in its highest (and practically impossible) intensity would be a reflector reflecting external light only, presenting the image of a mock-life by means of organic imitation of alien lives.

There is certainly a wide difference between the servant girl who, without knowing it, acquires the symptoms of the disease of the child whose nurse she is, and a Veronia Giuliana, who in a state of convulsions receives full stigmatization: still, they agree in one point—with all their symptoms they merely repeat external impressions. Imitation is the common characteristic of *all* hysterical phenomena. If reports are read about the monks and nuns of the Middle Ages, who were declared blessed, or saints, and especially if their own accounts are read, then one is amazed at the extraordinary similarity in the ecstasies experienced, and at the absurd lack of mythopoetic imagination. Thus in the sphere of stigmatization we meet again and again the following: the Saviour appears, either in the shape of a child, or as crucified, and offers the choice of a crown of flowers and a crown of thorns, of which, of course, the latter is chosen; he then touches the region of the heart with a rod, a spear, or a ray of light (in order to impress the lateral wound), and later grants full stigmatization by the well-known five rays emanating from the stigmata (from the lateral wound, the hands, and the feet). The rays vary between blood-red and dazzling white. The impression of wounds reaches its peak on Good Friday. Briefly, the same series of imaginative events is repeated again and again, and always in the closest observance of the scriptural history laid down by the Church.

But further, such phenomena in periods which were stirred to the very depths (which are but the incubation periods of the hysterical mechanism) throw light, not so much on this mechanism as on the condition, based on racial history, of its origin. These "saints" will to be as like to their Saviour as possible, they wish to suffer his sufferings; above all, they will to be tormented by him. But such events of willing would be incapable of producing the internal image unless that, of which the event of willing is only a conscious symptom, had already happened in a vital manner, namely, the internal cleavage or schism, which now, however, we can study very conveniently in its conscious consequences. Why do the saints wish to suffer torments and pains? Because they wish to mortify the body; because they oppose an extreme resistance to its needs, claims, and wants. Let us reflect on the significance of this for a moment.

Every unit of life is a totality having two poles, body and soul—body the manifestation of soul, soul the meaning of the manifested body; the movements (partly locomotor and partly formative) are expressions, urges, and intuitions of that which is expressed in them. The central experience of the body is sensuous joy, the central experience of the soul the joy of creative exaltation. The condition for the loftiest development of the body, as well as of the soul, is contained alone in the equipoise of the two poles. To make war upon the body means inevitably to make war upon such joy, and to make war upon joy inevitably also means to expel the soul and to make it homeless, to dissipate its creative enthusiasm, to dry the source of creative force. But why do those saints *wish* to make war upon the body, and why do they pursue (at least unintentionally) what is the inevitable consequence: to expel the soul, to dissipate the creative exaltation, to paralyse creative force? It is because their soul was cloven by the acosmic power of Spirit (Logos, Pneuma, Nous), whose essence is will, the enemy and slayer of life. Either this is understood, and then the supernatural visions, instances of possessedness, hysteria, and finally personality itself, are understood; or else it is not understood, and then nothing at all of this will be understood and nothing will result but further confusion of speech by means of that Babylonian tower of emergency concepts which necessity forces us to develop by way of substitute. A hundred attempts have been made to derive the negation of body and life from life itself —an attempt a hundred times more blind than would be the attempt to prove of the flame which is put out by pouring water on it that the flame has extinguished itself by changing a part of itself into that water which is being used to extinguish it.

But in the Saint, too, we can follow part of the road which spirit was forced to follow in the past in order to reach its next goal: the expulsion of the soul, and the subjection of the body (which had become weak in images) beneath the domination of the will. In our days, when the will has largely usurped the place of the urges, and is no longer forced to veil its object, which is the absorption of the whole of life on the surface of this planet; when the mechanization of vital processes by means of the universal compulsion of men's professions is almost perfect—at least in civilized man; when the power of intuition lies at death's door—in our day instincts and moods can be suppressed, switched off and starved, and the bare rest can be used as a store of energy to feed the machine of will; but in those days it was otherwise. In Asia, where by comparison sleep dominates more, Buddhism could undertake to kill desires by deadening stimuli; but Christianity could hope to lay hold of the full-blooded thirst after life of the heroic peoples of the still semi-barbarous North only by perverting the direction of desires by means of phantoms and by using the vehemence of the urges themselves in order to kill the soul of the urges. The Moloch spirit, dressed in the mask of the appearance of sense, played the part of the images, sucking dry, like a vampire, every enthusiasm, and converting it into orgies of self-mutilation. The joy of bodies, the joy of creative exaltations, the joys of pregnancies were changed by it into the joys of mortification of desires, of castigation and torturing of the flesh, of the enslavement and degradation of the soul by sacred "obedience", of cruel bleeding to death, and, in the end, of complete self-annihilation.[38] We need not here further discuss the fact—for in the main it has already been "discovered"—that the executioner who served Spirit in those times—the head priest and prince of the Church— knew how to make the polarity of the sexes serve the enslavement of the soul, for example, by developing the "heavenly bridegroom" for nuns (and women in general) and the Mother of the gods for monks (and men in general). In this way, unintentionally and by way of interlude, there was occasioned that greater inner intensity of life which, increasingly since the so-called Renaissance, appeared as exclusive and world-excluded passion between person and person. To-day we are witnessing the end of this too, now that all along the line the last scene but one has begun: man as the slave of the machine of will (which has become its own master) on the one side, and of the Mask (which has become its own master) on the other, and often enough the slave of both at once.

It is monstrous folly to suppose that the civilized man of today is of the same material as man during the periods of the Caesars or of a St. Catharine, St. Cecilia or St. Lidwina, when one glance at the condensations of consciousness in buildings, pictures, and costumes could teach us that the mankind of heathen temples and festivals, of Gothic cathedrals and glowing twilights, of pomp of robes and sounding organs is finished, and has given way to a generation which manifests itself in Stock Exchange, Wireless, Aeroplane, Telephone, Cinematograph, factories, poison gases, instruments of precision, and newspapers. The pilgrim's path has its stations, which end at Golgotha, and similarly the path of Spirit in European man has its main chapters, which may be headed as follows: war of body and soul—decorporization of the soul, or condemnation of joy, or paralysis of creative force—extinction of the soul in body, or blinding of intuition, or, the body as machine—man as the instrument of the will to power—in place of the soul, soul mimicry, the phantom, or Mask. But, if it should seem altogether too strange that a mere mental discipline should strike at the germ-cell and should, as generations succeed one another, produce new varieties, then it must be remembered that Spirit, if not consciousness, is a metaphysical power—that each new change of mankind is accompanied by changes in economic conditions which make servants of former masters, and produce a bloodless and gradual extinction of all who cannot adapt themselves to this new mode—and finally, that the selection is aided and completed by simultaneous intervention of most ruthless force. We only mention the slaughter of the Knights Templar, Stedings, Hussites, etc., the Inquisition with its burnings of witches and Auto-da-fé, a St. Bartholomew's night, the horrible religious wars, not to speak of the French Revolution. Such feasts of death are biological necessities, and are chiefly directed against those who embody and will not relinquish *old* substances. We now return to the "hysterical mechanism" as the present knows it, as a finished fact.

If anyone were to raise the obvious question, why it is just symptoms of *disease* for which the living entity which has

LUDWIG KLAGES

become paralysed in images forms the reflector, then we would reply:—

(1) Symptoms of disease are by no means imitated alone, although they do preponderate.

(2) On one occasion above we opposed the It and the Ego, thereby indicating in advance that we must leave a relative independence to that aspect of vitality by virtue of which the entity which it inhabits has experiences as a thinking and willing Ego, if there is to be any further question at all of personality and its symptoms of whatever kind. The "perfect reflector" would be a biological spectre, a monstrosity no longer capable of life; for, after all, it would no longer have any interest in simulating life. Thus we are still obliged to assume a personal system of driving forces having the Ego or Self for centre, which never wholly lacks attractive or repulsive selection: and in relation to this the process of imagination would then appear as a process of disturbance, even if it was not by any means a copy of symptoms of disease; for in every case it would have taken place by reason of the unstable equilibrium of the It, which is poor in images; it would hence have taken place without touching consciousness and would not have been created out of the original reciprocal relation between the organism and the world.

(3) Finally, there are at least two reasons why the hysterical interest in representing life is turned upon the vital imitation of symptoms of disease, and these two complete its character. First, nothing is more definitely felt to be an unfortunate experience than disease; secondly, nothing rouses more intensely the sympathetic attention of fellow humans. We, each of whom is an Ego, not only experience, but also are spectators of experiences. If for a moment we play the part of spectators of ourselves, and if we assume that we are denied the power of experiencing passions, exaltations, and enthusiasms, then we shall be hard put to it to find something to give us more convincing evidence that we *are* alive than an interruption of the texture of our life. If we think that we experience and feel nothing

else remarkable, there still is the thought that we are plagued by disease. And the certainty of this belief precisely meets with no contradiction: it is underlined, supported, and strengthened by the ready help of others which takes care of us.

Now, however, we have already passed from the character of hysteria to the hysterical character.

The Hysterical Personality.—We were at first obliged to disregard the hysterical will-structure in order to render intelligible the hysterical symptoms; similarly now we neglect the hysterical symptoms in order to render intelligible the hysterical personality, which, for the rest, need not necessarily suffer from these any more than it is necessary that one who does suffer from them is a hysterical personality. We saw that where there are hysterical symptoms, they are due to a cleavage, which causes a part of the vitality of the person in question to be relatively co-ordinated to another part; in the hysterical personality the whole of the system remains subordinated to the system of driving forces. Herein, then, there lies no distinction from the normal Ego. The over-emphasis of the aspect of will as against the cognitive aspect for example (which is very common, though not essential) characterizes the man of will too, with his faculty for the easy transformation of all feelings into feelings of will: and though he can be, he is not necessarily, a hysterical person. We therefore ask after the distinction between the normal man of will and the man whose character makes him hysterical.

It will be remembered that we equated driving forces with dispositions of feeling, and in doing so we made clear that the urges, too, participate in the chief directions of volition. It is indifferent which directions are given preference, whether they are rather general interests (interests in things) or personal (interests in self) which prescribe its aims to the personality; it is indifferent, for example, whether a man acts from desire after knowledge, or from lust after power: always it is the subjective value of the goal from which his volition and action are derived; and it is precisely this fascination of the goal and its desirability for the person that express the identity of the foundations of his will with the foundations of his feelings, and hence the connection of his interests with a more vital stratum, namely that of the urges. If now we reflect upon what it means for our opinion of a man if we consider him to be very greedy of possessions, or of admiration, or very vain, then we shall see that we consider his actions as internally conditioned, necessary, and determined in exactly the same proportion, and that we can forecast his behaviour from case to case, although we can never calculate it exactly.

Intended movements are also called movements of caprice; but the name of caprice is also used in a deeper significance when we say that somebody has acted according to the caprice* of a mood, or that a commander abuses his position in a regiment from despotic caprice. Here the volition is not due to any pleasure in the goal, but the goal comes from a pleasure in volition, as an occasion which accidentally and most obviously offers itself for the exercise of will, and that most commonly in that purposeless direction which challenges and then breaks a powerless resistance. If we compare with the driving forces enumerated above the demand for action, the occasion being perfectly indifferent, or the bare will to power without any selection of the field where power is to act, or the admiration of success for its own sake and whatever kind of success be attained—then we find no remnant of the urges except the remnant of energy which remains after deduction of the attractive force of images, and we see that it is only within the sphere of capricious volition that the final separation of the spiritual from the vital personality takes place; which would be the beginning of a cleavage similar to that which we saw above, although with different results. But, however often such madmen of caprice may be hysterical (such are most record-breakers) and however often, conversely, hysterical persons may be the fools of their caprice, still

* German "Willkür", etymologically, choice of will.

these two are not the same. It is true that in both types formative power is paralysed, that in both a capriciousness which has become quite senseless is called upon to fill the gap, and that both feel stimulated to excel the performances of any will other than their own: but still, so long as an independent pleasure is connected with this one form of self-representation, there still remains a definite motive force, and, with it, a certain computability of behaviour, although for the most part this is largely incalculable. In the *Elective Affinities* Goethe draws with unparalleled mastery the will-caprice of Luciane, moving at a hair's-breadth along the limit of hysteria.

But now let the greatest conceivable severance take place between will and vitality, or between the stratum of driving forces and that of urges, or again let caprice, which has broken all bounds, be coupled with an interest (acting as irresistibly as an urge) in the representation, not of a person's own glory, power, or thrust, but simply of experiences in general, and in fact of such experiences as are most likely to excite attention—and the hysterical personage is perfect. The reaction of the desire to represent against the feeling of impotence to experience (which is far from being an impotence of self assertion) is common to the person who exhibits hysterical symptoms, and to the hysterical personality; but the former, by reason of the readiness in imagining of a comparatively severed stratum of his vitality, undergoes impacts of imagination, the consequences of which, partly bodily and partly psychical, meet his consciousness as something alien, and, generally, in the shape of morbid disturbances; whereas in the latter the impulse after representation has become the dominant and chief driving force which determines what shall be his action and what his volition. We now glance cursorily at some of his main characteristics, which are immediately explained in this manner.

The typical hysterical person is incapable of not following his longing to represent; but that does not mean at all that he cannot control himself. If, for example, it is necessary to represent self-control, then he can endure with remarkable equanimity insults, mockery, degradations, and bodily torments of the severest kind. One thing only he can never repress—his desire to represent. For he has not a single substantial interest of real importance to oppose to this desire, and the rich store of energy at his disposal pours undivided and not to be dammed into this one craving. If one wanted to call him a mere actor, it would be necessary to add that he suffers from a passion to simulate passions, and that no genuine passion could be more irresistible, overpowering, and consistent (that is, like an impulse) than this. And if one wanted to call him thoroughly sophisticated, then it would have to be considered again that a permanent spice of intentionality does in fact flavour his every attitude, but in a different manner, and in one much harder to recognize than in a man who has ceased to be naive merely because he has inhibitions; for here the mask itself has become sovereign. He is not an actor so much as a man wearing a mask which has grown into his flesh; or rather, he carries behind the mask no living being but a clockwork, ready to follow the suggestions of the mask. In *Klein Zaches oder Zinnober*, Amadeus Hoffmann has prophetically dealt with the reflective nature which assimilates everything, and, by excelling makes it valueless; and, in the *Sandmann,* has given a fantastic treatment to the life-mimicking automaton.

The definite characteristic of the hysterical attitude is, that there is a relationship to the spectator. Those who must represent something, represent it for the benefit of a spectator; by choice a real stranger, if not an imaginary one, or as a last resource the spectator within himself. Accordingly no hysterical person is ever attentive to the matter in hand, and whatever he does or leaves undone is not done or left undone with a view to the effect, but is itself the effect by anticipation which itself suggests the idea of the goal from moment to moment; hence a change of surroundings may be accompanied by a change in behaviour of a kind which shows some points of similarity with that of a medium.

Here the type of hysterical exaltation is sharply distinguished from the vain man and from those who require to please or to win approval. The latter wish to appear superior in some respect, or to evoke affection or gain esteem: but the hysterical type wishes to excite attention either by creating amazement or admiration, or by challenging those other feelings, which are even more suitable for the purpose, of aversion, loathing, disgust, horror, indignation, contempt, and fury. It happens quite commonly that faults are invented, that a hysterical woman claims to have been raped, and a man to have raped, and even fictitious confessions of alleged murder have been known. The typically hysterical crime of Herostratus may here be recalled.

Finally we now understand his capacity for deceiving himself as well as others—a capacity which reaches its peak in so-called pseudologia phantastica. We must not infer from this any mental defect, and, indeed, the intelligence and methodical cunning of many who suffer from this trouble, which often are considerable, are in conflict with such a view. But it must be considered that, with regard to feelings, the distinction which we know between genuine and false is nonexistent, or at any rate of no importance for the hysterical type, simply because at bottom he cannot experience genuine feelings. But those whose disposition allows them to confuse false with genuine feelings have lost the capacity to distinguish exactly between real and fictitious events, however excellent their intellect may be in other respects. A lengthy investigation into the science of consciousness would be required to prove beyond objection what is here merely asserted, namely, that in so far as we do not rely merely on the demands of logic (or laws of thought) in order to discover truth, but must fall back on the knowledge of actually existing facts, in so far our knowledge depends on a dimension of our feeling which is properly called its actuality-weight, or (if it is given independence) the feeling of actuality. Whenever those vital processes are weakened which underlie the character of actuality in the contents of experience, the soundness of the "judgment of existence" is impaired, and with it inevitably the capacity for distinguishing between the actual and the merely imaginary. In a work which we have not yet completed we derive from a weakening of the feeling for actuality a tendency not only for self-deception, but also for the gravest deceptions with regard to facts. Here we confine ourselves to the remark that in the victim of hysterical *pseudologia* the lie is of essentially the same quality as error, and the converse too is true: and both because of a morbidly reduced feeling for actuality.

CHAPTER VIII NOTES

34 First in *Graphologische Monatshefte*, 1904, pp. 53-80, later in *Probleme* (1910), pp. 68-101.

35 It might appear as though this favoured depressive at the expense of euphoric states, since the former particularly are considered as forms of ill-temper; but such an appearance would be deceptive. Ordinary depression (as its name shows), and also moroseness and surliness are characterized primarily by a general inhibition of impulses and dullness, and by no means by a gloomy mood-colouring. Quite different from this is the youthful sadness of the years of transition, the poet's melancholy, sorrow, deep resignation, the mourning of love, and so on. These moods are rich in images compared with which any concomitant inhibitions of impulse are of small importance.

36 Staudenmaier, *Die Magie als experimentelle Naturwissenschaft*, Leipzig, 1912. We are indebted for a knowledge of this remarkable book, which we recommend to all psychologists, to the excellent *Allgemeine Psychopathologie* by Jaspers, which among the murky flood of attempts made by contemporary neurologists to build psychologies on this or that special clinical experience stands unique (unless we are mistaken) by virtue of its eminently critical attitude.

37 So-called psycho-analysis is, in the development of spirit, the strange bastard of an even stranger misalliance—that between Herbart's atomism of imagination and Nietzsche's philosophy of self-deception. It is true that the misshapen creature also bears traces of certain influences of a comparatively exotic nature, for example, in the shape of the doctrine that the whole of man and, indeed, the whole world is sex, or, to express it more modestly, that the living individual is a mere appendix to his germ-cells, a variable dependent in relation to them; an idea of which traces are found already with Schopenhauer, cultivated later by various biologists, and copied from a doctrine which was favoured by medicine long ago (certain scholastic doctors, for example, taught that *sperma virile*, if not spent, rises into the brain and there becomes spirit). But this kind of theory really has only a popular interest, and is a mere belief; a proof cannot even be attempted from the nature of the case. (If, in accordance with this theory, the equation is set up, God = sex, then we have one of the main directions of the psycho-analytic view of the world; if the equation is reversed, sex = God, we have the other direction.) We do not pursue this further.

The tradition of Herbart was never quite broken off in Austria, and to him is due the idea of species of atoms of imagination which struggle for admission on the "threshold of consciousness", now inhibiting and again aiding one another, and also the idea of repression, for, according to him, all strivings are due to repressions. "In exact proportion as the imaginations are converted into strivings, they are repressed from consciousness" *(Lehrbuch zur Psychologie*, 1816, p. 118). When this was compounded with Nietzsche's view, which attributes a decisive influence upon the course of the activity of consciousness to the urges, and not least to the urges of self-esteem, a mythology of the so-called unconscious arose to which we must allow the charm of the sensational, had not its inventors been wholly smitten with imaginative blindness. For this unconscious has a curious resemblance to a thorough-paced hedge-lawyer; it has the sole function to use every kind of dodge in order to cause consciousness to believe in whatever would be advantageous to the obvious, and even more to the secret interests of the conscious entity, and especially to undermine its belief in everything calculated to disturb his self-esteem. Nietzsche's subtle and profound investigations of the tactics of self-deception are here translated into the language of the vulgar intrigues which may be studied in modern business life, including the diplomatic devices of politicians, a method which seeks compensation by calling itself psychology of the depths.

But whatever may be the origin of all this, the psychoanalyst asserts that he is in possession of the truth, and points for confirmation to the innumerable "cases" of which he disposes, that is, his patients. Here, however, two aspects of the case must be distinguished, the confession which the analyst draws from the patient by examination based on what he imagines to be so-called associations, and successful cures by means of what is described by the pretty word "Abreaktion" (i.e. recall of repressions into consciousness). With regard to the confessions, the past history of psychoanalysis really spares us the proof that they neither have nor can have demonstrative force. At first the data obtained by this kind of confessional were taken at their face value, that is, as being events which really had taken place in the life of the confesser: but later it was found necessary to take them partly for fiction, although they might have symptomatic value; and today even this symptomatic value has undergone a change, because it is clear that they often merely express how the "conscious" of the patient would like to see the meaning of his trouble (and hence himself) interpreted. But whatever is the proportion of demonstrable events, of supplementary matter, and of pure fiction, the view that this method will lead to the discovery of the conditions of the disease overlooks that these are already presupposed as an x, if this confessional method (which often is extended through years) is to be possible at all. Further, it is necessary only to look more closely at any complicated piece of analysis to see that the meaning of the case which the examiner requires for the confirmation of his doctrine is imported by him, and that by virtue of a method which has the rare advantage that it never fails: so far as the data which he obtains suit his view, he takes them literally, so far as they do not, he takes them metaphorically, or, rather, as imaginations substituted for wholly different contents of imagination. For this purpose he has prepared a system of a sexual symbolic language which, without exaggeration, can be applied to any single object in the universe. (For, after all, it must be possible of every object to take it as being convex or concave in some manner.) One must share this faith in order to believe in this kind of imaginary demonstration.

There remain, then, the cures. In order not to lose our way we will take them point by point.

(1) If we possessed statistics of unassailable accuracy about all patients who were treated by psycho-analysis, we *might* become sceptical about these healers. Apart from a certain proportion of persons who were relieved of the disturbing symptoms, we would find a large proportion of those who ran away from their examiners, and no small proportion of those who were all the worse for the confessional. (We are aware of most serious cases of this kind.)

(2) It is certain that these classes exist; but the proportions remain uncertain, for we do not possess statistics. We will therefore confine ourselves to the cures. We disregard the fact that in the treatment of every patient, but especially of a neurotic, the personal influence of the healer (whether he is a declared suggester, or magnetopath, or homoeopath, or internist, or psycho-analyst, etc.) plays an incalculable part. We also disregard the fact that psycho-analysis was fashionable for a time and still is so to some extent, and therefore, for reasons which will easily be understood, carries with it, in the eyes of the neurotic patient, an aura which assists the cure. On the other hand, it does something which would retain its curative value, even if all the reasons which determine it alone to do it were false: it gives the patient a full opportunity of "having a good talk". Here it follows the approved methods of the Roman Catholic confessional.

(3) Further, it deals chiefly with hysterical patients. If we were right in saying that the hysterical type possesses abnormally small formative force combined with a highly developed desire to represent, then it encourages his formative desires, and encourages him even to tell tales, to lie, and to invent; it affords him an opportunity of forming his inner life.

(4) But it effects something greater besides. Probably most neurotic types, and certainly all hysterical, suffer from secret feelings of inferiority, although they are not always aware of the fact. Although the psycho-analytical confessional may be a plague, it offers him a tenfold recompense by showing him new possibilities of taking himself seriously—very seriously—internally. Whatever bug of notion or thought may creep through his consciousness, it is significant and perhaps an enchanted prince. A curious method, though none the less efficient, for strengthening self-esteem.

(5) But psycho-analysis also has its secret, which, however, we are unwilling to publish, for perhaps it is effective only because the psycho-analysts do not know it. Also, in order to reveal it, we would have to unfold the psychologist's psychology, which, though somewhat more entertaining than psychoanalysis, would also require a more lengthy exposition. If the author of these lines were a neurologist, he too would occasionally prycho-analyse his patients, and perhaps he too would be successsful: not because he considers there is any truth in the psycho-analytic chat, but because he holds that this prescription fits with amazing exactness a contemporary variety of neurosis. The two arise together necessarily, and will vanish together, for every epoch has its own neurosis, and no epoch that of another.

We trust that none of our readers will harbour the absurd suspicion that this effusion upon psycho-analysis is meant as an attack on psycho-analysts. A real psycho-analyst cannot be refuted, and he is a fool who makes the attempt. It is true that there are many psycho-analysts who are not psycho-analysts at all. They do as Rome does—as the author too would do if he specialized in nervous cases. (In this matter the purse too can play a part.) But the real psycho-analyst—the man who holds the psycho-analytic world-view—is the true member of a religion, and as such cannot be assailed. If objections to personal immortality are raised before a strict Christian, he would not pay a moment's attention to them, but would ask himself what faults or even sins of the speaker prevented the light of the truth from illuminating him. If objections are raised before a true psycho-analyst, he does not attend to their value as proofs for a moment, but only asks himself what complexes or "repressions" (of sexual origin, of course) can be preventing the speaker from seeing and recognizing the light of truth—of psycho-analytic truth. Predestination, beginning at the germ-plasm, determines the genuine psychoanalyst as it determines the strict Christian. We therefore do not touch upon this matter; but we considered it proper to say a word about this scientific fashion, because we ourselves had an opinion to offer upon the nature of hysteria.

We would add expressly that there is one psycho-analyst to whom the above remarks about psycho-analysts do not apply unreservedly, namely, Freud. The man who founds a religion or initiates a new direction—and every direction has one initiator only—is of a very different stamp from his disciples. All psycho-analysts without exception are disciples, a fact which is not altered by feeble attempts at insubordination such as occur among all bodies of disciples; but Freud is a pioneer, and if any part of his work should survive, it will be associated with his name, and with his name alone. If he believes in the doctrine of psycho-analysis, he does so because he made, or, if it be preferred, created it: and although a pioneer can neither be taught nor converted, it requires no common degree of simplicity in order to confuse his obstinacy with that of a disciple. The psychology of the pioneer is of a different class, and does not here concern us. But we would say that this man has some of the true speculative spirit, together with temperament and stubborn tenacity. Unfortunately, he has no superior spirit, and a narrow horizon (we found similar qualities worth mentioning in Lipps above). This is to be regretted for other than merely practical reasons; for such thoroughbred energy deserved to make real and not only imaginary discoveries.

It is to be remembered finally that mankind is by no means divided into leaders and followers: only one definite type of man has for poles "master" and "disciples". The other types of mankind are mere spectators of this variety, which has been known to exist for three thousand years, and of its various disputations. For them it is a curious piece of history. We could make some observations on the question how it arose, what is its origin (especially its racial origin), and what its significance, but this is not the proper place.

---

[38]   We have the most inexhaustible store of information about this and kindred phenomena in the monumental work of Görres, *Christliche Mystik* (see especially vol. ii, pp. 410-56). If we penetrate into the facts there laid before us (which include his profound meditations upon them) we shall not escape the conviction that these phenomena were blood-mysteries, which

may be resumed under the single notion that the body was to be drained of blood by means of perverted ecstasies. A mist of sweat and blood surrounds the brow of these strange sufferers, streams of blood flow from mouth and nostrils, and the open wounds of the stigmata (especially the lateral wound) involve an incessant loss of blood. Of St. Francis of Assisi it is said (vol. ii, p. 423): "It is a marvel that he remained alive for two years in spite of the incessant pain and loss of blood caused to him by them" (the stigmata). The spiritual principle which had seized upon the Christian saints appears here in its most immediate shape: as a blood-sucking vampire.

CHAPTER IX

OF THE METAPHYSICS OF DISTINCTIONS OF PERSONALITY

If those great thinkers of the past who undertook to explain the world by some governing principle had first tested their formulae on human character, it is likely that many of them would have discovered the inadequacy of their attempts at explanation; and if, conversely, those students of character who attempt to classify personalities, relying on a store of experience and observations which often is rich enough, had sought after a supreme principle of explanation, then no doubt a good many of them would have themselves discovered that their explanations, to say the least, are merely preliminary. All such attempts either serve as personal guiding lines, or at best are valuable because stimulating, in so far as they are not derived from an analysis of the nature of man which pierces down to the central stratum of vitality. Such attempts, too, have not been lacking —as witness the Sceptics, Stoics, Epicureans, the French Moralists, Schopenhauer and his followers, and, finally and above all, Nietzsche; but all suffer more or less from the monistic prejudice which causes them to overlook that an Ego like historical man cannot be explained solely by means of his vitality, nor by means of his spirituality. The great thinkers of the romantic period did, indeed, eagerly take up the threefold division of the Greeks—body, soul, spirit, and thereby did gain a considerable lead over English sensualism as well as over French and Kantian Rationalism; but not one of these saw that here they were dealing not with three storeys of human nature, but with the irreconcilable opposition between life with its two poles, and spirit which is outside space and time. Granted that the author of these lines should have devised a whole system of errors by means of faulty conclusions, still one fundamental piece of knowledge would remain unshaken and unshakable, whether recognized sooner or later or never, namely, that there is an antipathy between Life and Spirit, and consequently between Soul and Spirit, whence results the postulate that every future study of character must be based upon this, if it is to claim to be knowledge and not a mere stimulant.

The elementary notions upon which we rely have for the most part already been used in the course of our exposition, and have been explained by examples; we will now, however, define them exactly one after the other, though we will not yet justify them. The dogmatic formulation must be taken merely as a definition of names designed to facilitate further discussion, or as a programme which will be fulfilled in the course of our investigation, at least in so far as is demanded of the process of laying the foundation of characterology.[39]

It has been known since Aristotle that the living entity is a being which receives and acts. If it be considered from the point of view that it is forced ever to renew itself, then the absorption of food, and breathing, would have to be placed in the foreground, together with the assimilation of what is needed and the discarding of the superfluous, and it must be emphasized expressly that this fundamental process takes place on the side of the soul as well as on that of the body. It is a grave lack in European thought that it never made nutrition seriously the object of metaphysical study. If we too confine ourselves to cursory glances upon it, this is due to the fact that we can throw light into the organism only from the point of consciousness, and that nutritive processes are the lowest depth, and as it were the foundation of vitality, which the rays of consciousness and of reflection reach last of all. In the zone of sensuousness, which is a little brighter, the contrast between receptive and executive capacity is seen in the shape of two polar and connected systems, which it is now usual to call the sensor and the motor system, although hitherto the degree of independence in the motor system which belongs to it as being one of the two poles has not been emphasized.[40] Hence every fundamental concept in psychology has twofold characteristics, and it is necessary to give a sensor terminology as well as a motor terminology to the experiences of the body and of the Soul, and to the acts of the Spirit. The whole of psychology rests upon three times two (that is, six) fundamental concepts. We enumerate them before explaining them.

The body finds expression in the process of sensation and in the impulse towards movement, the Soul in the process of contemplation, and in the impulse to formation (= to the magical *or* mechanical realization of images), the Spirit in the act of apprehension and the act of willing. Sensation (1), impulse to motion (2), contemplation (3), impulse to formation (4), act of apprehension (5), and act of will (6) are the six fundamental concepts. Of these, the third and fourth have escaped school-science, while the remaining four have been more or less misinterpreted by it in consequence, and the common concepts of perception, imagination, sensation, and action are not among the fundamental concepts. "Imagination" in its present usage is untenable; perception may be resolved into three chief components, sensation, contemplation, act of apprehension; action takes place automatically as the result of the act of will, in so far as it is not prevented by a contrary act of will; with regard to sensation, we shall deal with it in this chapter; the main facts will have been correctly anticipated from what has been said in the previous chapter.

The fundamental concepts (1) to (4) relate to genuine processes, and these in their totality constitute animal and human vitality, whence none of them can take place without the participation of the other three, though the corporeal experience sometimes predominates over the soul-experience, and conversely, and again the sensory experience over the motor experience and conversely. The last two concepts, on the other hand, relate to acts having no temporal extension, and these constitute personal spirituality, whose new centre is the Ego or self. And now it must be noted that the Ego or spiritual centre is incapable of existence without a coordinated life-centre, while a life-centre may well exist without an Ego. Not only all animals lack Ego, but original man also lacked it. But, as surely as the four vital processes *can* take place entirely without consciousness, so surely is it impossible that they should take place only when we are capable of relating ourselves to them by means of spiritual acts.

We have already stated what is essential about the impulse to motion and to formation, and we shall soon proceed to give the more exact details of spirituality; but we must still give an explanation about sensation and contemplation. By sensation we mean exclusively the component of contact in the sense-impression; this component is strongest in the act of touching, and weakest in that of seeing; it is thus our conviction that in any sense-impression the corporeal experience of body-contact merges into the sensory soul-experience of the intuition of an image; in animals the seeing of the image is under the control of bodily sensation, and in man the bodily sensation under the control of the seeing of the image. The current view of five (or six or seven, etc.) specific sense-energies subsisting independent, side by side, is demonstrably false. The experience of corporeal contact is the receiving function of the body which is graded in the different senses by degrees of sensitiveness, and the experience of seeing the image is the receiving function of the soul which in the individual senses has a sensory differentiation. A perfectly soul-less sensuousness is unthinkable, because if we were to assume it we would be compelled to imagine actual differences in pressure without any spatial or temporal characterization. A perfectly bodiless sensuousness is not indeed unthinkable, but it is unimaginable, because to assume it would require us to imagine distance removed from the world we know— which goes far beyond what we have experienced even in dreams. "Now" would coincide with "then" and "there" with "here", and the body would differ in no way from its reflections. This much must here suffice.[41]

We now proceed to unfold the metaphysics of personality so far as is demanded, in order that we may find in the classification of driving forces a supreme principle drawn from out of human nature and not applied to it like an external measure. In doing so, we are inclined, in view of all the results which we have already gained, and especially of those gained in the last chapter, to see the decisive deed of the spirit not in the act of apprehension, but in that of will, and to use it as the standpoint from which to understand spirituality itself, that is, the essence of consciousness, and to posit vitality as its reflection. Herein we follow these schoolmen who taught the primacy of will over cognition; further, Schopenhauer, who spoilt the profound idea by the illusionary presupposition that the world is "imagination" of the experiencing subject, and, finally and above all, Nietzsche, who was the man to carry this idea to a finish, but that he was upset by an inner conflict which caused him in his interpretation to classify the nature of Spirit, which he had correctly seen, under Vitality.

If the driving forces are in fact what we have taken them to be, namely, partly causes of will and partly dispositions of feeling, then will is connected by virtue of them with the impulses in such a way that, under certain conditions (which we have not yet fully elaborated), each driving impulse should be capable of occasioning, through the stratum of driving forces, an act of will. Any given example shows that this is in fact the case. In the state of hunger, which is invariably accompanied by a feeling, the impulse towards union (by incorporation) with something eatable, which this state contains, drives the animal to look for food and, similarly, man finds himself caused by the same condition to aim at the acquisition of food and, if necessary, to go through whole chains of will-acts, each of which stands to the next in the relation of means tending to bring about the final success. Thus here the animal impulse of hunger would have changed into the driving force of care about food, and conversely we find no driving force (whether envy, jealousy, business interest, thirst for knowledge, or conscience) which could not make itself felt by means of a feeling of lack, thus leading back to a vital substratum, although at the moment we may be unable to point to animal impulses corresponding to it. Men certainly act from hate as well as love, from jealousy as well as from admiration, and from ruthless selfishness as well as from adoring self-sacrifice: but another consideration shows us that there appears to be a contradiction between feeling and willing which can be aggravated to the point where one negates the existence of the other.

If I judge that somebody is a giant of action, the unbiased hearer does not expect that he is also warm-hearted and impulsive, and if I judge that he is warm-hearted and impulsive, it is not expected that he is also a giant of action. A remark that he is both at the same time would cause surprise. In order to understand the reason of this unreflected astonishment, we recollect that the word "feeling" is used in current talk much more narrowly than in science. By it we do not mean feelings of hatred, envy, or jealousy, still less will-feelings or logical feelings, and least of all the feeling of indifference: we do mean feelings of sympathy, especially of compassion and love. A man of feeling means nearly, if not exactly, the same as a man of heart, and such a person has sympathy and, frequently, pliability. But a man of will and action requires power to force his way, steadiness, ruthlessness, and hardness; in short, more or less complete *lack* of feeling (again in the narrower sense).

Here the contrast between heart and head is very instructive. The former in numerous phrases and words stands for a capacity for feelings of affirmative affection, the latter for intellectual acumen or for obstinacy of will. Feeling = feeling of affection = heart, for example, in warm-hearted, cold-hearted, heartless, tender-hearted, to take something to heart, a broken heart, the voice of the heart, to pour out one's heart, to lose one's heart to somebody, etc. Intellect = head, for example, in thick-headed, to lose one's head, etc. Will (obstinacy or self-control) = head, in hard-headed, to run one's head against a wall, etc.* In such words and phrases

---

* Several untranslatable locutions have here been omitted.—TRANSLATOR'S NOTE.

instinctive assumptions find expression which deserve the attention of the investigator, namely, that the essence of feeling is to be looked for in the feelings of affirmative affection and in the last analysis in love, and the assumption that there is a profound opposition between inclination and self-assertion. But if we look upon the bloody battlefield of so-called history, upon the competitive wars of business life, and the totality of the action of any individual life, then we must admit that a thousand times a thousand more acts of will arise from love of power, self-seeking, and rivalry, in short, from selfishness, than from sympathy, love, and admiration: and we find a relation of attraction between active force and feelings of attack, repulse, and flight, and a relation of repulsion between active force and the affirmative feelings of affection. If the latter were, so to speak, the soul of feeling, then there would be an essential difference between feeling in general and will in general. But this does exist in fact and in a more radical manner, though from other reasons.

I never possess a feeling, of whatever nature, but the feeling possesses me; an event of willing never possesses me, but it is I who generate it. I can forbid myself to give way to feelings of hunger, love, or jealousy, but I cannot order the feeling to come and be here, or order it to go away. No one will say that his will urges him to pluck the rose; he will say that he wants to or, perhaps, that his desire drives him. Desire "compels", admiration "seizes", grief "convulses", hate "blinds", rage "seizes"—briefly, the emotion (so to speak an It, or something external to the Ego) moves me, and I in turn move my will. The will can either follow or resist the feeling, but cannot by itself provoke it, which (if activity were given up) would rather mean that things were allowed just to happen, or, a passivity. A resolution is "taken", but feeling "overpowers", one "sticks to" an intention, but "cannot get rid of" a feeling, emotion "sweeps us along", but one displays "iron" energy of will. Thus in each feeling without exception the Ego is the passive part, and each event of willing, without exception, the active part, and there is no transition of feeling into will: and all theories which make bold to represent event of willing and emotion as two phases of one process are evidence only of an amazing lack of reflection in their authors. The event of willing, far from emerging out of feeling, usurps its place, and not only as a different, but as an essentially opposite condition— obviously by reason of some change of government in the depths of the living entity. But the event of willing is never merely a spiritual act, but also is a vital state, the quality of which we sought previously to define by the expression "feeling of will", and therefore we can ask for a more exact characterization of the feeling of will, and prepare the reply while concentrating the keenest light upon the generic distinction with which we have just become acquainted between feelings of attack and feelings of affection.

I am possessed of feelings of hatred as well as by those of love, but the impulse inherent in the feeling of love must be called a process of being attracted to the goal of the impulse, while the impulse inherent in hatred appears to urge to the destruction of the goal; thus, compared with the former, it is rather active, while in turn compared with it the former is seen to be an extreme passivity. If a very malicious person is mentioned, we are inclined to consider him active and, for example, also credit him with energy; but if a very good-natured person is mentioned, we are inclined to consider him very passive and lacking in energy. The expression that somebody is a "good old sheep" betrays that we expect of good-naturedness to suffer much before it rouses itself to act. If, then, the feelings of affection bear this character of vital passivity, and those of repulse and of attack the character of vital activity, then the latter at any rate resemble that activity of the Ego which in volition is experienced as active force and is manifested in action. The similarity goes still further. For the experience of willing force is the naked movement of impulse which remains over after its quality (as of being an impulse of hatred, rage, anger, etc.) has been deducted from the feelings of attack or repulsion by the act of Spirit: thus it is negative activity "in itself". The obvious question, how will can ever serve such goals as are set by love and sympathy, is answered thus: it has the sole function of removing obstacles which stand in the way of realization. It is aimed at a goal mediatedly, but immediately is turned against the resistance of the "world".

When a great artist carves the image of a god with chisel and hammer out of a block of marble, it is by no means his will which has inspired him with the outline of the divine image: it is the capacity for intuition, to which life has given its blessing, and to this capacity the will-act of carving is related exactly like the chisel, which can never do anything but destroy the stone. The example shows perfectly clearly why the destructive nature of volition does not preclude the employment of volition in the service of affirmative movements and creative impulses after formation, but it also shows that the event of willing itself always consists in a series of acts which are simply destructive, and that will is a completely negative power. It is easy to imagine the terrible consequences which must arise if the will were to become autonomous by having severed itself from the directive power of vitality which lies at its back, transforming its force —the only one remaining—into blind energies, becoming the murderous intent of an instrument of irrational destruction. What, however, is the meaning of being afflicted with the fatal capacity of willing, and how could it really arise in man?

It might here be objected that, considered for itself, will is like an engine of destruction; still, without the engine, it would be impossible to reach even "good" objects, so that it would seem improper to make this indispensable instrument responsible for the fact that sometimes it serves a negative disposition: in which case we would reply that it is erroneous to assume that volition is indispensable to the realization of an end, since there are as many as two methods to realize an end which are quite free of will: the magic and the impulsive manner. The fairy-tales and legends of every people on earth know the theme of the fulfilment of wishes, as, for example, in the self-covering table. The mere wish suffices for this table to cover itself with delicious foods, and no effort at all of volition is required. If it is replied that these are just fictions, we would ask how they could arise and why (especially in earlier ages) they were believed by innumerable men. Evidently this would be impossible unless innumerable men had *experienced* will-less realization of wishes, and we, too, experience it sometimes in day-dreams and especially in nightly dreams, when severe thirst is gratified by the choicest drinks without effort on the part of the dreamer, and severe hunger by the most savoury dishes, and he is transplanted in a twinkling to the distant place of his desire. It may be replied that these are "just" dreams, and instead of refuting this assertion, the mind is better prepared for a profounder view if we consider once more, and more impressively, the second kind of will-less realization of ends, namely, that which obeys an urge, the fact of whose existence can be disputed by nobody.

The bee which leaves the hive in order to gather honey has made no resolutions, formed no plans, and possesses no end. It does not reflect on the fact that there are such and such honey-bearing blossoms, and knows neither tasks nor duties nor maxims. It sets itself in motion because it has experienced a lack, a need, and that which inwardly drives it is of such a nature that the movements and processes which it causes end as soon as the end is reached, that is, as soon as the need or lack is satisfied. This is unintelligible unless we understand it in the following manner: the odour of the flowering lime, or of the field of clover, or of heather, *draws* the bee. Without any intervention of volition the attraction of the end is translated into the flying motion of the bee, and finally leads it, flying, to the end.[42] It is true that for human interests, too, we have occasionally made use of the attractive force of the end: but in man it occasions decisions of the will, which in their turn allow the impulses of movement to become active in the direction of the end which now only has come "in view", whereas in the whole of the animal world it acts *immediately* upon the impulses of movement. How is it that the one is possible, and the other requisite?

The one is possible because, and in so far as, in the whole of the animal world, there is, between the soul of the animal and the images of the world, a life-magnetic connection. The duckling could not dash joyfully into the water unless between the sight of water and its soul there existed a connection at least analogous to that between the positive pole of one magnet and the negative pole of another; and the hen which hatched the duckling would not be frightened by its dive unless between the hen and water as an element there existed, once more, a connection analogous to that between the positive poles of two magnets. Now if man is entirely incapable of realizing ends by magic, and only partially incapable of realizing them by urge, then something in him must have deserted the life-magnetic connection with world-images, or better still, in him, between his soul and the world-images, something must have intruded, like a wall which separates; and now we see the necessity of the destructive instrument of will in a new light; it is the salient partial expression of a breach with nature which has taken place, or of the exclusion of the willing entity from the communal life of the world. The being which is subject to impulses stands in the midst of the world-nexus, the being which must will stands beside it; and we can expect to have rightly understood the essence of the act of will only when we have traced it back to that power which snatches its victims out of the world-nexus.

The myths of many peoples tell us of a happy original state of man, which the Greeks called the Golden Age, and the Jews the Garden of Eden. Of these the Mosaic paradise-myth has the advantage for us that, while entirely unpicturesque, it expresses the secret and formative meaning of the images almost abstractly, and thus anticipates interpretation in a welcome manner. The first human couple exists in the Garden of Eden, living on fruits and in harmonious community (symbiosis) with all beasts, understanding the language of the "serpent", the sacred genius of the place, but soon, from transgression of the well-known commandment, they fall under the curse of Jahve, in which we must distinguish two parts. "Cursed", says the Daemon while expelling the two, "is the ground for thy sake; in sorrow shalt thou eat of it all the days of thy life. ... In the sweat of thy face shalt thou eat bread"; that is, the vital union with the planet is ended, and hence follows the compulsion of labour: man must will in order to continue life. But, further, a warning had been added to the prohibition, "For in the day on which thou eatest thereof thou shalt surely die", and accordingly the second part of the curse runs, "For dust thou art, and unto dust shalt thou return". And here Jahve's true motive is revealed: "Behold the man is become as one of us to know good and evil; and now lest he put forth his hand and take also of the tree of life and eat and live for ever ..." That is, severance from the tree of life means loss of "eternal life", and the doom of the compulsion to will goes hand in hand with this.

So long as man has been endowed with reason (*homo sapiens*), he has busied himself with the thought of eternal life, and so long, too, he has confused "eternal life" (for reasons which we shall immediately discuss) with existence of infinite duration. There are not, and there cannot be, any existences of infinite duration, but "eternal life" has a meaning nevertheless: all plants and animals live this life, and man alone has lost it. For no being ever was able to be aware of the moment when it fell asleep, still less of the moment of its death, and hence we must be convinced that death is a mere concept, and that it can be experienced merely in thoughts about death and in the foreknowledge of dying. A dying man may tremble at the thought of his impending death a minute before he dies: but at the moment when he dies he knows nothing whatever about it. "Death, the most dreadful evil", says Epicurus, "thus does not concern us, for while we are, death is not; and when death is there, we are no more". An animal does not die, but merely ends: but man dies, for the *thought* that he must end accompanies him wherever he goes: this is the loss of "eternal life". It is true that every living being lives through the prolongation of its past and the preparation of its future: but the animal experiences only the presence of its life-nexus in the shape of sensations and movements of urges, while man who is endowed with reason lives rather in the recollection of the past and in care about the future than in the present, and then, paradoxically, thinks of the one real moment far more often than he experiences it: that is the result of this loss. But here we must digress.

Surely the hunted stag flees in fear of death, and it is a distortion of the facts to deny that fear of death exists in the animal world? Our answer to such a question is no mere admission: every fear is fear of death, and fear, the antithesis of joy, is common to beasts and men. But fear is so far from being the same as the thought of death or the foreknowledge of dying, that a man may choose death for fear of death, as very frequently happens. Conversely a man may think about death without experiencing much fear, and he may even, in exceptional cases, long for death; which state again does not prevent a sudden and torturing fear from seizing him, from which he saves himself in extreme cases by voluntary death. In order to understand this we must clearly uphold the qualitative distinction between fear of a thing (timor) and bare fear (pavor). The former is always fear of something definite: fear of the dentist, of an examination, of loss of wealth, and this has nothing to do with the latter kind which is indeterminate fear, and as such, on the level of contemplation is horror, a state the nature or meaning of which can be understood only as the anticipation of that vital fact which we call death. The two feelings, the indeterminate and determinate fear, may coalesce in an actual experience, but still they remain feeling, and the feeling as such is never a thought. The fleeing stag is afraid of his pursuers: but only the prescience of death which mingles with this feeling lends to his definite fear an unusual depth and power, and to the movements of his flight the vehemence which can be obtained only in this manner. But what the grazing stag, or cow, never experiences is the thought of death and the fear of it which thence develops. The animal which flees in fear of death, even at that moment lives only through its immediate present, and as soon as it has succeeded in escaping has forgotten this fear: whereas man may be seized by the thought of death and hence by the fear of death in the midst of calm and safety, and, indeed, for at least three thousand years this has happened so often that unending illusions about "continued existence after death", together with that other ineradicable illusion about unlimited existence, grew out of it. Let us here bring to mind wherein exactly this fear consists.

Epicurus' dictum sounds wise, but will free nobody from his fear of death, because the question is not at all whether we feel or do not feel the process of dying. Men do not fear death because they fear the process of dying or the pain which goes with it, but because they fear the pangs of death, which means the revolt of their will to live against the certainty that they must cease to be: and the aim of so-called euthanasia is always to induce before death, if not a complete suspension of consciousness, at any rate the greatest possible dimming. Man undergoes during life far worse pains on a hundred occasions than death generally brings with it, without any fear of death, and in this respect is fundamentally superior to animals: but what can fill even the bravest, at least for a moment, with an unspeakable horror of death, and forces men again and again into some belief in immortality, is the thought of final parting, of a severance for ever: for every living being cleaves to life, and it is no small thing to know in advance that all this must be left behind and will never be seen again. The irremovable tragedy of death which of all living beings is the doom of man alone, is in the consciousness allotted only to him, that all things shall pass away; and the fear of death is far from being rooted in fear of dying: rather it is rooted in the thought of being, which struggles against death. But we are anticipating.

If we revert to the paradise-myth, we can now formulate the fall from life in this far stricter form: through an event which still remains to be explained some part of man was snatched from the stream of becoming and perishing, and in exchange he received knowledge of the perishable nature of (unconscious) life in him. No animal has consciousness of time, for it is itself a form in which the stream of time manifests itself: man has consciousness of time from moment to moment because he has the fatal gift of contemplating what happens from moment to moment; and he has obtained this gift through the fact that some part of him exists beyond the reach of time and alongside of it. Now the contradictory concept of happening is being. Only that which *is* is beside that which happens, and in actuality, all of which "happens", the only thing which *is* is the Ego. The expulsion from paradise is identical with the arising of the Ego: for only a being having an Ego is, as such, a being having existence, and hence a being having consciousness of temporality and a knowledge that it has begun and must end.

Those who would reflect upon this state of Ego must disregard the changing properties and conditions of their person: for the Ego is no property and no condition, but a something which persists through time, and, in relation to it, properties and conditions are *its* properties and conditions. But if they do this they will realize that the thought of their own Ego completely coincides with the thought, "I am", "I exist", and that, to feel that one is an Ego is identical with a feeling of being or of existence. If we take the word "consciousness" in its narrowest and proper meaning of consciousness of existence, and hence, inevitably, of time, then the Ego alone has consciousness, and this is the form in which timelessly existing Spirit reacts upon the experience of ever-happening actuality. Man lost "eternal life" because in him the temporal life-cell had opened itself to the irradiation of timelessly existing Spirit, which, according to the profound saying of Aristotle, burst into the cosmos θύραθεν, that is, from without, from a foreign place. Jahve fears that man might become as gods if he were to eat of the tree of life too. Here we are concerned, in this illuminating turn of the myth, with one point only: that man lost his original godhead because he ate of the tree of knowledge. The "tree" of knowledge, indeed, is a fiction, for there exists solely the tree of life: but the myth clearly and unequivocally expresses the fact that the loss of "eternal life" was the consequence of the arising of consciousness; for it is only in the new state of existing Ego that the glance can be turned upon life which shows life in the light of a devouring corruption, whose victim man knows himself, to his horror, to be in so far as he has any part in life. We shall forthwith reveal the reason why the will is not so much the instrument as the medium of a power which must deny life itself in denying the soul of life: the reason lies in the fact that its character is to be a happening which is in conflict with being; to be a destruction which without beginning or end ever renews itself.

We saw that will is rooted in the Ego, and with the help of volition the Ego operates upon the organism like an impulse: and the most universal thing, in which all urges of volition necessarily have a share, is the tendency of the Ego to assert itself against life in immutable independence, or, more briefly, the urge of self-preservation. But an existing entity can hold its place in universal change only by making incessant war upon the latter, whether by excluding disturbances which come to it thence, or by overcoming and eradicating the disturbing entity. If Nietzsche substitutes "will to power" for will, it is to be remarked that a will which should not be a will to power would no longer deserve the name of will; unless, indeed, the expression be given the much narrower meaning of a will to domination over one's fellows, or, more briefly, imperiousness. We cannot will without striving after power by that action, and even if we willed to cease to will we would still be serving its desire to enforce a wish. The artist who carves the image of the god is a masterful being of spirit and Ego, however true it may be that the artist who beheld it was able to make the man of action who holds the chisel (like a cheated devil) the servant of the Soul. If accordingly we set up the equation impulse for self-preservation = impulse for self-assertion = immediate foundation of will to power or will to success or, in short, of will, then we have stated that, without the participation of the impulse after self-assertion, events of willing cannot take place. Volition essentially is a fight with corruption, victorious in places, but finally hopeless and vain; and hence, in accordance with the curse of Jahve, it is labour, trouble, and care, with the final prospect that the willing entity must become dust, and that sooner or later his work must become dust.

The myth connects all the trouble with the acquisition of knowledge, or, in our language, with the origin of thinking consciousness: but it may perhaps be said that it is not clear what a self-asserting will has to do with knowledge, and why the act of apprehension and the activity of thought depend upon the act of will and upon action. It would take us far beyond the scope of this book to give a scientific proof of the primacy of will and the possibility of knowledge in spite of this.[43] But we need only collect together facts mentioned repeatedly, though in different places, in order to bring before the mind at least the connection of the willing Ego and the apprehensive Ego.

The Ego is the fundamental type of all existence, the ultimate ground of every fear of death and the birthplace of all our wishes for immortality: but no less is it the focus where that world arises which alone we can hope to make intelligible. I, as living entity, am in manifold connection with other living entities and with the planet which, a tree of life, caused me, a leaf, to grow upon it: but as Ego I am absolutely severed not only from every other Ego, but also from every segment of the world which I can experience, and this is why my state of reflection never coalesces with the content of my reflection, which, in fact, isolated like myself, stands over against me and even opposed to me; which is the reason why there are, strictly, no contents of thought, but only objects of thinking. It is true that the world of bodies and images already bears the character of strangeness, but of a strangeness which is either threatening or alluring, and which admits of union, as we shall see: but it is only the world of thought which bears a character of insurmountable and quite non-qualitative objectivity, not to say of resistance to the thinking entity; and the restlessness and worry of the seeking spirit exercises itself upon it in acts of distinction, resolution, and analysis no less than the lust for power of willing spirit exerts itself upon what has become part of it by the exercise of life-destruction.

But the exclusion of thought from life is revealed more drastically if we compare that which by thought (for example) we merely comprehend of the outer world, with that which we experience of this same world: more briefly, if we compare the thought-content with the experience-content of the external world. We experience, but we do not comprehend bodies and images, but only their relative distinctions, so that in thinking, we already presuppose as given the entire content of the world. If this were not so, then the expression of the judgment that the blotting-paper is red would afford an intuitive image of redness to a person blind from birth who should hear our statement; which, as everybody knows, is impossible. If finally, in view of this curious state of facts, the question, which for thought is crucial, was asked, What *are* the objects of thought? (or at any rate those which belong to the external world, or things) then their nature, as well as their origin and kinship with will is best revealed by the epigrammatic answer: things are Egos projected into the world.

The content of experience called "world" is certainly in a state of irresistible flux, for it is the stream of time having become image: it does not exist but happens. The world, on the other hand, which is the object of thought does exist, as I exist, who, by apprehending the world, have made it a self. The heaven which I comprehend is always the same heaven, the heaven which I experience in contemplation is already at the end of a minute a different heaven from what it was. We "comprehend" the actuality of happenings only by insinuating into them that false element of being which we, who comprehend, are in truth: and we are Egos, independent of time, self-identical, and therefore excluded from the world. Without a cleavage of images, a single step of thought would be as impossible as a single step of the will without a cleavage of happening: and volition, measured against the power of abstraction, is but the practice of the latter. Finally, let us briefly consider a fact which nowadays only they do not see who will not see it.

The huge whirl of eternal corruption and creation in the world is certainly no dream of paradise; but equally it does not resemble the foul orgy of destruction with which "civilized" or "moral" man defiles the face of the planet—the last offspring of the horrid drama which we are pleased to call the spiritual development or even progress of mankind. So true is this, that, in comparison, that whirl does, indeed, resemble a dream of paradise; and for proof, a European may look upon some surviving South Sea races which so far he has not yet poisoned with syphilis, murdered with high explosive, or worn down with compulsory labour.[44] If by contrast we consider the spiritual history of Asia, it shows, all things considered, a flight from actuality; if we consider that of Europe, it shows that horrible assault upon actuality which in a few centuries will have destroyed life completely on this planet—except perhaps the bacteria. The European spirit proceeded according to the prescription "Cursed is the field"—and it will reap as it has sown. And what enabled it to continue its murderous success? Applied Science. And what forged this instrument of murder? Pure science—numbering, measuring, and weighing. "By their fruits ye shall know them." But if these are the fruits of Galileo, Newton, and Faraday, then let us admit that to this moment reflection has in truth been led captive by Spirit which either flees or else hates life: and then let it be admitted that the course was set for investigative zeal, not by the powerless vision of Prometheus, but by the raging will of Hercules. This might, indeed, be different, however improbable the conditions, and we shall at least indicate how it might be brought about: but things *are* at any rate as has been stated, and the hour for returning has been missed; soon the last divine image will have fallen under the killing blows of will.[45]

We have here given some indications about the metaphysics of Spirit. Before giving some indications about the metaphysics of Life, we shall show how, by the help of the former alone, a supreme principle of classification for all the driving forces can be derived with logical compulsion, if we will consider the Ego exclusively in its relation to vitality. The Ego could not wish to assert itself against Life unless it had somehow undergone its power and influence, and it could not have undergone these if it had not been temporarily subordinated to Life. So far we have contrasted will with the feelings; now we say, more exactly, that these vital processes in which finally the act of will flashes out (self-assertion and affirmation of the Ego) must have been preceded at least by an intended subjection of the Ego. If this were to be completed, then a feeling could no longer emerge into that state in which acts of will are created: but the weaker participation in Life of the Ego, too, appears, from the side of the Ego, as a claim of Life; and exactly as the assertion of the Ego negates this claim, so it can be accepted and affirmed by self-negation of the Ego. Thus in the sphere of the Ego the urge of self-assertion is met by the urge of self-devotion, and the ultimate reason of every possible decision of the will must be found either on the side of assertion or on that of devotion. This, however, must be investigated in further detail.

If the Ego were the Spirit, it would be impossible to speak of any tendency to devotion, and also impossible to speak of any will to assertion, for assertion presupposes that that has been experienced to which it is the negative reaction. But the Ego is not the Spirit, it is Spirit coupled with Life, and in the peculiar life-sphere of the human individual it is the directive centre whence Spirit radiates action into the life for the influence of which it has become receptive. In Aristotelian phraseology the νους ποιητικός requires for complement the νους παθητικός, and the Ego which demands requires the Ego which is subject to demands, which can succumb to the claims of Life in three ways: it is overcome, stunned, and relieved by vegetative vital processes (that is, by those which are altogether incapable of consciousness), as happens with regular periodicity in sleep, and, exceptionally, in narcosis and fainting; or again, it is subordinated to vital processes capable of consciousness; sometimes to those which belong to sensitive and urge-driven corporeality (actions of urge) and sometimes to those which belong to the contemplating soul (drunkenness, ecstasy, with which we shall soon deal); or finally it falls under the power of Life because it is, so to speak, persuaded by its allurement, and consequently acts as the satellite of life, that is, in the service of self-devotion. In Chapter VI we distinguish between dependence on Spirit and dependence on Life in the act of apprehension, and now we similarly distinguish between dependence on Spirit and dependence on Life in volition. In life-dependent apprehension we could not permit ourselves to overlook the participation of Spirit, because that would have made impossible any further apprehensive activity, and similarly we must not now overlook it in life-dependent volition, because that would make impossible any activity of will. This at length leads us to an elucidation of the contrast between feelings which lie close to, and those which lie far from, the will.

Volition by nature is negative, and the immediate reason which makes it possible is the spiritual driving force, and never the infra-spiritual impulse. Consequently the tendency to devotion causes acts of will only with the help of self-assertion, and through it, and the paradox of an act of will which depends on Life is realized in every case through the negation of negation. Will which acts on behalf of self-devotion is turned destructively against the conditions of its own existence: this is true of acts of a genuine search after knowledge, with acts of a genuine formative impulse, and so too with acts of affirmative affection. Love, too, is transformed into acts, but only by bitter self-denial: for at the moment of action it is not love which acts. Let us imagine two persons of different sex and bound by reciprocal affection of passionate strength (whether it be Eros which binds their souls or sex which binds their bodies), and let us imagine that before the eyes of the lover the beloved falls from a narrow bridge into a torrent: he follows, without hesitation, to save her. It *might* here be a threatened sense of property which actuated him, but equally certainly it also was true love.[46] But the whole content of his action is struggle with the current, struggle with the weight which draws him down, struggle with the movements (which perhaps hinder his purpose) of the drowning girl: and the impulse-foundation of this is will to assertion, will to overcome, and will to power, and accordingly the rescuer would be lost if instead of struggling he would continue to love and to continue in loving devotion. And whenever acts of will break forth from devoted affection the case is similar to this. If we compare the action of a champion swimmer who tries to excel a competitor in speed, or of a wrestler whose one design in wrestling is to throw his opponent, then it is evident that every action is immediately occasioned by the impulse of self-assertion, and only in a mediated manner by the impulse of self-devotion.[47] But in this rather unnatural alliance with the interest of self-devotion the will runs a continual risk of being disarmed, and of giving place to a state of mere feeling; and this makes it intelligible why, in comparison with feelings of attack and defence, the affirmative feelings of affection have much slighter chances of enforcing , their claims by actions. But at the same time the feelings of will are also not identical with feelings of defence.

The contrast between feelings of affection which are of affirmative flavour and feelings of defence, which are of negative flavour ("flavour" because in pure vitality "yes" and "no" do not occur), gives way to the contrast between genuinely affirmative and genuinely negative feelings as soon as we imagine the union with Spirit completed and the kernel of urges covered with a stratum of interests. The contrast between feeling and volition furnished us with the instruments which served to make intelligible (so far as seemed desirable) the origin of the Ego; and now that we have the Ego at command and know its fundamental relation to Life, we may transfer the opposition into the feelings themselves, by distinguishing the feelings of devotion from those of assertion. From this it is now clear why there cannot be urges corresponding to the multiplicity of interests. Even if we left all the urges their power to act, still that power would be added to them by virtue of which the Ego would respond in each one of them with appropriate acts of self-assertion. But therewith the scene of Life has completely changed. The moment when (for example) the sexual urge in man is *immediately* active, that is, when all events of willing are excluded, is the moment of sexual union. But the steps which are taken by a suitor in order to reach the object of his desire and to render her pliable are no longer the urge-movements of the male pursuing the female, but are acts of will serially connected and executed in the interests of sex; and here it is not only possible but inevitable that there will come into play numerous assertive driving forces complicating the process—such as selfishness, self-esteem, sense of honour, pride, suspicion, prudence, downheartedness, vanity, obstinacy, and so on, whence results an infinitely various complex, not of urge-movements, but of actions. If we compare the sexual life of any animal with the hundreds of thousands of love-stories which amuse modern mankind, then we would be blind not to see that the animal plane has here been left behind.

We are now no longer in the sphere of urges but of driving forces, and no longer of vital feelings but of such feelings as invariably are *also* Ego-feelings; and, with regard to the Ego, we must henceforth look for every feeling either on the side of assertion or on the side of devotion. From this point of view we outline the system of driving forces, and pay attention to the urges only in so far as it appears expedient and possible to indicate the points of junction between them and the interests. If we use volition to throw light upon feeling, we use feeling, now better known to us to throw the light which still is needed on vitality. But first it seems needful to explain in a few words the relation of feeling to the elementary and fundamental concepts of our psychology.

Consciousness is no active power, but the token that in the sphere of life of the individual acts having no temporal extension have taken place, partly at the demand of Spirit and partly under the compulsion of vitality: and similarly the feelings (which here also include moods) are not active powers but, metaphorically expressed, are messengers bearing instructions; messengers, in the animal, of active images to the acting body-soul of the animal, and in man messengers of his active vitality to his active Ego. Man, too, of course, receives messages from his images, and even has the faculty of entering into communication with them by contemplation and without the intervention of messengers: but this state no longer is feeling, and those messages generally pass, by way of his vitality, to the new centre of his body, the Ego, where they receive an immediate response, being either accepted or declined, in such a manner that they must rather be considered as signals which inform us about the never resting traffic between the It and the Ego. Instructions given by the Ego to the It, when followed, manifest themselves in feelings of self-assertion, whose active side (that of urges) very often occasions acts of will; instructions given by the It to the Ego, when followed, manifest themselves in feelings of self-devotion, the urge-side of which can likewise occasion acts of will, but more often leads to a dethronement of the Ego, which has very different mental states for signal. How far this description is incomplete (because disturbances take place already in the sphere of the Ego, which also are signalled by feelings) is a question which we prefer to discuss after the fundamental principles have become familiar from examples and consequences.

We shall now introduce a considerable extract from a chapter bearing the same name in our earlier book, quoting almost verbally and indicating gaps by means of dots; although in details the extract does not fully agree with our present view, we still quote it because it aroused such enthusiastic echoes in the souls of the young that we would hesitate to omit it even if it varied from our doctrine of consciousness, which has made great strides since then, even more than in fact it does. But further it attempts to throw light upon the origin of feeling, and by this means draws the outlines of the plan which we require for the system of driving forces, using a straightness of outline which simplifies so remarkably that we could hardly hope to effect a similar performance in view of the far richer details which we believe ourselves to command today. We therefore believe we shall reach the goal more quickly if we reproduce it, and either complete or improve it in a final discussion, than by completely re-drafting it.

"Let us imagine that somebody is contemplating a gleaming jewel (for example, in a shop window), and is held fast in the contemplation. Let there be present in him at first only the feeling of himself and the image of the jewel. And now let there happen what in full strength is granted only to few, although its rudiments, if the object be suitably chosen (for example, the sight of the setting sun or the form of the beloved) are, after all, known to everybody: the contemplating subject is 'absorbed' in the contemplated object. Then consciousness has become a mirror, empty except for the blaze of the jewel, and the feeling of Ego is extinguished before the supreme power of the image. A man who has become pure contemplation knows of no 'existence', and 'has forgotten' himself, and nevertheless is in a state of ardour compared with which the loftiest content of thought grows pale. He is freed from the trammels of solitary existence and *becomes* the reflected content, and through it becomes that of which it is 'in itself' not part, but the vision and the symbol—the world, 'infinity', and 'universe'.

"For reasons which cannot here be discussed in detail such states have been experienced with intoxicating fervour only by the classical age. Such states were then, as they still are with certain races which are in a state of nature, the zone which gave birth to holy mysteries, which the dense shade of horrific myths hid from the eye of the uninitiated. Since the time of Nietzsche our knowledge of these matters is chiefly connected with the name of the Thraco-Grecian god Dionysus, who in truth was only one manifestation of this universal elementary power with certain peculiarities of partly barbarian and partly Hellenic origin. Our views of the psychical conditions of his 'epiphany' are confirmed by the fact that the mystic took the perfected degree to be not an 'exaltation' or 'purification' of the soul, but simply an 'ecstasy', to be taken literally as a 'being beside himself', and that he prepared for it by a profound excitement of the senses, whose deadly excess was softened only by the 'rage' of orgiastic dances. But, as being beside himself, the person who has been dissociated from himself has become 'enthousiasmos', that is, 'filled by the god' or 'possessed'. He sees no longer with the eyes of common day, bounded by space, but is beyond every barrier, even that of time; words which he utters have prophetic meaning, and his power is capable of magical effect at a distance. And when enthusiasm fertilizes knowledge, then, according to the belief of every age and race, there arises 'revelation', 'illumination', 'enlightenment', 'inspiration' ...

"The man who is wholly resolved in the contemplation of the jewel bears the world within himself, and therefore can possess neither striving nor feeling. The ruling state of profoundest fullness or highest exaltation is distinguished from feeling (however intense) by the satiety due to the state of being at one—the perfected presentation of moving or quiescent entity. He would be no man and no person, but what the ancients called a Daemon, if he could remain in the flux of ecstasy. But we assume that this is impossible; the man who a moment ago was 'far away' is awakened, for example, by some impact on his body, and must 'come back' to himself: and now, being cut off himself, he sees reduced to the dimensions of an object that in which he recently embraced the world. Then there has been forged between him and the object the link of a striving which aims at the possession of the object as a source of potential happiness.

Such a desire would include the complementary feeling of reluctance against any impediment to its satisfaction.

"The outline of the origin of feelings which has here been developed would be misunderstood if it were assumed that so commonplace a matter as the multiplicity of feelings and emotions is based upon the extremely rare and exceptional state of ecstasy. We gave the direction of an inner process by placing before it a possible goal at which it aims even when it has not the means of reaching it. In the striving of will the Ego experiences its own activity: and in the striving of feelings it succumbs to the attraction of the world-content which is turned against them; and if the former, with relation to the Ego, is the urge after its preservation, then the latter, seen from the same point, represents the urge towards a weakening and solution of the Ego, and towards its surrender to the allurement of the image. ... The power of the innermost of all feelings, of love, to free from self, has been felt and described in words partly full of illumination by the poetry and wisdom of all time; whereas philosophy (at least in the West, and apart from certain thinkers of the romantic period) almost always misunderstood it. Accustomed to consider the action of Reason as the prototype of every event, philosophers were inclined to subordinate feeling, with the rest, to the effects of Spirit, and have left to modern science, if nothing better, at any rate the incapacity to imagine the might, fullness, and power of the inner life otherwise than as a corresponding vehemence of self-assertion (whether egoistic or altruistic), in spite of the fact that language itself assigns a passive part to the Ego in every violent mental affection, as in 'pathos' or 'passion'. Modern thought, under the influence of a traditional inversion, has become blind for the entire sphere of self-sacrifice, and for the 'conception' which can be undergone in that sphere alone; and thinks to raise yet higher the true 'works' of an inspired artist or poet if it calls them 'deeds', and by the absurdity of its interpretation degrades the most splendid of all the marvels of the past: the tragic and the heroic. ...

"In principle every striving, like a straight line, may have a beginning, course, and necessary end, and consequently cannot last as striving: and this is especially true of sensitive striving. In volition the Ego tends straight to the final point, the act, but in feeling, while the Ego tends, there is also something which exerts a tendency against the Ego, and therefore feeling, which rests upon polarity, is extinguished in a twofold manner: both the Ego, and the content which is directed against it, are deprived of their force. The former happens in the process of getting beside oneself, the latter in the act of will. The feeling does not end, it rather oscillates between two ends—

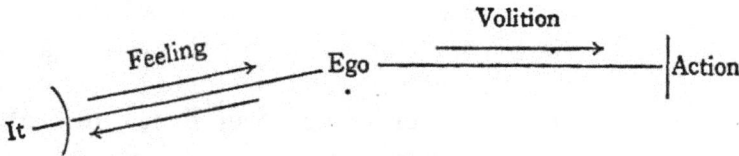

and whatever its nature may be otherwise, it is a state of inner conflict, which, if protracted, would prove destructive; which perhaps explains why the exalted feelings of love, admiration, and adoration are never without a hidden note of profound woe, and why the ethical desideratum of artificial equanimity (the ataraxia of the Ancients) does not owe its existence to the tutor Reason alone. ...

"It will be seen that our view leads to the necessary assumption that the nature of man has two substrata, one of which is active in the urge to exist, and the other in the urge to sacrifice existence. The exposition of the system of driving forces is much easier if we give a name to both, which, after what has already been said, can be done without too rash an incursion into the province of metaphysics. The principle of Ego, as is testified by the oldest human philosophies, lives in the Spirit, which is opposed (in popular language) by the 'world'. This principle was celebrated in the Apollo-worship of the Greeks in its praise of 'moderation' and 'know thyself' (the inner meaning of which is know *the* Self); the famous Judaeo-Christian demand for love of one's neighbour realizes it; and the systems of almost all philosophers confess it with a monumental onesidedness when they comprehend the prime cause of the world-content, under however diverse forms, by analogy of the Ego—as ultimate Ego, unmoved Mover, Will, Absolute, God, etc. ... The 'world', on the other hand, is not, as the philosophers falsely taught, a by-product and creature of the Spirit, although it *is* produced by Spirit in so far as the latter moulded it so that, from being an incomprehensible elementary world of experience, it became a world of objects comprehensible in principle. ..."

For the man of today the world agrees so perfectly with the actuality with which he is familiar that he cannot immediately understand why there was an abyss between the original world and Spirit. "But we need only turn to an age which, unlike ours, pursued no utilitarian but a truly spiritual direction in order to discover how profoundly it is in conflict with the world of the senses. Charitable gifts and altruistic long-suffering were not the supreme commandment of a Church militant of the Middle Ages, but a denial of the world and contempt of Eros. It took the coloured twilight of 'worldliness' with its heathen idolatry, which even now has not been wholly eradicated, for a far worse temptation of the devil than selfishness, which became a moral stigma much later. 'Cursed be all makers of images' is an anathema of the Church Fathers (or, in Tauler's words, 'Man must hide before all images and forms'); and the 'Bride of Heaven' renounced not only sex in her oath of chastity, but also condemned as sinful pleasure what, for the Ancients, had a sacred dignity—bodily perfection. Her God, by the witness of those who proclaim him, is Spirit, and the Kingdom of the Spirit was 'not of this world'.

"At the same time an appeal might be made to the arts, and especially to architecture, to the coloured glow of Gothic, and to the orgy of hues in books, robes, and public festivals of this particular period on the one hand, and on the other to the visionary states of so many ascetics, to the *unio mystica* and its symbol, the Eucharist: and in the end we might see in the Middle Ages the brightest flower so far known of the ecstatic capacity of man. In face of such a view it would take us far beyond our limit if we were here to undertake the proof that the sensuous aspect of these and similar phenomena, although certainly it is part of the history of Christianity, still in fact denotes a dissolution, the reluctant fall, and the death struggle of heathendom whose afterglow mingles its fires with the cold clarity of a spiritual Beyond. We will consider only the alleged ecstasy of anchorites and saints in a few words.

"Completely ignorant of the existence of *two* substances which are opposite and incompatible, certain essays in the description of ecstatic phenomena, partly of occultistic tenor and partly psychological, confound these uncritically with the 'convulsions' and 'visions' of hermits; and in doing so they remain behind ascertainable knowledge in a remarkable manner—by more than a thousand years. Augustine knew, and Benedict XIV finally applied fixed rules to the distinction between the elementary intoxication (which, according to our explanation, alone deserves the name of ecstasy) and the spiritual so-called ecstasy which alone, according to the perfectly appropriate views of the Church, gives proof of sanctity, whereas the other (and genuine) ecstasy is interpreted as a kind of vulgar possession, secular at least, but very often diabolical.[48] But in order to understand why the *unto mystica* could ever be taken for a kind of ecstasy, we must remember what is explained more fully below, that Spirit is not identical with the personal Ego: whence, in proportion as the latter is bound in it, there does take place a rejection of all personal interests, as is demanded by the well-known Rule of 'Poverty, Chastity, and Obedience'. The *Pater Ecstaticus* enjoys a closer proximity to God but, unlike the Dionysian mystic, he has not become God; he is freed from his person, but he is bound all the more tightly to the Spirit; and, on the other hand, he is not one with the content of the world, but is severed from it all the more sharply or raised above it in the mirror of his own experience (a process which is made objective, for example, in the overcoming of gravity by so-called levitation). And equally the absolute Ego or, more correctly, the Spirit, or even God (as is attempted by the feeble compromise of Pantheism, rightly condemned by the Church) never becomes one with the world: for Ego is only an alternative term for the consciousness of distinction, and the expression 'World-Spirit' hides a contradiction.

"We will return from these rather far-reaching explanations to closer and more familiar facts by pointing out that the contrast which we postulate was well known to classical as well as to romantic thought in the shape of the distinction between Spirit and Soul. For the former represents only the absolute Ego, the latter only the element of life, so that it must be imagined as having universal extension. There is no contrast between the Soul and the body: rather the Soul is the inner life which is one with and inseparable from the body; and therefore it changes, ever flows and never stays, like the becoming and perishing of living creatures; compared already by the ancients to the incessant waning and waxing of the moon, and hence called 'sublunary', and strictly banished by the founders of Christianity from the sphere of Spirit with the counter-threat of the fiction of the 'Kingdom of the Heavens'. Side by side (because fundamentally identical) with the antithesis of permanence and change there stands that of absolute activity and extreme passivity. Action belongs to the Spirit alone, it 'masters', 'rules', and 'overcomes', while the Soul suffers and undergoes. Action has a kinship with the arrow and the beam, and so the free God Apollo is at the same time god of light; while, according to German usage, the Spirit alone appears as 'wideawake' or, on the other hand, as 'benighted'; while combinations like 'sorrow', 'grief', and 'torment of the soul' bear witness to the passion (lower in the human scale) of the soul. The analogy of gender, too, between Spirit and man, and Soul and woman, has a deep foundation, and recurs in Greek in the analogous contrast between ὁ νοῦς and ἡγ φυχή.

"Now according to such a view each personality in its decisive kernel is built up of two substances, and the different species of character can all be traced back to different proportions in which Spirit and Soul are mixed. The former supports the urge to preservation, whose effects are the apprehension of things and the will; the latter supports the impulse to devotion—the desire to supplant self and to ebb away in contemplation. Soul without Spirit may be experienced, it may pulse rhythmically in the atmospheric 'elements', and it may at any rate preponderate in the animal world. Spirit without Soul, on the other hand, can neither be thought of nor imagined, it is acosmic and lies outside consciousness, and is revealed only by its influence (which, in fact, however, is incessant) upon the Element in ourselves, which, under its ray, is frozen and shattered. It is 'absolute' or 'excentric' externality, while Soul is natural interiority: and the latter is akin to darkness and night, as the former is to clarity which knows no twilight. Their struggle in the neutral ground of personality gives birth to specifically human consciousness with the characteristic symptom of a feeling of self. The philosophy of the romantic period called it 'day-consciousness', and its opposite pole 'night-consciousness'; in man only exceptional states are symptomatic of it, but in animals whole groups of symptoms, like a mysterious sense of locality, a magical power of scent and supernatural instincts of care for the young. ...

"Spirit and Element (or, Spirit and Life, or, Spirit and Soul) are by natural law antagonistic to each other; hence the former may wish to 'free' itself from the latter and shake it off completely, in which case the final goal of its endeavour would lie outside the world or *supra naturam*, the personal form of which is the spiritual character (in the narrowest sense)—which in the form of flagellant monks gives its peculiar mark to the Middle Ages, and in the shape of esoteric self-scrutiny to Buddhism. It has lost its importance in modern mankind, and we do not here discuss it. This is also true of the opposite mixture—of the Element, which not only offers a lively struggle, but also breaks the Spirit in

216

ecstasy: an example (which has become unfamiliar) of this we find only among peoples in a 'state of nature': and a crystallization of this notion (which has been universally misunderstood) in such mysticism as deserves the name. In these two composite forms the struggling substances tend apart, and the result consequently is not so much a wealth of varieties of personality as of suspension of personality. In spite of the complete difference in their respective governing substances, both spiritual and elementary eras show a certain scarcity in strongly marked personalities, and in feelings of personality and a preponderance of universal and, as it were, catholic ends of life which resemble one another in their tendency to break through the barriers of isolated existence. On the spiritual side this is arrived at by ascetic practices, by self-conquest, and even self-mutilation, and, generally, by a disciplined renunciation of an independent will. Certain Tibetan monastic organizations of the present day closely resemble in these respects the practices of mediaeval Christianity. On the elemental or vital side this end is reached by stimulation to intoxication, which likewise admits a peculiar technique and prefers to act through the means of crowds in a state of festive emotion—as, for example, in the orgiastic cults of the ancients, especially that of Dionysus. And both these tendencies meet even today in the cult-practices of Islamic Dervishes.

"On the other hand, an infinite multiplicity of character unfolds itself when we pass from the separate existence of substances to their co-existence. Spirit may turn to the Element, and the Element to Spirit: each with a deep indwelling need to imitate the opponent, which leads to processes of indefinite length in a twofold direction. For, while neither is submerged in the other, Spirit either forms a layer over Element (or conversely), and this with greatly varying completeness—at the same time surrendering a considerable part of its peculiar nature. Spirit seeks to tie down the stream of happening into the unity of Ego, and to dictate its 'law' to the content of the world, and thus become 'Reason'—that is, the vehicle of Logic which atomizes and conquers one part after the other, and yet can never read a riddle. The preponderance of the arithmetical intellect (which occurs in varying degrees) is the foundation of the third variety of character-types, which naturally has numerous subordinate forms. By its side there is the fourth and last variety in the shape of the enthusiastic character in which the Element charms the Spirit through the image and seeks to dissolve it in the image, and in exchange for its part assumes the form of feeling which (but for different reasons) can reach the goal no more than can the impulse of cognition.

"The two genera are rich in variants and spread simultaneously with only a slight displacement of the accent; they characterize the personal subdivisions of history, like the later age of Greece, the Renaissance, and the second half of the eighteenth century, and, without exception, they contain all that is greatest in historical mankind. Let us look with a clear eye at such periods of great individuals, and more especially at these themselves, with their restless tension of the will, their periodical attacks of deepest discouragement (to be interpreted as the reaction of violated 'nature'), and their self-torture (mostly ill-disguised), and we shall have to reject as intolerable the legend of the beneficent quality of action, and shall no longer doubt the schismatic dualism of personality. We must mention, however, that the relation between these substances is not necessarily one of antagonism, but may sometimes be a less painful co-existence. The former, in the most varied measure, results in the ill-centred and ill-balanced, the inconstant, inharmonious, contradictory, and finally the distracted character; the latter, in the harmonious, just, and well-proportioned, which, in exchange for the loss in complete immediacy with which it manifests its life, has acquired a 'style', and represents a short truce in the war, which in fact can never end in reconciliation, between the original powers. Hence results that happy show of synthesis and totality which (for example, in Goethe) attracts a naive spectator, and deceives him."

If now we look back to the beginning of this wide sweep of thought, we must add several restrictions to the attempted explanation of the origin of feelings. First, it does not deal with feelings in general, but only with psychical feelings of sympathy and antipathy in the narrower sense. These, and these alone, are the signals of an immediate connection of the soul of the vital entity with images, whether due to intuition or to fancy, and they are peculiar to man. On the other hand, the predominantly corporeal feelings of desire and repulsion, which are common to men and animals, serve to announce the "vegetative" processes of the body immediately, and images only in a mediated manner in so far as they are connected with the body in a manner which we have compared with magnetism; and even if phantasms originate in man even from these, the feeling is not perfected in them, but in the animal urge and the mutual pursuit and flight of bodies.

But further, all this studies only the relation of the Ego to Ego-less vitality, and not its relation to the world of objects and the emotions related to the latter. It is true that there can be no feeling of Ego quite without its vital side, and no vital feeling quite without Ego. Even in the intensest ardour of adoration there inheres some part of the struggle of the soul with the claim of the Ego, until it has passed over into self-oblivious intoxication; and even in the shallowest irritation at an offensive remark there inheres some part of the struggle of the Ego with the claims of life, until it has given way to a mere pondering of efficient causes or a volition aiming at their removal. But a single example, like that of irritation, suffices to convince us that a direction towards intoxication or against interruption of intoxication does not inhibit every feeling. This is true of feelings of devotion, but not of feelings of assertion, whose existence we could not clearly apprehend on that occasion because, instead of them, we could lay hold only of volition, which is cognate. The state of anger does not so much announce a commerce of the Ego with vitality as a disturbance of vitality by the commerce of the Ego with the object, which very frequently is an alien Ego. But not only an alien Ego, but any given object can be the occasion of a disturbance of the Ego, and among such objects there are our own interests. The anger which a man feels at his precipitation is obviously due to a struggle between his driving forces; and the It with which his Ego has commerce in such a state of anger, is not infra-spiritual vitality (the point where images are admitted and urges nurtured), but one side of that same vitalized Ego or sphere of the Ego, as we called it above, of which another side at this moment has become of "topical" importance in him. It is true that this "commerce" could not be signalled by any feelings (and hence not by the feeling of irritation) unless there were some disturbance of his vitality as such: but these disturbances are only the consequences of processes within the vitalized Ego. We here introduce two observations.

The personal Ego is spiritual fact *and* vital fact, and is never *only* one or *only* the other. As spiritual fact, it is the ground on which all acts arise; as vital fact it is, first, the vitalized crystallization of all acts which have taken place (or more exactly, of their effects), and, secondly, their connection with infra-spiritual vitality. The second point is not often properly appreciated, and we will therefore use an example (for instance, the irritation which we chose above) to make it clear. If I am irritated at a fatuous remark, vital processes are needed in order that I shall have any understanding of the question, and still more of its significance for me; there is needed the process of hearing (which is altogether infra-conscious and infra-spiritual), and further, the equally unconscious processes by which I apprehend the meaning of what is heard, processes in which now my vital as well as my spiritual past takes part; and finally processes of which, by their nature, consciousness is capable, by virtue of which the relation of the meaning to my awareness is revealed to me. Of all this at the moment it is the irritation which forces its way "into my consciousness"; and the past history of my life accordingly is "virtually" present in it in the same manner as the content of the three hundred preceding pages is present when the last page of a long novel is read with intelligent appreciation. Hence it is clear that the centre of action which happens to be of immediate interest must never be imagined as separable from the vitalized Ego, nor the latter from infra-spiritual vitality. Thus we reach a second observation.

It does not much matter whether we imagine the immediate Ego as a mathematical, that is, as a non-extended point, like the true centre of a sphere or some other figure, where now one and now another driving force exerts a compulsive or an exacting action, or whether we allow the Ego-point, which is capable of action, to change its place according as now one and now another driving force has attracted and bound it; for the result in both cases is the same, for it is always the victorious one of two conflicting driving forces which determines the actions of the Ego. Hence it follows that in principle every distinct driving force can enter into conflict with any other in the same Ego; whence in fact most internal struggles take place, not so much between the Ego and infra-spiritual vitality, as between the different interests of the personality. When the Ego is playing its isolated and isolating part, every driving force is under a natural necessity of participating, in so far as it is capable of filling the part of the Ego. A man's selfishness may quarrel with his ambition, and both with his desire for domination, and the feelings of assertion which accompany one relate themselves immediately to the opposite feelings of assertion, even although they do so in the shape of feelings only, because they must at the same time assert themselves against the disturbances of vitality thereby occasioned. The Ego atomizes, and this is the reason why rationalistic psychology (of which Herbart is the classical instance) discovered instead of vital processes only an infinity of points, mostly called "imagination", which throng unpleasantly at the "threshold of consciousness", and either force an entry or else creep in after having misled the "guardian" of the threshold by a skilful disguise. At bottom this is nothing but the competition of interests, exactly as in ordinary life, but the object of this competition is not a fictitious space which exists only in the imagination of minds incapable of thought, but the role of Ego. Accordingly we must treat all the driving forces as mutual competitors: but we would never reach a supreme principle of classification and allotment of precedence unless we had penetrated to the reason which makes possible the inner strife—namely the hostile division of every personal individual into a spiritual and a vital half. We now return to our main subject.

Our theory of the origin of feeling was only half correct; but it works its way through to this foundation, and therefore can act at each step as though it were already acquainted with our modifications; and, besides, it has drawn a twofold advantage from its incompleteness: first, it can correctly point the extreme contrast between contemplating Soul (world of images) and Spirit (which is all action without image), and secondly it can describe the four possible forms in which Spirit can be connected with Soul as an equal number of variations of human vitality. The consequences for the system of driving forces are described in the next chapter: here we only premise in what respect the fundamental outline of the driving forces must be complemented (the predominantly corporeal strivings being duly considered); and in doing so we intentionally alternate in our use of words and phrases, and for short call the properties of feelings, feelings themselves. Thus, instead of speaking continually of an Ego-side and a vital side of feelings, we speak of Ego-feelings and vital feelings.

If now we first contrast the Ego-feelings in the widest sense, or the feelings of assertion, with the vital or elemental feelings, then we must divide the latter into preponderantly corporeal or sensuous, and into the preponderantly psychical vital feelings; and it goes without saying that the interest of assertion takes a different shape according as it operates in opposition to a vital demand which is mainly sensuous or mainly psychical. Among the feelings of assertion we distinguish (as the above outline has already done) Ego-feelings of the narrower meaning from spiritual feelings. The former manifest the tendency to assertion of the personal

Ego, the latter that of Spirit within the Ego. The feelings of assertion lie close to will and far from urges, the feelings of devotion far from will and close to urges; and therefore the domination of personal as well as of spiritual interests in preservation is accompanied by a more or less considerable repression of the impulses; whereas the domination of sensuous and psychical interests in devotion favours a return to power of the urges, which involves the danger that will in general may to a large extent be deprived of its power. Finally, we will give an example to explain sensuous devotion too, partly in order to render vividly clear its difference from psychical devotion, and partly in order to anticipate a misunderstanding into which a reader untrained in biological thought might easily fall.

We have already stated that no sense-impression can occur which is not also soul-impression, but we added that among the senses the most sensory is touch, and the most intuitive is sight. In a doubtful case, and circumstances being otherwise similar, we shall have to consider an emotion all the more sensuous the more the impression which occasioned it is a near process: and another more psychical, the more the impression is a distant process. Sight is the typical sense of distance, hearing is chiefly so, while smell is chiefly a near sense, and taste and feeling are typically near senses. Now if we assume that somebody intoxicates himself with the taste of peaches and desires peaches for the sake of such intoxication, then the ultimate motive of his action lies in a sensuous devotional driving force; just as it was a psychical devotional driving force which caused the lover to save the beloved from drowning, and the person who was fascinated by the sight of the jewel to desire its possession for that reason. Equally it is a sensuous, and perhaps a quite predominantly psychical devotion-interest which can cause somebody who grows intoxicated at the smell of a flowering branch of lilac to break off the branch and take it with him. It should be clear from this that a distinction having for principle the difference between assertive driving forces and devoted driving forces is by no means the same thing as the distinction between moral unselfishness and moral egoism. The desire to possess the jewel, the lilac, or the peach would be classed as an egoistic emotion in the ethical sense, but not in the biological sense, although no Ego-assertion took any part in it. We need only put by the side of the cases which we have discussed the other case, that somebody takes the lilac in order to put it in his hat, or that he takes the jewel in order to sell it or to add it to a collection of curios, and we see immediately that only now the determining motive comes biologically too from self-assertion, and that it does not do so in the former cases.

Now what is the case where somebody takes food because he is hungry? Hunger, like the sexual urge, is an urge after union which in itself has nothing to do with self-preservation, although it may have grown to the intensity of an irresistible need. But the animal needs act immediately in man only on exceptional occasions, while normally they are in the service of the egoistic will to preservation and to power; and, accordingly, as a rule, we shall have to look for the source of actions done for the purpose of getting food and satisfying sexual desire on the side of assertion, and, more exactly, within the sphere of the will to possess. So much we premise in order to make more easily intelligible our tables of the driving forces, of which an account must now be rendered.

CHAPTER IX NOTES

[39] We have shown why scientific study cannot do without concepts of properties and of substrata and, further, why, if properties and substrata are to be defined, we must have recourse to characteristics of phenomena which are of the nature of states or processes, and are supposed for certain reasons to be the effects of the substrata which have such properties. In the sequel we confine ourselves to processes. If we use such substratum-concepts as body, Soul, or Spirit, then if we wish to state what each of them is we must state what are the processes in which body, Soul, and Spirit manifest themselves, and with such exactness that in every actual event (for example, the process of perception) not the slightest doubt could exist what share is due to the body, what to the Soul, and what to the Spirit. In doing this it will be well to use an abbreviating terminology, which we will first explain to obviate misunderstandings later.

If we speak of the properties of a body, of a sphere, for example, the properties are distinguished from one another and also from the sphere: but there can hardly be any danger that the distinguished terms shall also be considered separable. If next we speak of the progressive movement of the sphere, it is well to bear in mind the inseparability, because the process of moving is in turn, and rightly, taken as an event in which again distinct properties emerge which again can be separated neither from it nor from one another. Every progressive movement has a definite direction and a definite rate of speed (other than zero), and each of these is variable by itself. Direction can vary while velocity remains the same, and velocity can vary while direction remains the same; and, again, the bodies in motion may be of different mass, but have similar characteristics of motion or, conversely, may be of the same mass, but have different characteristics of motion.

Now the vital process (or, more exactly, the process of experience) is always vitally "given"; and if in spite of this we treat the details which may be distinguished in it as though they were processes themselves, we do so merely because our exposition would be made intolerably clumsy if we were to call to mind in each case every other aspect of experiences. Thus if we distinguish between experiences of the body and those of the Soul, it must be noted that the former cannot take place without the latter, nor the latter without the former, and if, further, we distinguish different traits in body-experiences as though these were independent processes, and apply the same treatment to soul-experiences, it is still our opinion that neither could subsist by itself. But in fact, they all are in principle as variable relatively to one another as the direction is relatively to the velocity of a movement, and emphasis will appear to rest now on one and now on the other.

If a physical image be desired for this, let a mental comparison be made between a bullet which has been fired and a falling avalanche; and it will be admitted that we find conspicuous and noticeable, in the latter its mass, and in the former its velocity.

40   So far this has been done with complete thoroughness by one thinker alone—Melchior Palagyi, whose *Naturphilosophische Vorlesungen* must be emphatically recommended alike to biologists and psychologists.

41   Further details in *Vom Wesen des Bewusstseins*.

42   We are here not so much concerned with the facts themselves, which are far more complicated, as with the formula of the emotions which come into play. It is known, for example, that bees returning with rich spoils perform dances in which the bees which remained in the hive participate, and these dances also have a symbolic meaning, etc. But however far our analysis penetrates into such events, the same formula will have to be applied to each part as was applied in the main text to the whole event.

43   A detailed demonstration of the supremacy of the will is given in our *Geist und Seele.*

44   For example, the inhabitants of the island of Bali (Sunda Straits), whose customs have become widely known through the Volkwang publications.

45   To satisfy quibblers, we state that these words neither are meant for a "prophecy", nor are in conflict with Chapter III. Here we are simply making use, to describe a state of affairs which has already been reached, of the thought of its inevitable results. The possibility of a "miraculous" change remains. But *only* something which, compared with a clearly prescribed course, would seem a miracle, could produce the saving change.

46   Of course, the action which we chose for example could bear many more interpretations than we assumed in the interests of our exposition. The rescuer might have jumped after the drowning girl from dash or recklessness, or from a need of self-esteem, or because he feared that he must charge himself with cowardice should he refrain, or (when there are spectators) from vanity and desire for distinction, etc.

47   Most assertive actions, too, are, of course, only means to an end. A man may devote a year, or decades, or a lifetime to the founding of a business, an invention, an engineering works, a title, the hurt of an enemy, etc., and in such a case the hundreds and hundreds of actions which he does with this end in view are related to the final end as so many means to that end. But none the less each of them shares the assertive character of the attainment of the end, whereas where action is based on love, the end will be to make some kind of devotion possible, so that it would be essentially of opposite nature to the actions which mediate it.

48   Important documents will be found in Görres' *Christliche Mystik*, vol. ii, pp. 288-304. Görres, for his part, calls the elementary ecstasy the "magic", and the spiritual the "mystic", and quotes as distinctive characteristic of the former its periodicity which corresponds to the cycles of nature.

CHAPTER X

OUTLINE OF THE SYSTEM OF DRIVING FORCES

After our very exhaustive consideration of the metaphysics of personality, this chapter is intended in the main to be a commentary on our Tables of Driving Forces, although still a not inconsiderable number of fresh considerations will be indispensable. It is to be noted immediately that it is a classification of driving forces and not of personalities. There is not, and there cannot be, any man having driving forces of devotion only, or of assertion only, and even a preponderance of one or the other side can occur only exceptionally: normally the one or the other takes place only within definite classes of objects of desire.

Further, no driving force of the one side becomes active without at the same time causing to exist an occasion for the rejection of the activity of a driving force of the other side. If I am dominated by an assertive interest, then it dominates, among other things, a possible tendency towards devotion, and accordingly every stimulus to devotion is felt as an irritant serving to intensify the assertive interest. If conversely I am dominated by a tendency towards devotion, then it also dominates my assertive interest, and my strongest reluctance will be turned against assertive desires; and the assertive functions of my will (which, of course, are indispensable) serve merely the realization of such ends as satisfy desires of devotion. If we do justice to this fact, it will lead us on both sides to a curious duplication of the driving forces, for as soon as each has arisen, we must distinguish within it attitudes due to strength of interest from attitudes (which look exactly similar) due to weakness of counter-interest.

Finally we introduce two terms which make it much easier to distinguish between spiritual and personal self-assertion. We have seen that Spirit is a power which seeks after assertion (fixation, or existence), and that the Ego is the best habitation of the Spirit within vitality; hence our meaning will be clear when we say that every impulse towards assertion (whether spiritual or personal) is, with regard to vitality, an impulse *binding* certain vital processes; and that every impulse towards devotion, in relation towards the spiritual as well as to the personal Ego, is an impulse which unbinds or loosens certain vital processes from it. Accordingly we alternatively call assertive driving forces binding, and devotional driving forces releasing. Thus all driving forces are divided into binding and releasing, with a cross-division into spiritual and personal, and accordingly we have four chief groups: spiritual bonds, spiritual releases, personal bonds, personal releases. In the first place we turn to the spiritual bonds.

We adopt the threefold division of all spiritual bonds into theoretic, aesthetic, and ethical reason—a division which was developed early in the history of European thought for the main objects of philosophy, and has predominated for over a century; but we do so only because this division does in fact conceal a difference in spiritual interests, whose clear elaboration, however, involves a considerable change in the meanings of the words. We begin with theoretic Reason (Table I, A, I).

Activity in its totality, that is, the outer and the inner world without restriction, challenges Spirit to take up an attitude which in these days under the name of interest in cognition must be set by the side of its personal counterpart —love of news—as an independent faculty. If in place of this we say will to truth, this means a will to the discovery of truth, in relation to which will to truthfulness would be a will to make truth, as it is held to be proved and known, the guiding line of personal conduct. We are not here concerned to know whether interest in cognition is historically original or whether it depends on an interest of the will; we are concerned with the interest in cognition which now does in fact exist beyond dispute. But we need only to recollect facts which have already been established in order to know that genuine interest in cognition need by no means be looked for on the side of Spirit alone.

Spirit under no conditions whatever could translate actuality into the language of a correct judgment, that is, into truth, unless in each detail it had become aware of the truth: and then it could not even will to bring about this translation. But it does become aware of actuality in so far as it has for a moment come under its power within the vital range of personality: and to that vital faculty which allows this to happen we have already given the name, with reference to its consequences for the attitude of Spirit, of sense of actuality, or feeling for actuality. But if the feeling for actuality which lies on the side of life, or Release, takes a part in the interest for cognition, then we shall know what takes a part in the latter on the side of Spirit, if we consider what attitude must be added to the feeling for actuality in order that it shall fulfil itself in discoveries of truth. The answer is, that there must be added to the sense for actuality the one and only principle which Spirit, as a capacity which apprehends actuality, has at its disposal, that is, the principle of identity. Feelings for actuality may become truths in so far as the entity inhabited by Spirit succeeds in measuring the content which it feels against non-temporal concepts. If we give the form of the law of the excluded middle to the principle of identity, and further frame the former with reference to actuality to mean that something can only be or not be, then a breach of this law may be called that incompatibility by whose existence a possibility of thinking the world would be absolutely precluded; and we understand immediately the struggle of Spirit vitalized within us against this logical contradiction. Sensitiveness for it, and a tendency to remove it, are the sole content of Theoretic Reason.

Interest in cognition cannot exist without the latter; but with it alone it is like a mill without grist. As Theoretic Reason begins to outweigh the sense for actuality, so the probability that the truth will be discovered diminishes; and the place of a true passion for discovery is taken by formalistic extravagance, pride of subjectivism which fondly believes that the world-problems depend on its caprice like chess-problems which we set ourselves, and by understanding in the part of juggler and gambler whose cards are *mere* concepts, whose applicability to actual events is of no interest. In our days of financial and mathematical formalism there is no scarcity of minds possessed by Theoretic Reason which has been divorced from nature. If, on the other hand, we consider the positive part of the logical impulse in the process of cognition, then we shall find it, in the first place, in a love of facts and tendency to criticism; and the word *criticism* serves to assure us that the Bond in question is antagonistic not only to the Release which threatens the seeking mind with transcendental nebulousness, but also to every illusion and readiness for belief which the self-assertions of the personal Ego would desire to make acceptable to Reason.

Sensible actuality, in the widest sense of the word, is an essential part of the totality of actuality; thus, on the one hand (among other things), it denotes everything that can be heard, smelt, tasted, and felt, and on the other hand, everything of which fancy and imagination are capable—in short, everything that can be made present by imagination. If we imagine the spiritual entity placed in the world of sensibilia, and, once more, concentrate our attention upon the demands which he should feel himself bound to make in order to assert his spirituality, then it is clear that these are not identical with the formative desire whose origin we have already found to be in the Soul, but with that side of it which causes every conflict between the image of the world and the spiritual conditions of perception to be felt as an interruption and to be met by reprisals. Now the Spirit is disturbed, and its perceptive apprehension is diminished by lack of clarity, by contingency, and by lawless confusion in the images, for which it seeks to substitute uniformity, rule, and, as an extreme case, the machine whose action is pure repetition. A sensitiveness for absence of law in sensibilia, and a tendency to transform them into a mould where they are subject to rule (both temporally and spatially), or—

according to the favourite formula of the schools, to create unity in multiplicity—is the sole content of Aesthetic Reason (A, II).

If the formative desire does succeed to emerge as will to form in a spirit-burdened vitality it can no longer exist without it, but must relegate it to an auxiliary part unless it is to run the risk of perishing in a will to mechanize. That part of Aesthetic Reason in it which is compatible with Life we call a sense of order, or of simplification, or a need of correct style. The risk of a conflict between Aesthetic Reason and the personal driving forces is small, and that of a conflict with devotion, and of succumbing to the enticement of the "wilderness", are proportionately great. The struggle between the call of the blood and the stereotyped form can be traced through the history of art and poetry (including the work of craftsmen) for nearly three thousand years, sometimes secret and sometimes open, appeased only in the rarest creations of the greatest Masters.

There is one side of the whole of actuality of which, in itself, the importance could hardly be under-estimated; but for men it has become of the utmost importance, and on this planet it has reached a terrible domination: man, not as animal, which would not justify separate treatment, but as vessel of the Ego. If we take the two spiritual Bonds which have just been discussed as two foundations in the formation of values, and if we ask why we find ourselves bound to prefer the logical to the non-logical, and rule to absence of rule, then the immediate reason is given in the reply— Because we are Egos, or Existences; for it is the understood and not the unintelligible world which is the medium of the Ego, and regulation and not approximation is the means by which it spreads its power. This already implies that a consideration inspired by Spirit alone must have for supreme value, or rather for determinant of all values, the fact of Ego. Something which actually exists has value in so far as it is an Ego, and apart from this it has no position, or rather, has a negative value. Hence it is possible to deduce the share of Spirit in every series of values which ever was set up, and from this again there follows the will to the equality of all persons before the principle of the Ego. A sensitiveness for disturbances which Life causes to the principle of equality, and a tendency to root up the disturbing cause at any price— these are the sole content of Ethical Reason (A, III).

We had to treat Theoretic Reason as participating in cognitive interest and Aesthetic Reason in formative interest, but it would be somewhat bold to grant to Ethical Reason any share in love of justice, whose foundations should be vital: for its guiding principle, the equal rights of every being which has an Ego, stands in absolute negation over against the world of Life (to which Nietzsche's, "Like to like, and unlike to unlike" would apply): although it is true that, by declining all privileges, it has in common with true justice the subordination of personal interest beneath a supra-personal (but anti-vital) power. It has, on the other hand, a share in so-called humanity, or in that view which makes of the cosmos the pedestal on which stands the statue called mankind.

It is Ethical Reason, or reason of will, which finally unfolds to us the ultimate meaning of reason in general, showing the terrific goal of the domination of Spirit. Called upon to assign a value to man, reason must esteem him for being the vehicle of Ego or of Spirit, and for nothing else. High breeding, race, nobility of sentiments, soul, profundity, blood, intensity, beauty, and strength count accordingly for nothing, and man as such counts alone; privilege is accorded only to greater power to affirm the Ego such as, for example, lies at the bottom of the extermination of "natural races" by "civilization". In the service of practical ethics, the Judaeo-Christian formula of "love of one's neighbour" proved particularly efficacious; a formula which hides under the most powerful of all feelings that which flourishes only by its destruction: undifferentiating respect of humanity. To love a thing means to love it more: the feeling of inclination cannot be imagined without that of less, or of negative, inclination. Love prefers and hate makes war, and both are equal partisans. Ethics, on the other hand, demands the suppression of both, and asks for our judgment "without respect of persons", that is, without the feeling of a tribunal which stands beyond instinctive decisions. Hence the conflict between "duty and inclination", which is never quite to be removed, it is to the credit of Kant's acumen that he discovered the inner schism here at least, and that he used the command of Reason in the shape of categorical imperative or pure Ought to deprive the heart's desires of their right; but unfortunately he was unable to eradicate the belief (which at the moment is even "scientific") in the origin of conscience in feelings of sympathy.

Kant appropriately derives his imperative from feelings of self-respect (that is, unconditional respect of the Ego, whence also respect of the "dignity of Man"); he thus strips the stoic concept of Duty of its eudaemonistic character, and the Christian love of God (that is, fear of God) of its merely pretended sentimental quality. But if he puts his imperative in the formula: Act as though the maximum of your action should by your will become a general law of nature, then the monumental example of Stirner saves us the detailed proof that will to equality and respect of the law clothe with the appearance of affirmation only the will to destruction (which certainly is supra-personal). Stirner uses the same formula, although he does not admit it, to demonstrate the sanctity of unrestrained egoism. For even if we neglect the fact that such a formula leaves it entirely to me what I am inclined to consider a "general law of nature", it still means, by virtue of the autonomy of the Ego which stands behind it, that each Ego has the same right to seize power. Here the hidden meaning of the ideals of Christianity come to light, which put in the place of the gods the "Son of Man", that is Man possessed by the Ego—the practical results of which may be seen in the French Revolution. "The freedom recommended by Christianity is perfected in the suffix 'less'—sinless, godless, mannerless, and so on" (Stirner). But fifteen hundred years ago the heathens, too, knew this when they charged the Christians with atheism, and they knew it by virtue of the principle opposite, not only logically but substantially—the principle of world-joy which takes away self.

Stirner's solipsistic formulation has the advantage that it is perfectly candid, because it openly expresses the implicit idea that I have exactly the same rights as anybody else; that is, my rights extend as far as my power. Kant, on the other hand, has in mind the Authorities, collective man, or the state where Government is facilitated more than everything by the readiness of the subjects to believe in an absolute Law, and accordingly his view is, your right extends no further than that of anybody else, and you must not wish to interfere with his. The hostility to Life of Stirner's solipsism manifests itself in his elevation to a world-principle of the will to power of isolated subjects (and in this respect he goes far beyond Nietzsche)—a will which is unbounded, and in its action infallibly destructive (the Ego *is* not all, but *destroys* all): the hostility to Life of Kant's duty manifests itself in the demand which cleaves to it that all feelings, and especially the affirmative feelings of affection, shall be rejected. An action due to affection quite rightly has no positive if it has not actually a negative value, for the champion of bare Ought.

Schiller (a follower of Kant), in a well-known and brilliant epigram, lays his finger not so much on a sore spot, as it might be thought, as on a gap in Kantian Ethics.

> I like to serve my friends; but alas, I do it from inclination,
> And therefore my lack of virtue often distresses me.
> Nothing else will serve, I must try to despise them,
> And then do with reluctance what duty commands.

Socrates had overlooked that a knowledge about virtue, however thorough, was no guarantee of virtuous actions unless what was known was also approved; and such approval is conditioned by feeling; and Kant overlooks that in order that his imperative shall become active in man, it requires the readiness to acquiesce (which is coloured by feeling) of the person who hears it; it requires Ethical Reason. The man who acts from obedience, even against a principle within him, does so because he cannot do otherwise: and it is equally certain that if he did not do so he must experience the reaction of disobedience, for example, in the shape of the famous "Pangs of Conscience"; and the disposition which causes him to act in this manner is an interest as much as is selfishness or love of domination; only it is of a general nature. But it does remain true that he sides against the whole of his vitality, sacrificing the interests of Releases as well as all merely personal Bonds to the tyranny of one single Bond. The disastrous consequences up to the penultimate act have been understood and set out by Nietzsche with incomparable acumen and brilliance. The theme of the last act is this (as we have already said in Chapter VIII): Man completely deprived of Soul and a pure machine of the will, and (as we may now add), the slave of a relatively small minority of unscrupulous exploiters. This is the end of the "Ethical process" of mankind.

Our conceptual mechanism gives the meaning of *self-control* with amazing clearness; a word which, rightly considered, would betray of itself the existence of two selves (F). If the everyday expression that one must control oneself (or master, overcome, conquer, subdue, etc.) has any sense at all, then it is the appeal of one Ego (imagined as multiple and changing) in man to another and stable Ego. And language also reveals that the latter is the general Ego, when it judges of the man who exercises self-control that he consults his *Reason*, or sees *Reason*. We speak of moderation where this takes place chiefly at the expense of egoism, and of self-conquest or self-abnegation when a passion is suppressed whose unrestrained domination, on the other hand, is described by saying that a man forgets himself. We now turn to the personal Bonds.

Egoism is the true stage where human behaviour plays its part; consequently an approximately complete enumeration of the egoisms to which language has given a name would overload and distort our main Table; accordingly we enumerate them on a second Table and refer chiefly to this latter in the text. When the Ego stands contrasted to a world of eternal change isolated and itself incapable of change, then its will to exist becomes, in relation to the totality, a will to devour, and, since it has not the power to swallow up, it becomes will to destroy. In order that an affirmative will to destroy shall actually occur, three conditions must be fulfilled which are rarely found together; extensive atrophy of all releasing driving forces, complete or nearly complete lack of spiritual Bonds, and, finally, untrammelled activity, which, in turn demands urges which are strong, but are almost bare of quality. To Egoism which cannot be further determined, we give the epithet of "neutral" or "general". When it does happen to exist, then we have the essentially wicked man of whom Shakespeare drew the prototype in Richard III; and this wicked man is simply inhabited by a will "in itself" which utilizes energies of which a steady current is supplied by a vitality which has strong impulses, but wholly lacks Soul (I, 1, *a*). "History" provides scattered examples among temporal and spiritual politicians, among captains, conquerors, Caesars, and despots (for example, Ivan called the Terrible); among such scourges as Trenck, Colonel of Pandoors, and among great criminals of the grand style where such classical poisoners as Gesche and Brinvilliers must not be forgotten. A smaller portion of this will is very common, and that not only among criminals, but among perfectly respectable servants of Mammon. An interesting and not too rare combination is that of a slight element of negation with the hysterical character, an excellent sample of which may be consulted in Dostoievsky's "Stepantchikovo Village".

Here, as elsewhere, the limits are variable in practice because the relation between every driving force and the contrary driving forces is variable from degree to degree; however, we must carefully distinguish from the variant of neutral Egoism which we have just been considering, the other variant which results when strong spiritual Bonds are added: for in this case specimens of the variant, in so far as they are reasonably well characterized, have a very different appearance. Activity, enterprise, and the urge to do have their place here—typical properties of all record-breakers (among whom are many engineers and discoverers with their will to "conquer" the highest peaks, the deepest depths of the sea, the inhospitable poles and deserts, the air, the moon, and so forth), and of most *entrepreneurs* (I, 1, *b*). The former would not be rightly understood if they were to be derived from a preponderance of ambition, and the latter would be wholly misunderstood if they were derived from preponderant selfishness. In both it is the hunger of will which craves satisfaction, often at the expense of personal safety: releasing driving forces naturally participate in greatly varying degrees, but within the range of spiritual, and especially of ethical, Bonds. The choice of a field of activity, on the other hand, generally depends partly on accident and partly on the talents of the willing entity.

It must also be mentioned that the power of will may strike inwards, and can thus produce fanatics of abnegation and of self-torture and fakirs. If we compare what has been set out in Chapter VIII about the evolutionary history of the hysterical character (or at least of the European variety) and set by the side of this our observations on the "categorical imperative", then we shall know why of the three spiritual Bonds the ethical Bond stands nearest to neutral Egoism, and shall hold a clue which will allow us to understand a series of facts which occur again and again, and never fail to baffle ethical theorists: namely, the readiness to will of ethical natures and their tendency (disguised under illusions about perfecting the world) to act upon men (zeal to convert, pious agitation, proselytizing activity, Christian missionary ardour, Salvation Army, and so forth); and we shall also understand their usually remarkable incapacity to take even a faintly independent interest in the extra-human world. "Ethical" man and "wicked" man are two divergent branches on one tree, the tree of will, and theoretical Ethics in the end provide us with a corroboration, since its central problem is precisely the avoidance of evil. ("The good—this is certain—is the evil we omit to do.")

If the question were asked, What must be the nature of the stratum of urges in order that it shall provide the best soil for the development of neutral Egoisms? then we have already furnished the most general answer in showing that there is soul-less strength of urges, which, according to our former explanation, is manifested also in the ease with which qualities can split off. We now, however, define it more closely by its main symptom, which is never lacking—the exclusion of sex. When impulses can be, and have been, split, the surest sign is sexuality which has lost the element of love, and this must not be looked for among "natural men" or cannibals, but among degenerate members of "civilization".49 This suggestion must suffice, for a proof would take us further into pure biology than is allowed by the scope of this book. Those who know how to use it will easily discover why all European Ethics, at least, aim first at the extermination of evil, and next at the excommunication of sexuality, or, more exactly, its degradation to the place of instrument of common utility which alone is held to justify it.

Hitherto we have dealt with will so to speak in the abstract, and consequently we were obliged to bring into play the relation of vitality, with its foundation, to certain contrary driving forces, in order to be able to name certain qualities which are common in current speech. Accordingly we have set out, on the Table of Egoisms, the relative weakness of contrary interests (namely, lack of spiritual Bonds and lack of Releases) under Section V as "facilitative driving forces", in contrast to the main Table, where the lack in Releases at least forms an independent group. This is done in order to throw light on Egoism in general from the point of view of a weakness of capacity for devotion. Now when we would judge individual cases it is necessary, in order to estimate driving forces, also to estimate the respective contrary driving forces: but such an estimation is not required where interests are merely to be designated, as soon as we enter the sphere of particular Egoisms.

It need no longer be emphasized that each particular driving force demands a corresponding vital substratum, and it is understood from the beginning that for this reason it can threaten its bearer with subjection and may counteract his "liberty". But before we discuss this we must adapt our definition of Egoism to the far more common occurrence where it is bound to the world, and therefore is no longer capable of supporting a will to destruction, a case of which we have already given an instance in the urge to action. Essentially negative will, in proportion as it is attached to the world of the senses, becomes will to power, and since for Ego all non-Ego is an antagonistic power, becomes will to overpower. For vital reasons the latter sometimes takes the form of the wish to have, and sometimes of the wish to excel.

The wish to have is based upon acquisitive animal urges such as are manifested in the satisfaction of hunger, thirst, and sexual desire; hence among the Egoisms which have a place here we must look for the search for food and numerous conditions governing behaviour in the relations of the sexes. But possessive impulses, having the nature of urges, come and go in rhythmical intervals, and give way to indifference as soon as they have been satisfied, whereas acquisitive interests aim at possession, which has nothing to do with the satisfaction of urges: any interference is experienced as an interference with the personal sphere of power, and there is a corresponding reaction. And here we must note once for all that the wish to have is one side of *all* specialized Egoisms, and so is the wish to excel, and if in spite of this we distinguish between the two respective classes of interests, we do so with regard merely to a more or less noticeable preponderance of one or the other side; and in doing so we follow the names which language has prepared, and whose sensitiveness for shades of meaning has been reached by no thinker, still less excelled.

In the animal world the possessive impulses have as wide a habitat as the animal world itself, whereas cases of unconscious urge to excel (which do occur) play a modest part; and the most original form of all human Egoism is the will to appropriate which (apart from the need for food) awakens already in a child of one year, and never is lacking even in the communal organizations of ancient village life with their apparently communistic concepts of property. If we imagine the primitive will to possess raised to the power of dominant driving force, then its aim is revealed in those actions of collecting, gathering, and saving which can be traced far back in racial history, and are (for example) the foundation of the saga-motif of fights for treasuries of gold, whereas they are far from being the foundation of a businesslike utilization of the accumulated hoards. Thus every urge to collect has its place here, among them such qualities as curiosity or desire for knowledge, as also, of course, those impulses which partake of avarice and greed (I, 2, *a*; second Table in each case).

This offers us an opportunity of correcting a mistake contained in earlier editions of this work. Even among primitive peoples, who are not acquainted with our ideas of property, a great warrior's bow and spear accompany him into the grave and his charger is sacrificed; but the ultimate cause of such a practice is not egoistic will to possess, any more than it was an egoistic will to possess that could cause the man who was fascinated by the jewel to take it: the cause is Eros. There is an Eros of home and ground, of habitation, household animal, of memory of the tool which we made and which by long handling has become bound to us, of the tree which we planted and cultivated, and so forth; and in principle there may be an Eros of any object of perception which has become the symbol of some happy or some sorrowful stage in our life's pilgrimage. Hence any dependence which can be derived therefrom has as much to do with Egoism as has maternal love—that is, nothing. If they are to be called Bonds, they are erotic Bonds, that is, Bonds not on the side of the Ego (whether spiritual or personal), but of Life. With facts of this class we juxtaposed the other fact, that in certain circumstances the passionate miser will rather allow himself to be killed than surrender his treasures, and thence came to the faulty conclusion that not avarice only, but every so-called Passion* is to be explained by some form or other of the subordination to Life, and to look for its foundation on the side of the Releases. We shall now show what is the truth of the matter.

The word "Sucht", which formerly meant disease, has an ambiguous meaning in modern usage. It is used sometimes to denote passions whose objects are considered ethically worthless, and sometimes to denote an incurable dependence of their victim upon them (which could equally well be expressed by "servitude"), while the objects are comparatively indifferent. The first meaning gives us no cause to distinguish between "Sucht" and other passions, but the other leads us to a totally different set of facts which have nothing to do with the capacity for passion even when in an individual case they are complicated by passions.

However great are the differences between them, Stirner and Nietzsche (in spite of a tempting appearance to the contrary) betray their fundamentally ethical orientation by the demand which each makes, that we must hold ourselves in hand. Neither would "be the slave of any appetite", to use Byron's expression, and each would have declined to make another poet's saucy aphorism—"If 'tis our wish, it is our duty"—the guiding line of his actions. In *Beyond Good and Evil* Nietzsche pronounces himself as follows: "Cleave to no person, however beloved—every person is a prison. ... Cleave not to your country, however much it suffers or may need you. ... Cleave to no commiseration ... cleave to no science, though it should entice with the most precious ... discoveries. Cleave not to your own detachment. ... Cleave not to your virtues, and do not sacrifice your whole self to one part—for instance, to your 'hospitality'. ... Know to preserve yourself—the hardest test of independence". And Stirner asks: "Who makes sacrifices? Only he does so completely who sacrifices every thing to one passion. Does not the lover who leaves father and mother, and faces every danger and deprivation in order to reach his end, make

---

* German, "Sucht".

sacrifices? Or the ambitious man who sacrifices all things to one passion, or the miser who denies himself everything in order to amass a hoard, or the lover of pleasure, and so forth? ... And again, while making their sacrifice, are they not selfish, or egoists? They have only one ruling passion, and therefore they care only to satisfy one, but for that they care all the more zealously: they are absorbed in it. All their actions are Egoism, but they are a limited Egoism—they are possession." For, according to Stirner, I can pursue my end with the most passionate eagerness, and can yet know this about myself: "I remain at the same time chilly, cold, and incredulous towards my end, and am its most implacable foe: I am its owner, and therefore its judge."[50]

It will be noted that both these thinkers demand of man that same peculiar "freedom" and autonomy which, from Pythagoras to Kant, has been demanded by every teacher of ethics; but the extreme individualistic turn which they give to their demand allows us an important insight, apart from all imperatives. Stirner, with his examples, makes the same mistake which we made, only conversely: he counts acts of love as part of "limited Egoism", just as we attempted to count acts of avarice as one of the love-like kinds of subjection to Life. But, apart from this, he agrees with Nietzsche in the curious view that one should be able to command one's driving forces instead of following them. Can this be? The answer is yes and no. No, because that which commands is itself in turn a driving force which we have not acquired and whose presence we have not ordered, but which we find as a datum like the driving forces which we command. Yes, because with an action like that of a driving force there does co-exist something like a band which holds together our being, whether it has taken the form of a maxim (in the ethical teacher, whether a Kant, a Stirner, or a Nietzsche), or merely acts without principle (in the unreflected man of deeds). If we call it our personality we must, however, call it personality only in so far as it happens to culminate in the will to assert precisely this personality: for it can also mean a deliberate surrender of this will, when (as with many women) we make the sacrifice of living for another; although this too could be possible only by virtue of a driving force which had proved stronger than the will to preserve our own nature. If we had wished to give a place to assertion of personality in our first Table, it would have been inserted between right and left side, but with a considerable displacement towards the right, because it is the will which comes next to the neutral Egoisms—the will to unconditional retention of one's own vitality. It is the unique nature of our being which, in this vitality, awakes and makes violent claims to consideration and to *Being*.[51] The right of self-determination, the love of freedom and of independence are the properties most closely related to the assertion of personality, and those which serve it best.

But it is clear from this that there are other kinds of possession besides that which is denoted by the Greek Enthusiasm—possession not in the sense of the domination of a vital force which bursts the Ego, but of utter servitude to the tyrannical despotism of a single driving force. And here we reflect that, if it is certain that passions are apt to turn into servitudes, it is equally certain that it is not the element of devotion in the passion but the violence of the will of the Ego with which it awakens, which gives to the goal of the passion the powers of a despot, bearing the form of an Ego, to whom the being of the victim of the passion is surrendered unresisting. If this is how we are to understand a Passion—and perhaps this agrees best with the modern meaning of the word—then every Passion without exception is an Egoism, but a "limited Egoism" as Stirner calls them or, less ambiguously, an Egoism of this or that side of character to which the being of a man may surrender, often to the degree of self-annihilation. In "Passion" the craving has become an affair of the egoistic will, and the will has become a fanatic having one goal, and one goal only in mind. To explain the "servitude" of a Passion, we must say, not that character has become subjected to Life, but that the equilibrium of its component parts has been profoundly shaken.

If now we revert to the collecting urge, it is clear that compared with it selfishness, sense of gain, and aptitude for business (I, 2, *b*) must be called far more abstract forms of the appropriative interest which can flourish only under a capital system of economics, while the primitive collecting urge flourishes under a hand-to-mouth system. We have been unable to discover differences between the sexes with regard to the degree of appropriative interest; but it seems to us that among women parsimonious economy prevails, and, among men, greed. We now pass over to the interests to excel, but must first remark that the urge to domination (I, 2, *c*) has a far smaller share in them than in the appropriative will. Dominative personalities desire to dispose of alien spheres of volition much as an owner disposes of his "property", and in typical cases care very little whether their claims to domination are approved or not—in accordance with Caligula's defiant motto: *Oderint dum metuant.* On the other hand, rivalries immediately come into play when one dominative character collides with another of approximately the same power, since in each the desire is raised to excel the other in demonstrating his power. In principle, the will to excel extends to every possible object. If a child is given a present, his companion also wants a present, and feels a peculiar kind of satisfaction if his own present turns out to be even bigger—and so on. First we must open an approach to an understanding to the will to excel in general.

The person as Ego is essentially will, and its self-assertion grows with the effective radius of the will; thus, its power and capacity allow it to experience among other things a superiority (in whatever direction); and the tendency to compare the size of different spheres of power is inseparable from the existence of an Ego as such. But the egoistic feeling of self-importance is complicated with this fact. The popular division of all feelings into feelings of pleasure and of displeasure is as instructive as it is far removed from the truth in its complete blindness for other varieties of feeling. The learned observers paid attention only to the Ego-aspect of feelings, and accordingly they could not but reach a series in the form of a scale with definite polar ends, since will (alike in greatest and least things) is either satisfied (in success) or else is foiled (in failure). The so-called feelings of pleasure are feelings of success, and those of displeasure are feelings of failure. The greater the success, the more satisfied and coloured with pleasure is the feeling which announces it; and the greater the failure, the more dissatisfied, disturbed, disappointed, and coloured the displeasure. But success is a proof of the power, as failure is a proof of the impotence, of the Ego, and therefore the feeling of success is the basis of self-esteem, and the feeling of failure the basis of every diminution of self-esteem. Hence it emerges that every entity possessing Ego must needs strive after self-esteem, and strive against every diminution of it. Hence human will to excel achieves a scope which is unknown (for example) to the whole animal world; and hence its supreme importance for the world of Egoisms, of which a few examples will now convince us.

Even the most complete rogue runs a risk of losing part of his self-confidence, and consequently of his self-esteem, if several of his misdeeds fail in quick succession, and the displeasure which goes with such reverses becomes more acute by comparison with a "colleague" who was brilliantly successful in similar enterprises. It may be a point of honour with a burglar not to make some elementary blunder which may lead to his capture. This contains one condition of the practice of assigning values to which it is due that, in order to value, we must grade the object of our valuation. The other condition which causes us to value what in itself does not admit of valuation, namely, qualities, is based upon demands of the Spirit which in turn lead us back to compulsions of experience. This can be tested upon any object of valuation. If we contrast with the perfect rogue the virtuous person (and by virtue anybody is free to imagine whatever the word conveys to him), then it is equally true of the latter that he loses self-esteem whenever he has swerved in the least from virtue; and again, in view of this, the most painful sting in his displeasure will be the knowledge that there are people of greater merit than he. Even if virtue is his only aim, still each person of greater virtue is a diminution of his merit, as conversely his more tested virtue diminishes the merit of the other. We have treated elsewhere in detail of the psychology of the urge of self-esteem, and therefore confine ourselves here to a summary Table (No. III).[52] It is enough if our examples show why the egoistic will might feel itself compelled (among other things) to desire to excel in *every* field of activity.

Meanwhile we distinguish, in Striving, between the *immediate* participation of the urge of self-esteem, and of the desire to excel, and that which is merely *mediated*. Who strives after virtue is immediately directed upon virtue or, if he is directed upon the virtuous man, then the latter is simply his model; and he is in a position to compare the value of his virtuousness with that of others only incidentally. On the other hand, if a man strives after recognition, his immediate aim is the increase or confirmation of his self-esteem, and to effect this he uses a peculiar instrument at which we must look somewhat more closely. We need only say the words, "I think I may respect myself for such and such qualities", and it becomes obvious that in self-esteem the Ego is duplicated, the estimating Ego taking up the part of judge over an Ego which is to be estimated; and accordingly in the state of self-estimation, our Ego has taken up the position of the foreign Ego. The impossibility of estimating personality without at least an imaginary pluralization of personalities becomes finally clear when we consider that values in general demand distinctions of value, and similarly values of Ego, Egos different in value. Hence self-valuation is self-comparison even if the other Ego with which the comparison is made is only the desired image (ideal) of our Ego, or the Ego of our own past, or the phantasm of the Ego of a god. But evidently this assumes a standard common to a plurality of Egos, or, in other words, a capacity whose validity in fact is recognized by two Egos, and in principle might be recognized by any number; and in so far the impulse of self-estimation already is a kind of impulse to be recognized as standard. If we add that, apart from rarest and most exceptional spirits, man does not generally determine the standard (= the criterion), but takes it over from the social unit in which he grew up, we shall understand why his self-esteem could flourish upon such approval, or conversely could be impaired by the expressed disapproval of members of the group. In appraising himself, he thus plays the part of a foreign Ego over against himself, and he will be likely to confuse the foreign Ego, whose approval cannot be suspected of the partiality of the proper Ego when the latter appraises, with the latter in so far as its praise and approval go to meet his interest of self-exaltation. To this is added an immediate result of his will to power: for recognized superiority is, in *some* respect, actual superior power. This is proved by the opposite case; we have only to consider the actual disadvantages which may result when a man has obviously "made a fool of himself".

Nobody is completely indifferent to the approval and disapproval of every man; but different characters vary enormously in the degree in which they stand in need of recognition. Pathic cases, cases of possessedness (both on the grand scale) and extremely blasé persons are almost completely immune from applause. For we may remark here that there exists a *Pathos* of self-estimation having pride and humility for poles, before which, while receptivity for applause is undiminished, the satisfaction of the desire for distinction sinks until it is barely agreeable, and barely accepted for that reason. On the other hand, where a man is the slave of a single driving force, receptivity for applause degenerates into indifference, and the same applies to the blase type. The following types of character consequently do not, or hardly, require recognition: those who serve a "destiny" or "mission" (whether in fact they have or only imagine that they have one), those who are wholly bound by love of their task, who are filled by their "work in life", those whose life is devoted to a memory or to their "God"; but those also who are victims of a Passion or of fanaticism and those who seek only quiet, whether dissolution or extreme

THE SCIENCE OF CHARACTER

concentration be their aim. In spite of all the differences between them, they have a certain unsociability (or nonsociability) in common, and hence their self-esteem (of which they too are not devoid) depends on the success or failure of some undertaking, or on the undisturbed duration of a state which has displaced in them almost every other movement of life; and hardly, if at all, depends on a comparison of their own active and passive powers with other persons of a somewhat similar nature. They, too, do not escape numerous fluctuations in self-estimation, nor do they escape the need to compare; but the drama has become internal instead of external; one state is measured against the other, and the man's own Ego is still his chief rival. Much the same is true of the dominating type, which is essentially lonely.[53] Conversely the need for applause grows with sociable tendencies or (to put it with Nietzschean lack of politeness) with the herd nature in man; two arteries feed it, either of which may prevail: feelings of personal inadequacy which are generally not confessed and put self-esteem in need of an external prop, and the will to superiority over others who afford a criterion for comparison (I, 2, *d*). Which artery has the fuller flow results from the reactive forms of the driving force, to which we shall soon return.

In respect to the will to dominate, sexual distinctions cannot be shown to exist in characters: but ambition is a typically masculine Egoism, as also, of course, is vanity. One has only to stay in a school playing-ground where the boys are playing and fighting, until they notice that attention is being paid to them, and immediately one or the other will show off, whether in noisiness, running, or wrestling with a companion, and, on succeeding, will not spare glances which silently demand applause. The unconscious precursor to active will for distinction is found in the animal world in the striking gorgeousness of the male (cock's crest, lion's mane, many colours of the drake, etc.), which is generally misinterpreted as beauty, while in fact it serves the pride of the male and puts the accent, so to speak, on his superior strength. Accordingly among primitive races self-adornment flourishes entirely on the male side, and is practised quite without regard to our ideas of beauty (artificial distortion of the head, knocking out of the front teeth, piercing of nose and lobes of the ears, placing pegs in the lips, bizarre and exceedingly clumsy crowns of hair, excessively painful tattooing, etc.): it denotes distinction, victory, rank, dignity, privilege, power, and superiority. It is decoration which provides the distinction between the different ages—and between warriors, chieftains, and priests. It is a trophy which draws attention, talisman, and proof of capability, and is analogous to military signs of rank or such honourable marks as students' scars. The road from primitive to civilized man was, for the male, a road of desensualization or of internalization (if that be preferred) of his ambition: formerly he was proud of the feathers which decorated him, now he is proud of his Spirit; an unpleasant and dangerous exchange which, far more than the appropriative instinct, selfishness, or love of domination threatens the gravest injury to the interest in things.

To the masculine desire for distinction there corresponds on the feminine side the desire to please, which must not be confused with it (I, 2, e). The urge for recognition does not say, and does not generally even mean, but does act in conformity with the judgment, "I am more than you", and in conformity with the demand, "Bow before my superiority". The desire to please does not say and does not generally even mean, but does act in conformity with the judgment, "I am more attractive than others", and in conformity with the demand, "Like and prefer me". It is not easy to determine whether, and if so how much of, this property belonged to woman rather than to man originally: but it is certain that the germ contained in woman was nourished and reared by a social order where marriage customs are based upon a veiled purchase of husbands. This produced an essential change in the form in which the desire to please manifested itself. The original desire of adornment in women is (in our opinion) closely related to the desire for beauty (which is quite obscure as yet) which, however, during and since the

Hellenic period became the occupation of artists, and has since been passed on to Western men in a vastly more abstract form. We do not here approach more closely to the Greek idea of beauty which has dominated to this day, and merely remark that in opposition to it, the feminine joy in beauty, together with an urge for neatness, comfort, and homeliness merges into a relation, which can be derived from the profoundest depths, to certain peculiar objects, such as the world of flowers in particular. A woman who crowns herself with wreaths or otherwise adorns herself with flowers is not following the desire to please but, if we like to put it that way, a feminine artistic impulse. Now, in accordance with the development which we have just indicated, the element of wooing, which is of a totally different nature, has become attached to this, and inevitably caused adornment and finally the wish for adornment to be adapted to masculine tastes, whence there resulted a state of affairs which may most briefly be described by saying that women are the fancies of men. This fact, too, offers a plus-aspect beside the minus-aspect. The latter is clear: woman, as the toy of ever more rapidly changing fashions, and as the mannequin of man has lost that preserving sense which particularly enabled her to be the depository of customs and habits; and has cultivated her imitativeness immoderately, and to the degree of slavishness, losing at the same time independence of judgment, and in the first place independence of judgment of beauty. On the other side woman excels man in the descending road of evolution at each point and in many respects by as much as fancies are apt to be more precious and perfect than the mind which originates them. If he desires her modest and draped, she will be so; if he desires her bold and appearing in dressed nudity, she will fulfil the wish: but she will always wear that aura which is peculiar to phantasms, and alone allows one style or the other to become erotic stimulus. Remarkably little has been changed in this by the growing compulsion to work, and by their masculinization, due to a profound change in male instincts. This might tempt us to peculiar considerations about the nature of femininity; but these would take us away from our subject. In a more *spiritual* form the desire to please presents itself as the will for popularity, which also forms no inconsiderable or unimportant proportion of masculine vanity. Those in whom this desire exists are far more easily moved by flatteries by reason of the Egoisms *d* and *e*, than by *a*, *b*, and *c*.

Here we must make good an omission. Our present classification of Egoism, according to its objects, crosses an entirely different classification according to the different kinds of egoistic activity. In this respect we distinguish between spontaneous, passive, and reactive Egoism as the main groups, to which must be added a subsidiary group, the isolated Egoisms, of which we shall speak below. Spontaneous Egoisms aim at the extension of the power of the proper person or at the extensions of the Ego (I), the passive at preservation of power = driving forces, and preservation of the Ego (II), and the reactive at the recovery of losses of power = driving forces for recovery of Ego (III). The impulses for the extension of the Ego with which so far we have exclusively concerned ourselves, of course, never occur without impulses for preservation and recovery; only sometimes one class, and sometimes the other, unmistakably preponderates.

With regard to the preservative driving forces, the Table is self-explanatory. It is obvious that prudence, watchfulness, and calculation can serve personal Ego-assertion in a general manner, while timidity, suspicion, and cunning, etc., do so in a particular direction with particular means, and as the result of an evidently particular mental adaptation. In order that the driving forces for recovery of Ego shall be correctly understood, it must first be remarked that of all the Egoisms, they are most closely intertwined with self-estimations, because no loss of power can take place, or be suspected or anticipated without a concomitant loss of self-confidence. This intertwining makes the reactive Egoisms the most intractable, persistent, and dangerous of all. We must again

distinguish between the general (or neutral) and the
particular forms.

Whether an action takes place under the influence of
enterprise or appropriativeness or selfishness or will to
domination or ambition or desire to please, depends always
upon the goal to reach which was "interesting" for the entity
who willed. The greater the lack of "interest" (the less, that
is, one of the driving forces which we have enumerated, or a
releasing driving force, would have power to bring about the
decision) the more actions should normally be suspended. If,
in spite of this, there persists an interest in the evolution,
then the event of willing becomes dependent and reactive,
for now a stimulus (in the shape of a foreign will, or a
resistance which is experienced like a will) is required in
order that the man's own will shall become actual event—in
the shape of resisting will. Caprice, which was discussed
already in Chapter VIII, does not wholly belong here—its
other half must be classed under the spontaneous impulse
after activity: the classical form of a volition which is wholly
determined from outside and from contradictoriness is
obstinacy (III, 1). "The unconscious aim of obstinacy is to
prove to oneself (and thence to others) that it can, in fact,
will. To supply the lack of a definite striving, and as a
substitute, an undirected urge of this kind achieves reality
only against the striving of another, or, more rarely, against a
man's own desires. The decision of a foreign will here acts as
a challenge to consider not the fact with which it deals, but
to prove that I have a will of my own; and so this will
develops in resistance, and it is overlooked that this, too (but
in a converse manner), is a compliance with a foreign will."⁵⁴
Within reactivity in general (or the reactivity of will as such)
it is possible to distinguish between spontaneous forms like
love of opposition or contradiction, or opinionativeness,
with kindred forms like moody, disagreeable, or pugnacious
tendencies, and passive forms like obstinacy,
insubordination, defiance, mulishness.

We come to more particular forms (III, 2): by the
qualities of the sensitive group (quickness to take offence or

to be injured) we mean the conditions which govern the reaction to disturbances, or to deficient satisfaction, of qualities of the group of ambitions (1, 2, *d*) and of Egoism of the mind (1, 2, *e*); the latter is common with women, the former with men; both are due to secret feelings of inadequacy. It must expressly be emphasized that anybody who cannot forget small injuries, and continually chews the cud of them, is certainly suffering from reactive selfishness. Where there is a more active will to superiority and a corresponding urge to act, the reply to severe disturbances of vanity is given by vengefulness, which often is extremely enduring, but must not be confused with primitive customs of blood-vengeance (an explanation of which would here take us too far). In other respects it is best to begin with envy. Envy is the reply of selfishness to the shock which it suffers from a comparison of a man's own possessions (whether material or corporeal, mental or spiritual) with those (whether they be real or imaginary) of a foreign Ego: and the sting of envy lies in the fact that the perception of a man's own deficiency serves to hurt his self-esteem; and accordingly the excess of the object of envy is felt as a heavy reproach to his own inferiority. The most incurable kind of envy—life-envy—(Ressentiment) has already been dealt with. Now all properties which seek (even indirectly) to disturb, diminish, or end another's happiness or content are in part merely spiritualized forms of envy—like mockery, sarcasm, love of criticizing—and in part resultant symptoms—like the pleasure of another's distress, malice, and treachery. We will devote a short, separate treatment to jealousy.

There are a good many emotions which, though they differ considerably among themselves, must be counted as jealousy: two driving forces invariably have a share in these, but in extremely different degrees: the faculty of love (which lies on the side of the Releases) to some extent and, generally to a very much greater extent, the egoistic will to possess. Proportionately with the former, passionate jealousy will occur, easily leading to dramatic scenes and acts of violence; proportionately with the latter, a kind of jealousy which is akin to grudge and envy, and finds satisfaction in subtle torments which it inflicts on the object of love. In principle, jealousy is the reply which Egoism gives to any irritation of I, 2, *e*; and this means that it is far less a right to dispose of the object of love than the possession of the love which, when endangered (the cause being comparatively indifferent), awakens jealousy. A girl in love can become jealous of the books of her lover if she hears that he prefers to occupy himself with them rather than with her. But when jealousy is caused by a disturbance of the claim to possess love, then it need not be emphasized that a love which is wholly devoted would be incapable of jealousy. ("If I love you, what is that to you?")

Jealousies which are purely of the nature of urges play a great part in the animal kingdom, and allow us to answer two questions in a sense which contradicts the current view. If I stroke a strange dog with whom my own dog has just been romping, then my dog will turn on the strange dog to tear him. Accordingly we cannot restrict jealousy to the field of sexual attraction. It is rather co-extensive with the feelings of attraction, although it is true that in the sphere of sex it assumes a particular colour and an abnormal violence. And, farther, while in the exaltation of passion the jealous man may turn his rage against the object of his love, and Othello may kill his Desdemona, Ferdinand his Louisa, and Don José his Carmen; still, jealousy is not originally turned upon this object, but at the third party, who threatens to steal the love of the beloved object from the person who boasts that he had this love. My own dog, if I pat another, will bite not me but the other dog: and it is equally certain that jealousy is turned against everything which disturbs the possession of love and not against the object of affection. This is the reason why (especially between the sexes) to stimulate some jealousy is a proved method for causing a hesitant love to burst into passion. Jealousy is far from turning of necessity love of the object of affection into hate: it can even intensify love; partly because a belief in the preciousness of the object of love is strengthened when it is seen to be pursued, and partly because the idea of a possible loss of the other's love adds value to it by virtue of the well-known action of contrast.

As we hinted above, it is true that women even more than men tend to demand the possession of love: and if this is true, the faculty for jealousy must be looked for among women more than among men. This is in fact the case, and is generally overlooked chiefly because the jealousy of woman is more skilled in hiding itself than that of man, and manifests itself much less actively. Meanwhile, feminine inclination towards and capacity for intrigue in nine cases out of ten is rooted in jealousy.

Those readers who have followed our argument with any degree of attention will no longer doubt that the field in which all Egoisms alike develop is society. But social emotions presuppose not only spiritual relations, but also vital connections—or a living zone of contact between man and man. As this zone grows weaker and weaker, Egoism is restricted more and more to the person which it inhabits, and he tends increasingly towards self-observation, self-reference, and solitariness, and tends finally to take himself too seriously, and to indulge in a self-exaggeration which easily becomes morbid (IV). It is a curious play of the spirit of language that previously the word idiot, which originally denoted the man who lives privately or for himself, has become the name for simplicity, and even for mental hebetude. As was already stated in an observation, it is entirely the isolation and dissociation of vitalities which can explain this and similar phenomena. All Egoisms can act more easily when there is a lack of spiritual Bonds (that is, where there exist such qualities as unscrupulousness, lack of dignity, or vacillation), and a lack of releasing driving forces (that is, where there exist such qualities as prosiness, lack of sensuousness or of sympathy, coldness, and severity) (V, 1 and 2).

After our somewhat exhaustive consideration of the Bonds, the chief Releases result automatically. If we comprehend them all under the one name of love, then we must distinguish spiritual love (which always requires the mediation of one of the abstract terms—truth, beauty, justice), and love of the person, which always requires the mediation of concrete facts: the former is called enthusiasm, the latter love in the narrower sense or depth of feeling, or, finally, passion. Accordingly, there corresponds to logical reason the love of truth (that is, to the claim to validity of actuality), passionate desire after knowledge, and "love of the work" (main Table A', I); to aesthetic reason the love of beauty or, taken more widely, of the form whose motor aspect is the love of forming, or the creative enthusiasm of the ancients (A', II) and to ethical reason love of justice (but not of so-called levelling justice), and of truthfulness—which is inseparable from it—of which a most important consequence is true loyalty (A', III).

Here the impulse and the capacity must be clearly distinguished. Devotion to reason is no guarantee that we shall find truth, create beauty, or practise justice, any more than an inclination to logical, aesthetic, and ethical criticism guarantees such a discovery. A passionate thirst for truth, with its generalizations which gravitate towards first principles, has had its share in building up the most fatal and persistent heresies; love of beauty, unless ruled by trained good taste, will not escape aberration into mawkishness, exaggeration, or chaos; and an enthusiasm for justice, without adequate strictness against oneself, is always in danger of turning into romantic philanthropy and enthusiasm—an intellectual partiality characteristic of many of the friendships of the second half of the eighteenth century.

The Releases of the personal Ego naturally do not admit a particularization as extensive as that of the personal Bonds. Among their spontaneous forms we may distinguish between love of the extra-personal (B', I, 1) and the human-personal (B', I, 2) worlds. Under the former we cite ancestor-worship, which, in fact, invariably though unconsciously, participates in the enticement exercised by extra-personal images; and by this we do not mean piety towards family traditions and family portraits and the like (which are connected with it only distantly and loosely), still less any belief in ghosts, but the more concrete form of a coherence with the past. Because of its profoundest meaning, Nietzsche would like to call spontaneous love "giving love"; we would prefer to call it surrender, for the gift which it gives is always a gift of self. Thus devotion *can* be the result of every love, but we must not conclude conversely that devotion is always a symptom of love; for, as we know, it may equally well be the symptom of Spiritual Bonds. Among the passive faculties of love, kindness, and benevolence may be expressly noted (B', II). By reactive devotion we mean that love is awakened only by participation in foreign feelings, and develops as it responds to these. This, then, is the place for sympathy, mercy, and compassion and, more or less, for all behaviour-faculties for which the German language has prepared the word "Gemüt"* in the narrower sense.

Our division of Releases into those of the person and those of the spirit of the person has brought us to the lowest, or, if it is preferred, profoundest cause of all the sexual distinctions between characters, upon which we had cause to touch in the course of our work. The typical form in which the male takes part in life is a capacity for inspiration and creative enthusiasm which sacrifices itself in a work and to a cause: the typically feminine form is personal love and motherliness, which is ready to sacrifice its own will to the object of love. Thus when there is mutual love, the woman would have cause to pay a tribute of highest reverence to the inspired flight of the man's spirituality, unattainable to her: and the man to the depth and unselfishness of the woman's soul, which he cannot reach. The reflecting reader will be able to derive from this the difference in the intelligences of each, most of which have already been mentioned.

There are driving forces which facilitate personal self-assertion, and similarly there are driving forces which facilitate personal self-surrender. Among the former, we

* Untranslatable. The nearest equivalent, perhaps, is "heart". —TRANSLATOR'S NOTE.

mentioned the weakness of the dispositions for Releases, and, similarly, among the latter, the weakness of the dispositions for Bonds. We refer to the Table, and here confine ourselves to giving the key-word "selflessness" (C', D'). Finally, as has already been remarked, the side of the Releases is that which is close to impulses and the side of the Bonds that which is distant from them: accordingly, there is an affinity between the former and self-control—like moderation, powers of resistance, self-conquest, restraint, steadfastness (F); and between the latter and weaknesses of self-control, like lack of moderation, of restraint and steadiness, instability and licence. Already the ancients knew that in this human world of Egoisms (which, as things are, have become indispensable), the character which surrenders to nature and the world is endangered by the ἐπικίνδυνον τῆς ἀκολασίας (= danger of licence). But in fact self-indulgence threatens equally the Egoisms, and more especially egoistic sensuousness; we have, therefore, bracketed the two groups, in order to indicate that we merely express kinship of nature without attempting to classify actual events. To classify definitely sensuous driving forces would be an infinite task: we therefore confine ourselves to enumerating a few chief forms, which are self-explanatory (E, E'). The two poles, joy and pain, are common to the right and left side—an indication of the fact that it is the body and not, as is commonly thought, the Soul on which the Spirit immediately rests, and of which those processes which are most important to life are reported by consciousness.[55] The dispositions for emotions proper we have neglected—such as irascibility, poor temper, timidity, and so on, partly because they half belong to properties of structure (excitability of feelings), and partly because their specific half belongs to the outermost circle of character, and, while their influence upon habits of action is quite slight, they are manifested chiefly in properties of behaviour.

The vital background of the man in whom Releases dominate is passivity, in the man in whom Bonds dominate, it is activity. The poles of *Pathos* are horror and bliss, or, in a slighter form, joy (serenity) and grief (gloom); the poles of activity, joy at success, and displeasure at failure; the poles of pathic self-consciousness are pride and humility, and those of active self-consciousness, self-esteem, and diffidence. Now although it is certain that the light pole can never exist without the dark and conversely, still extremely great varieties of character emerge according to the preponderance of the light or the dark pole. Accordingly, we have on the side of Releases the melancholy and even gloomy bearers of metaphysical horror (for example, Lenau or Nietzsche), and the radiant bearers of metaphysical bliss (for example, Mozart and, in part, Goethe); and on the side of Bonds the ever morose and querulous bearers of personal ill-comfort—the depressive type—and the ever cheerful and, at times, actually jolly bearers of personal comfort—the euphoric type. Raised into consciousness, the world-feeling of the pathic type would be expressed in the conviction that actuality is a world of incessant coming and going of soul-bearing prototypes, and that of the active type in the conviction that it is a world of facts which, in principle, may be held fast, conquered, and possessed. The former is turned towards the perishable and the past, as the mother and fountain of his life, into which he shall return; the latter, virile and hostile to tradition, is turned towards the future in which he hopes to persist, whether in the descendants whom he leaves behind, or by virtue of any claims to immortality, or by deeds and achievements through which he thinks to control the future. The works of the pathic type are like the pyramids, memorials and monuments of the dead; those of the active type, useful works like machines.

In view of this, it may be proper to consider at the end how far this book may perhaps be counted a monument of modest scope. An age which is absolutely dependent on Life (and therefore averse from Spirit), and an age which is absolutely dependent on Spirit (and therefore averse from Life)—this was the sense of our ninth chapter—would never produce that kaleidoscopic confusion of personal characters which can result only when Spirit turns towards Life, and

Life towards Spirit, and both—so to say—engage in mutual struggle. But also we stated repeatedly what we now resume in the following words: Unless this struggle is interrupted by long pauses due to incalculable changes in the depths of Life, allowing Life to recover from its exertions, Life must become the victim of complete exhaustion, and before it finally succumbs to this, of a period, which may last a long time, of standardization. It is impossible not to see that "civilized" man, and with him man in general, is rapidly approaching that end.

Already those are exceptional spirits in whom we may look for any independence of judgment. The masses—never, since the existence of mankind, more completely the victims of suggestion than now—have become the toy of that "public opinion" which is produced by the daily Press in the service—it need hardly be said—of the ruling powers of finance. What is printed in the leading papers of the city in the morning is the opinion of nine-tenths of its readers in the evening. America, where more rapid "progress" allows us to foresee the future from day to day, has established a considerable lead in the standardization of thought, work, amusement, and so on. America made war on Germany in honest indignation because it was printed in the newspapers that Prussian militarism wanted to conquer the world and was rioting in devilish crimes: and this was printed in the newspapers because a few high priests of Mammon hoped that American intervention in the war would be a lucrative business for them. Americans thought that they were fighting for pretty phrases like liberty and justice: in fact they were fighting for the increase of the bank reserves. These "free citizens" are in fact puppets who imagine that they are free, and a single glance at American methods of work or American methods of amusement is enough to show that *l'homme machine* is no longer imminent, but has already become reality there.

Some students of genetics seem to be dimly aware that this will be the end, first of white man, and of black and yellow man only a few lengths later. (We do not speak of the primitive races; for they are already at their last gasp.) But this is of no particular interest, since in the end the destruction of all is inevitable. It is not this which depresses us here, for nobody can tell whether a completely mechanized mankind will last for hundreds or for thousands of years: we are concerned with mechanization itself. It is the tragic fate of knowledge—of true knowledge and not of imaginary, which merely furnishes the intellectual apparatus for engineers and mechanicians—that, so to speak, it plays the funeral march which accompanies the departure, if not the burial, of a vital essence. We know only that we are no longer. "Somnium narrare vigilantis est" (Seneca). It is like history, only, delving incomparably deeper, and, showing behind daily events their hidden sense, and between the pageant of "world-history" the stage manager, it is a sort of chronicle of what has been. And thus, unless we are mistaken, the process of giving an outline to characterology will also be the beginning of its end, and our successors must make haste: otherwise, instead of a world of human characters, they will grasp only a quickly fading memory.

CHAPTER X NOTES

[49] For although among primitive peoples sexuality generally shows slight and often shows no traces of the amatory passion with which we are familiar, still among their numerous customs and practices which govern sexual intercourse we shall find plenty which are direct enough: but we shall always find them related in the closest manner to a general craving for festivity, and therefore to genuine sensuality. But it is this precisely which the civilized sensualist lacks. His sensuality—in so far as any remains in him—is uprooted, and ranges the abstract peaks of an "art" (especially music) which has become an article of luxury and a fashion; and this deflowered sexuality has become (to put it bluntly and tangibly) a localized irritant (which is not incompatible with a craving for it which often is unceasing) felt as a "disturbance" by Spirit and, accordingly, approved of, if at all, not for its own sake, and not without side-glances of an "uneasy conscience".

[50] At bottom this is will to power, and even one form of the desire to dominate; as is irrefutably certain if we observe how Nietzsche uses the same idea in order to interpret his view of Frederick the Great, whom he admired. In *Beyond Good and Evil* (209) he attributes to Frederick the "scepticism of daring virility" which "is most closely akin to genius for war and conquest, and first made its entry into Germany in the shape of Frederick the Great". "This scepticism", he continues, "disdains and charms at once; it undermines and seizes; it has no faith, but does not at the same time lose itself; it gives a dangerous liberty to spirit, but sternly controls the heart; it is the German form of scepticism, which, in the shape of the spirit of Frederick, but developed and raised to its most spiritual form, subjects Europe for a long period to the German spirit and to its critical and historical doubt". But Nietzsche could not be the terrible sceptic and incorruptible self-student which he was without knowing the *real* facts, although thereby he once more renders doubtful all his triumphs of independence. For in *Daybreak* (109), under the heading "Self-control and moderation and their ultimate motive", he develops six "distinct methods to fight the violence of an urge", and then continues: "It is not in our power that we shall will to fight the violence of an urge, nor is the choice of the method in our power, or the success with which it meets. Rather, in the whole process our intellect obviously is the blind instrument of another urge which is the rival of that one of which the violence plagues us; whether it is the urge after quiet, or fear of shame and other evil results, or love. Thus, while 'we' think that we are complaining of the violence of an urge, it is at bottom the one urge which is complaining of another; that is, the fact that we perceive that we suffer from such a violence presupposes that there is another urge of equal or greater violence, and that a fight is impending in which our intellect must choose sides." We shall immediately revert to these facts.

[51] Nietzsche was unrivalled in objectifying and illustrating states of experience: perhaps he has given no finer (certainly he has no more vivid) presentation of this racial will, this will for the race's spread and

perpetuation, than in his praise of Genoa (*The Gay Science*, 291): "For some good while I have looked at this town, at its country houses and gardens, and the wide circle of habitable hills; and in the end I must say that I see visions of past generations. This region is haunted by the images of bold and self-reliant men. … I always see the builder; I see his eyes resting on all that has been built around him, far and near, on town, sea, and the lines of the hills; and I see his glance exerting power and conquest; all this he wishes to make part of *his* plan, and in the end to make his property by making it part of the plan. All this region is overrun by this glorious and insatiable love of possession and of booty; and, as these men acknowledged no boundary in the distance, and in their thirst for something new set a new world beside the old, so even at home each man revolted against his neighbour and invented a means to express his superiority, and to interpose between himself and his neighbour his personal infinity. Each made a second conquest of his country for himself: he overpowered it by his architectural thought and made it an object on which his house might feast its eyes. An admirable cunning of phantasy causes him to desire to found afresh all this, if only in thought; to lay his hand and to impress his mind upon it, if only for a moment on some sunny afternoon when his insatiable and melancholy soul is sated for once and nothing may show itself to his eyes but what is his own." Hence precisely it may be inferred how much will to power, that is will, that is Spirit, lies in the will to self.

52 *Die psychologischen Errungenschaften Nietzsches.* The modalities of self-consciousness on Table III are not enumerated quite irregularly, but with a certain amount of method: but this method does not claim to be so strict as to exclude other classifications. Especially—(to prevent a misunderstanding which we have known to occur)—the classification on each side of the Table is independent—so that the "forms of manifestation" enumerated on the right do not correspond to the "forms and degrees" on the left.

53 The pride of very proud men is perpetually at war with the urge after appreciation and applause which by natural necessity is part of their own need of self-esteem, and passionately looks for a solution. Is there such a solution? Careful reflection shows that with every attempted and every imaginable evasion we only deceive ourselves. It is probably clear why the forms just mentioned of a relative surrender of applause do not really lead out of the circle of the need of esteem. A mere dullness to applause, or a frigid indifference, does not prove that the inner claim to *value* has been overcome, but only that a certain deafness to its appeal has arisen. But the pathic and dominative nature carry their judge in their own hearts; and his claims are more rigorous than those of the Spirit of society, his approval and applause can be spared even less than the applause of group-mates. Both Nietzsche and Stirner were on the search for a solution, and expended the strongest powers of their spirit upon it; but they, too, achieved no more than subterfuges, which, however, may be counted truly splendid monuments of pride. For Nietzsche, under the stress of the struggle which we have indicated, invented the dictator of values; the "inventors of new values" are,

for him, truly autocratic and master spirits. But, although they may be autocratic in the art of invention, they straightway became slaves of their inventions, for no sooner has the new "table of values" been produced than it makes its threatening claims upon him who himself wrote the text upon it. Stirner again declares the whole world to be the property of the one, but cannot escape measuring all opinion by this one opinion: he thus postulates this opinion and despises all those who are the slaves of laws which are thrust upon them. And, if an attempt were made to cling to the consciousness of one's own uniqueness, a *value* could be wrung from it only at the price of a suppositious comparability with other unique entities; whereas any uniqueness which was thought to be part of it would have removed it altogether from the sphere of valuation. I am certainly unique, but that fact is not enough to give me the smallest claim to value. From all this it emerges that the fact of Ego is indissolubly connected with those other facts, the urge after self-esteem, and the desire for appreciation ; and we escape their demands only in proportion to our escape from the Ego itself, or, in other words, to an approach to states of ecstasy. The ecstatic man alone knows nothing of impulses of self-esteem and desire for appreciation; but this is so only because he is no longer conscious of his Ego.

[54]   *Graphologische Monatshefte*, 1903, p. 57. The *Graphologische Monatshefte* have been out of print for many years, and can hardly be bought even at second-hand. But certain passages to which we refer (for example, the present) are to be found in the treatises which we have published together in the volume called *Zur Ausdruckslehre und Charakterkunde*, published by Niels Kampmann, Heidelberg.

[55] *Vom Wesen des Bewusstseins.*

TABLE I

SYSTEM OF DRIVING FORCES

SPIRITUAL DRIVING FORCES

RELEASES.	BONDS.
A'. Spiritual Self-Devotion = Capacity for enthusiasm.	**A. Spiritual Self-Assertion = Reason.**
I. Thirst for Truth. Intellectual passion. Urge after knowledge. Devotion to the task.	I. Theoretic Reason = Will to make the world intelligible. Love of facts. Analytic will. Critical tendency.
II. Formative Impulse. Love of beauty. Creative urge. Formative urge (enthusiasm).	II. Æsthetic Reason = Will to make comprehensible the world of intuition. Tendency to uniformity and application of rules. Sense for organization, will to simplify, need of "style".
III. Love of Justice. Passion for truthfulness. "Spiritual nobility." Original loyalty. (Dangers: "Schwärmerei," utopianism.)	III. Ethical Reason = Will to equality (Humanity). Feeling of "Ought". "Categorical imperative." Sense of duty. Conscience (sense of remorse). Impartiality.

PERSONAL DRIVING FORCES

B'. Personal Self-Devotion = Depth of feeling (capacity for passion).

I. Spontaneous Tendencies Towards Devotion.

1. To the extra-personal world. Love of nature, of home and country, of animals, of plants. Love of a made article, of a memory. Ancestor worship (pietas). Love of the universe ("cosmic passion").

2. To the human-personal world. Passionateness. "Capacity for love." Urge to admire and to venerate. Tendency to adoration. Ardour, self-surrender, love which gives itself. (Liberality, love of giving, prodigality.) Motherliness. Tendency to self-immolation.

B. Personal Self-Assertion = Egoism (selfishness).

I. Driving Forces Towards the Extension of the Ego. (Spontaneous Egoisms.)

1. Neutral or general. Enterprise. Lust of success. Love of action. Aggressiveness. Reforming zeal. (Partly on the side of Releases; Impulse after self-determination and liberty, love of independence.)

2. Particular.
   (a) Acquisitiveness, possessiveness.
   (b) Selfishness, love of earning.
   (c) Will to dominate, to patronize.
   (d) Ambition; urge after recognition (vanity).
   (e) Egoism of the "Heart". Desire to please.

II. Passive Tendencies Towards Devotion.
Benevolence, kindliness, clemency, warmth, faithfulness, gentleness.
(Contemplation, retrospectivity.)
III. Reactive Tendencies Towards Devotion.
Capacity for sympathy; to share joy and sorrow. Mercy; readiness to self-denial. "Heart."

C'. *Lack of Spiritual Bonds.*
Unreasonableness. Rashness, "lightheartedness".

D'. *Lack of Egoisms.*
Unselfishness, selflessness.
Compliance, long suffering, patience (modesty). Carelessness, unsuspecting nature, confidence.

E'. *Sensuous Need of Devotion.*
Love of living, desire of intoxication (or of narcosis).
Passion of self-surrender.

F'. [*Weaknesses of Self-Control.*]
Inflammability, immoderation, lack of restraint or bond. Instability.

Fundamental note of life: Passivity. Belief in the past. Reverence.
Poles of moods: Horror (melancholy)—Bliss (serenity).
Poles of self-estimation: Pride—Humility.
Fundamental conviction: Actuality = a world of appearances having souls: it happens and cannot be possessed.

II. Driving Forces for Preservation of the Ego. (Passive Egoisms.)
Prudence. Watchfulness. Calculation. Suspicion. Distrust. Timidity (Shame). Artfulness. Cunning. Hypocrisy.
III. Driving Forces for Rehabilitation of the Ego (Reactive Egoisms). Obstinacy. Headstrongness. Argumentativeness. Obduracy. Indocility. Insubordination. Refractoriness. Readiness to take offence, to bear ill will. Craving for retaliation, for revenge. Spite, mockery, love of intrigue. Envy, malice, pleasure in distress. "Resentment", rancour, insidiousness.

C. *Lack of Capacity for Enthusiasm.*
Dryness, prosiness. Predominance of cold reason. Strictness, coldness, impatience. Rigour, intolerance.

D. *Lack of Capacity for Love.*
Hardness. Lack of compassion, of mercy. Insensitiveness. Lack of sympathy.

SENSUOUS DRIVING FORCES

E. *Sensuous Need of Pleasure.*
Love of pleasure, of enjoyment. Sybaritism, drunkenness (morphia-habit, etc.), Sexual craving. Ruttishness. Lecherousness. Wantonness. "Sweet tooth."

F. [*Forms of Self-Control.*]
Moderation. Resistance. "Self-domination." Restraint. Steadfastness, firmness.

Activity. Belief in future. Will to seize (Utilitarianism). Pleasure in success (Euphoria)—Displeasure in failure (Dejection). Self-esteem—Self-doubt. Actuality = World of facts (which can be seized and held).

266

TABLE II

PERSONAL SELF-ASSERTION OR EGOISM

I. Personal Driving Forces for Extension of the Ego (Spontaneous Egoisms).

  1. Neutral: General predominance of will.

    (*a*) Without spiritual Bonds.
      Malignance. Hatred. Cruelty. Destructiveness. Satanism.

    (*b*) With spiritual Bonds.
      Enterprise. Love of activity. Lust of success. Love of actions.
      (Ambition. "Caprice." Reforming zeal.)
      (Will to self-determination.)

  2. Particular.

    (*a*) Acquisitiveness.
      Love of property. Parsimoniousness. Mammonism.
      (Rapacity.) Collecting impulse. Meanness. Stinginess.
      Avarice. (Inquisitiveness. Desire to learn, to know.)

    (*b*) Selfishness.
      Love of earning. Sense of gain. Business instinct. (Rapacity.)

    (*c*) Dominativeness.
      Domineering nature. Will to superiority. Sense of standing.
      Sense of rank. Patronizing nature.

    (*d*) Ambition.
      Desire for recognition, for distinction, to "be somebody".
      Need of applause. Love of glory. (Vanity.) Need of spiritual
        standing.
      Primitive form: Masculine desire for adornments.

    (*e*) Egoism of the "Heart".
      Desire to please. Coquettishness. Will for popularity.
      In its primitive form has a part in feminine desire for
        adornment.

II. Personal Driving Forces for Preservation of the Ego (Passive Egoisms).

  1. Neutral.
    Prudence. Caution. Wakefulness. Calculation.

  2. Particular.
    Timidity. Suspicion. Distrust. (Shame.)
    Atfulness. Cunning. Foxiness.
    Duplicity. Deceit, it. Hypocrisy.

III. Personal Driving Forces for Rehabilitation of the Ego
(Reactive Egoisms).

   1. Neutral.
Contradictoriness. Love of opposition. Disputatiousness.
(Caprice. Quarrelsomeness.)
Obstinacy. Stubbornness. Obduracy. Refractoriness.
Mulishness. Indocility. Insubordination. Incompliance.

   2. Particular.
Sensitiveness. Readiness to take offence, to bear malice,
     reluctance to be reconciled.
Vengefulness. Resentfulness.
Quarrelsomeness, litigiousness, difficult nature.
Mockery, love of criticism, sarcasm.
Love of scandal, of intrigue.
Envy. Grudge. Malevolence. "Resentment."
Pleasure at distress. Spite. Rancour.
(Jealousy.)

IV. Personal Driving Forces for Self-Exaggeration (Isolated Egoisms).
Love of isolation. Solitariness.
Tendency to self-attention, self-observation.
Self-reference. Ego-centricity.
"Ideas of Reference"—Idiotism.
(Sentimentality. Maudlin disposition.)

V. Facilitative Driving Forces.

   1. Lack of spiritual Bonds.
Partiality. Lack of thoroughness. Superficiality.
Unreliability. Independability. Carelessness. Unscrupulousness.
Fickleness. Lack of conviction, of dignity.

   2. Lack of Releases.
Prosiness. Dryness. Lack of sensuality.
Coldness. Hardness. Lack of sympathy.
Insensibility. Mercilessness. Lack of "Heart".

TABLE III

SELF-ESTIMATION

FORMS AND DEGREES	MANIFESTATIONS
Self-esteem. Self-consciousness. Sense (exaggerated sense) of worth.	Arrogance Authoritative manner. Dictatorial manner.
Self-confidence. Assurance. Self-glorification ("Lording it").	Overbearing nature. Imperiousness.
Sense of inferiority. Self-doubt. Faintheartedness. Self-torture. (Penitence.)	Modesty. Unassuming manner. Subjection. Servility. Obsequiousness ("Second fiddle".
Megalomania. "Micromania."	Lack of dignity. Sycophancy.
Self-sufficiency. Self-satisfaction. Self-righteousness. Self-complacency. Superciliousness.	Caprice. Brazenness. Impudence. "Cheek". "Pose" (Blasé manner). Disdainful manner.
Self-love. Self-admiration. Self-adoration. Self-deification.	Pretentiousness Bragging. "Talking big". Boastfulness. Self-praise. Self-glorification.
Vanity. Conceit. Vaingloriousness (Bloatedness).	
Self-exaltation. Pride. (Hubris.) Self-conceit. Self-sufficiency.	Insolence. Condescension. Presumptuousness. Haughtiness. Officiousness.
Sense of honour.	Dignity.
Pride. Dignity. Humility.	Reverence.

www.ingramcontent.com/pod-product-compliance
Lightning Source LLC
Chambersburg PA
CBHW062120020426
42335CB00013B/1040